LIGHT-HORSE HARRY LEE

AND THE LEGACY

OF THE AMERICAN REVOLUTION

Also by Charles Royster

A REVOLUTIONARY PEOPLE AT WAR:
THE CONTINENTAL ARMY
AND AMERICAN CHARACTER,
1775–1783

LIGHT-HORSE HARRY LEE

AND THE

LEGACY

OF THE

AMERICAN REVOLUTION

CHARLES ROYSTER

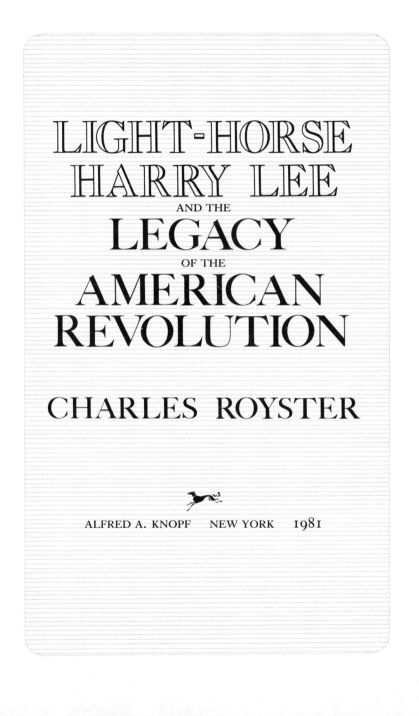

ALFRED A. KNOPF   NEW YORK   1981

THIS IS A BORZOI BOOK
PUBLISHED BY ALFRED A. KNOPF, INC.

Library of Congress Cataloging in Publication Data
Royster, Charles [date]
Light-Horse Harry Lee and the legacy of the American Revolution
Bibliography: p.
Includes index.
1. Lee, Henry, 1756–1818. 2. United States—History—Revolution,
1775–1783—Influence.
3. Generals—United States—Biography. 4. United States. Army.
Continental Army—Biography.
5. Virginia—Governors—Biography. I. Title
E207.L5R69   973.3′092′4 [B]   80-2706
ISBN 0-394-51337-1

MANUFACTURED IN THE UNITED STATES OF AMERICA
FIRST EDITION

To
Lester J. Cappon
&
Philip and Charlotte Partain

CONTENTS

ILLUSTRATIONS

PREFACE

THIS BOOK IS A STUDY OF THE EFFECT OF THE AMERICAN Revolutionary War on the character and career of Henry Lee. As a soldier, politician, investor, and historian, Lee touched many of the major events of American history between 1776 and 1815, and the eight-year war gave the dominant themes to this forty-year story. I do not tell that story in full; nor do I undertake a complete account of Lee's times, his family, or childhood. Instead, I try to trace the legacy of the war in Lee's life and to analyze the ways in which the American Revolution dominated the period that came after it.

Because this account deals with themes in Lee's career rather than telling the story of his life, it departs from chronology at several points within a broadly chronological framework. I begin by studying the effect of the Revolutionary War on Lee. Then I examine what he expected from peace. Both accounts prefigure the defeats that he experienced later in life. The remaining chapters discuss those defeats, as Lee tried to shape his career and, through it, the American Revolution, in order to bring his country the promise of the Revolution without its worst flaws. In describing Lee's mind and character, I do not apply clinical psychological analyses. I lack the professional competence to do this, and have not found ways in which such an analysis would satisfactorily explain the connection between Lee and the Revolutionary War that is my main concern.

Writing this account, I had before me the example of several scholars who have pursued thematic studies as an alternative to full-scale biography. Three recent works are Peter Shaw's *The Character of John Adams* (Chapel Hill, N.C., 1976), Robert Dawidoff's *The Education of John Randolph* (New York, 1979), and Richard M. Rollins's *The Long Journey of Noah Webster* (Philadelphia, 1980). These works demonstrate the value of studying one man's character, alike for its intrinsic interest and for its usefulness as a reflection of, influence in, or commentary on his era. And all three explore the lasting effect of the American Revolution on the participants and their posterity.

However, I seek a still more concentrated focus: a focus not only on character but on the connection between character and war. What did a revolutionary strive for in war? How did the war affect his understanding of the Revolution? In what ways did his experience in the Revolution and its war shape his life and, through him, his country? These questions bear with special force on the study of Henry Lee. Revealing events, issues, and statements from his career can help in framing answers.

I believe that these answers in turn suggest insights that go beyond the character of Lee. The Revolutionary War became a crucial experience in defining a nation, a generation, and a legacy for posterity. Each question one asks about Lee can be asked about his contemporaries. If the study of Lee were to prove useful for understanding his contemporaries, the reason would not be that he was typical—even of leaders or of army officers. Few Americans saw as much of the Revolutionary War as Lee did; few Americans suffered reverses so complete in the years that followed; and few Americans grew so isolated from their country. Yet Lee's distinctiveness might also make his career fruitful for analysis; the extremes of his conduct and fortunes might set questions in bolder relief.

Many of his countrymen, like Lee, tried to emulate and re-enact the victories of the Revolutionary War. And many Americans, like Lee, feared that the Revolution might still fail—lost or betrayed by weak revolutionaries or by posterity. Lee's distinctiveness arose partly from his pursuing these shared concerns to uncommon extremes. He may have suffered not only from a flawed character but also from devoting his life to revolution. The tragedy of such a life was not confined to Lee alone.

PROLOGUE

On Cumberland Island, Georgia, late in the afternoon of March 10, 1818, a fifteen-year-old boy was playing near the beach. He saw a ship approach the island and drop anchor not far beyond the wharf that served his aunt's plantation. A boat was lowered from the vessel, and two sailors rowed it toward the landing. The boy went down to meet them. At the wharf the sailors lifted an old man out of the boat and bore him in their locked arms to the beach.

He looked poor and sick—plainly, almost scantily dressed, pale and thin. He gave signs of suffering much pain. He called the boy to him, and in reply to the old man's questions the boy said that he was Phineas Miller Nightingale, that his aunt was Mrs. Louisa Shaw and she was at home, and that he was a grandson of General Nathanael Greene. The old man hugged Phineas. Then Phineas supported him as they walked a short distance to a log and sat down. It was easy to tell that the old man had once been used to giving orders and making speeches. He told Phineas to go to the house and say to Mrs. Shaw that General Lee was at the wharf and wished her to send a carriage for him. "Tell her," he said, "I am come purposely to die in the house and in the arms of the daughter of my old friend and compatriot."

Phineas hurried to the house. No one had known that General Lee was coming, but the Shaws were glad to hear it.

After returning to the beach, Phineas rode back in the carriage with the general and the possessions that the sailors had left on the wharf: a worn-out trunk and a cask of Madeira. The carriage went down a sandy avenue between dense groves of live oak trees choked with scrub palmetto. The live oaks dangled Spanish moss and shaded the avenue with branches interlocking overhead, encircled and bound together by long, thick grapevines.

A short ride brought them to the home that General Greene had planned but had not lived to see—Dungeness, a four-story mansion surrounded by twelve terraced acres of gardens and groves: flowers, vegetables, and spices; olives, oranges, and tropical plants. At the door General Lee had to be helped out of the carriage and up the steps. Mr. and Mrs. Shaw welcomed him cordially; he excused himself at once and was taken to a third-floor bedroom in the southeast corner of the house. It was a solid, comfortable mansion with hard outer walls of composite shell, lime, and gravel laid four feet thick. Indoors, most of the twenty rooms were richly appointed; some, however, still remained unfinished.

The old general stayed in his room. From it he could see the southern tip of Cumberland Island, the coasts of Georgia and Florida, and the thousands of acres of silvery-green salt marsh that separated the island from the mainland; to the east lay the dunes, the beach, and the Atlantic. The prospect aroused the orator in Lee, and he often praised "the wide-spreading sea, the charming groves, the flowers and the songbirds which filled his chamber with their early spring notes of joy and gladness."

But General Lee suffered intensely. Soon after his arrival he sent for a naval surgeon and gave the doctor a clear, detailed description of his condition. Keen pain in his bladder was compounded by an intermittent fever. The surgeon conjectured that "little could be done particularly at his time of life."

Yet Lee was not as ready to die as he had sounded when he first met Phineas. He still hoped to reach home in Alexandria, Virginia, where his wife and youngest children lived; his health would mend, he said, "as the spring advances." For a long time he had put faith in warm weather to alleviate his lingering disease. He had spent the last five years in the West Indies; the night before reaching Cumberland Island he had suffered "excruciating torture," which had alarmed the ship's captain, who warned him against the sudden change to a cooler climate. But "his anxiety to get to America was so great" that he had ignored the captain's advice and "repeatedly expressed his conviction of improving health."

In his first days at Dungeness, General Lee liked to leave his room once a day for a short walk on the grounds. Phineas always accompanied him. Lee put his arm around the boy's neck, then slowly and with difficulty went down the steps of the mansion. They moved southward, along a broad walk that led to the lower garden. There they could see the flowers and the many kinds of trees—citrus, camphor, coffee, rubber, fig, and palm. They walked along an avenue through one of the orange groves. The general, as usual, liked to talk. He celebrated the beauty of nature, and he recalled his youth. "Often did he allude in glowing terms to the glorious memories of the revolution." He spoke with greatest enthusiasm about the two men who had been his commanders in those days and whom he had most admired throughout his life: George Washington and Nathanael Greene. But walking soon tired Lee; so Phineas helped him back to the house and up to his room.

After a week or ten days at Dungeness, General Lee quit taking walks. He stayed in his room, reading a book that described the resources of the Ohio and Mississippi valleys. Since his arrival he had seldom come downstairs to dine with the family. Now he took all his meals in his room, never leaving it and spending most of his time lying down. He was not mending; instead, he was growing weaker. Spasms of pain overwhelmed him intermittently. Someone stayed with him all the time. The army officers from Amelia Island and the naval officers from the squadron in Cumberland Sound had jointly visited Lee soon after his arrival. Now one or two of them came by turns to sit up with him each night. Many of the officers had known him in earlier days, and among them Lee was "beloved & venerated as having been one of the patriots who had acted so conspicuous a part during the memorable Struggle which immortalized America." Lee told them that he had not seen one well day since a mob in Baltimore had severely beaten him and others who opposed the War of 1812 almost six years ago. He said that he was "absorbed in misery & tortured with pain."

It was hard to tell exactly how long after reaching Dungeness Lee came to know for sure that he was about to die. After his second or third day on the island, he had spoken to the officers even more dramatically than he first addressed Phineas on the beach. He had told them of his "constant prayer that he might be suffered to die." Yet even then he had still hoped to get home in the spring, and he had still taken his daily walk in the garden. Now, after another seven days—weaker, more gaunt, at last bedridden—Lee could no longer look forward to leaving Dungeness. Without hope, riven by his disease, he was overcome by depression and anger. He raged at the healthy people who tended him. His seizures came more often and lasted longer. Whenever they let up for a while, he talked. Still eloquent, Lee spoke of the Revolutionary War, of issues from the past, and of the political questions now before the public. "He was a decided Federalist, and avowed his utter detestation of all Democrats." He felt anxiety about the lapse of virtue in America. He wrote to President James Monroe in mid-March, urging him to try to diffuse virtue for the common good. He reminded the President of the fate of the

Roman Empire, in which even the most dedicated rulers only checked for a while the "torrent of vice" that "ultimately subverted the government & let loose on the fairest portion of the world all the scourges of the human race." Throughout his years in the West Indies Lee had prayed for the "prosperity & glory" of the United States. Now he knew he would no longer live to see how America fared.

Before the end, the pain grew worse. As Lee became more feeble and emaciated, his paroxysms went on and on, unintermitted, newly severe. "His countenance and voice gave fearful token of the most intense agony." He did not converse any more but uttered only expressions of his pain. Some of his last intelligible words blamed his coming death on the Baltimore mob. During his final few days he was kept alive by "the aid of constant stimulants." When the Shaws were in the drawing room on the second floor, they could hear the sound of the waves on the beach and the screams of General Lee in the room above. The old man stayed at Dungeness for two weeks; but when Phineas remembered that time, it seemed like two months.

The corruption of Lee's body began before his death. Still he retained his senses. On Tuesday, March 24, he became unable to speak. At six o'clock in the evening of Wednesday, the fourth day of spring, Lee died.

1

PARTISAN WAR

LIGHT-HORSE HARRY LEE AND HIS CAVALRYMEN WERE getting their breakfast later than usual on Tuesday morning, February 13, 1781. On an "abundant farm" near the border between North Carolina and Virginia, the unbridled horses had plenty of provender, while the owner of the farm and his slaves handed out generous helpings of corn meal and bacon for the men to cook. Lord Cornwallis's army was not far away—earlier in the morning, instead of eating breakfast, Lee and his cavalrymen had been killing eighteen of Banastre Tarleton's British dragoons—but Lee's Legion of one hundred cavalry and more than one hundred infantry felt safe at the farm. It lay on an out-of-the-way narrow road through woods known to Lee's guides. He was taking the road as a short cut north to Irwin's Ferry across the Dan River. While the Legion relaxed, Lee posted a few mounted sentries to tell him when the British passed by at a distance along the road to Dix's Ferry, farther upriver on the Dan.

Through days of midwinter forced marches, Lord Cornwallis had been trying to catch the Continental Army of the Southern Department, led by its young commander, the thirty-eight-year-old General Nathanael Greene. Cornwallis believed that, if his nearly three thousand men could force Greene's two thousand to fight, he could destroy Greene as he had destroyed another American army the summer before. By doing so, he would avenge the Americans' defeat of Tarleton at Cowpens in January and come much closer to re-establishing royal government in the South. Greene, on the other hand, meant to keep his army intact to fight again and, by retreating north to Virginia, get closer to the source of his supplies while drawing the British farther from their own. To cross the rising Dan, leaving no boats on the south bank, would secure Greene's retreat. Between the main body of Americans and their pursuing enemy, the general posted the thirty-one-year-old Colonel Otho Holland Williams and his élite light infantry and cavalry. Between the light troops and the enemy, Williams posted the Legion of the twenty-five-year-old Lee.

Lee planned to rejoin Williams after the Legion cavalry finished breakfast. The time for taking short cuts had come because the end of the retreat was near. Williams and the light troops were no longer trying to decoy Cornwallis by making him think that the American army was headed for Dix's Ferry. Now all the Americans were hurrying toward their true goal downstream: Irwin's Ferry, more than forty miles ahead.

But Cornwallis knew where Williams was going, and Cornwallis too had guides, and now the British Army was coming up Lee's short cut. The Legion's sentries, instead of watching the British pass by on the main road, saw them coming head on and fired warning shots. Lee and his outnumbered men would have to run. Across the path of his retreat from the farm ran a creek, swollen by recent rains. To pass the creek swiftly, he would have to use the one bridge that crossed it, and the bridge was as close to the British as to the Legion. Lee ordered his infantry to head for it "in full run," while he and the cavalry—quickly arrayed but still with empty stomachs—went to support the sentries. The British light troops who came upon Lee while chasing Williams were as surprised as he was. Instead of attacking, they halted, sent back a report, and waited for orders. This delay gave Lee's cavalry time to race for the bridge and follow the infantry across before the enemy started to chase them.

Before them lay a mile-long road through open farm land, leading to high ground and the road to Irwin's Ferry. Covering that mile between the cleared fields, Lee's Legion stayed ahead of the pursuing army of Cornwallis. As they reached the high point where they entered the road to the Dan, the more than two hundred Americans could turn and look back at over two thousand of the enemy spread out below.

For the next twenty-four hours Williams's men, covered by the Legion, were following the trail of Greene's retreat, never far from the British. Williams, to ensure Greene's escape, or Lee, to ensure Williams's, must if needed turn and fight a sacrificial delaying action. But between eight and nine o'clock on the night of February 14, Lee's troopers drove their horses into the river and accompanied them across in boats. Lee followed in the last boat left on the south bank of the Dan.

When Lee later remembered his narrow escape from the farm, he censured himself with words that he did not apply to the many other close calls experienced by units he commanded. For this instance of nearness to capture or death had occurred not because the Legion took a daring risk on purpose, with hope of commensurate gain, but because Lee had relaxed his vigilance by resting so confidently at the farm. "Criminal improvidence!" he said of his conduct. "A soldier is always in danger, when his conviction of security leads him to dispense with the most vigilant precautions."[1] Such mistakes were rare with Lee, who had attained the most coveted post open to a young officer—command of an independent legion—by the exercise of exceptional discipline and foresight. His professionalism was famous. In drafting a proposal to create a corps of light troops in 1778, General Charles Lee, a retired English officer who had joined the Continental Army, wrote of him: "Major Lee . . . seems to have come out of his mother's womb a soldier."[2]

Lee spent only seven of his sixty-two years as a soldier. Those years loomed disproportionately large in his life because of his aptitude for warfare and because the American Revolution shaped his subsequent career. Throughout the Revolutionary War, Lee was given commands that enabled him to exercise independent initiative outside of routine military operations and the ordinary hierarchy of command. His success as a commandant first of cavalry, then of a combined legion of cavalry and infantry, won him promotion, a gold medal, an augmented force, and special assignments. These assignments—especially the raid on the British garrison at Paulus Hook, New Jersey, in 1779 and the capture of British and loyalist garrisons in South Carolina in 1781—gave him uniquely conspicuous fame as a soldier and a patriot at an early age.

When Lee left the army in 1782, he married his rich cousin, Matilda Lee, and entered politics, in which he remained active for fifteen years. In the 1780s and 1790s he served successively as a delegate to the Continental Congress, as a member of the Virginia constitutional ratifying convention and the Virginia General Assembly, as governor of Virginia for three one-year terms, again as a member of the General Assembly, and finally as a member of the United States House of Representatives for one term. During his tenure in all of these offices, Lee and the people who spoke about him often referred to his Revolutionary War experiences. His years in the army contributed to both his peacetime stature and his postwar concerns.

However, despite Lee's early popularity as a military patriot, he sustained many disappointments in both private and public life. After only eight years of marriage, Matilda Lee died in 1790. Harry's years with his second wife—Ann Hill Carter, whom he married in 1793—were marred almost from the beginning by the failure of his many investments, especially his speculations in land. A few weeks before their sixteenth wedding anniversary in 1809, Harry went to jail because he could not pay his debts. His political career as a Federalist had already ended with the rise to power of Thomas Jefferson and the Republicans—first in Virginia, then in the national government.

Looking back over his own and his country's history, Lee believed that the American Revolution had gone awry. Its promise of national grandeur and individual happiness, which his initial military skill had promoted so ably, seemed to have been lost or purposely thwarted in the postwar years. Finally, while aiding Federalist opponents of the War of 1812, Lee was beaten and maimed by a Republican mob in Baltimore, which attacked him as a traitor. Soon afterward, in 1813, he left the United States and spent the last five years of his life in exile in the West Indies.

Few of Lee's contemporaries underwent so sharp a change of fortunes or so complete a ruin. Yet in the later careers of many American leaders—Thomas Jefferson as well as John Adams, Patrick Henry as well as Alexander Hamilton, Samuel Adams as well as Robert Morris, Charles Thomson as well as George Washington—lies a vein of disappointment over the outcome of the American Revolution. With differing concerns and in varying degrees, they found the years of peace falling short of the promises evoked to justify the Revolutionary War, and they warned that America might yet lose the cause it seemed to have won. The lives of all of them were continually shaped, if not completely dominated, by preoccupation with perpetuating the gains of the American Revolution.

In Lee, both the preoccupation and the disappointment attained a unique intensity. Having come out of his mother's womb a soldier, he came of age a revolutionary. In both undertakings his successes were flawed. Those who knew him regretted or scorned a career which betrayed its early promise. Yet in peacetime Lee redoubled the ambitious striving of the revolutionary soldier to bring prosperity to both his country and himself. Repeatedly and, at last, irreparably, he failed. Lee was neither a leading nor a typical figure in war or politics or enterprise. Rather, he combined in singular concentration the aspirations and the defeat that touched many of his contemporaries.

Henry Lee's father sent him to Princeton at the age of fourteen and intended to send him, after his graduation in 1773, to London and make him a lawyer.[3] But the crisis with Britain intervened, and within three weeks of the Battle of Bunker Hill the nineteen-year-old Harry was writing to General Charles Lee "to ask a permit to enlist under your banner in order to acquaint myself with the art of war." Not until the following year, 1776, did Harry join the army with other Virginians under the command of Colonel Theodorick Bland. He made up for the delay by quickly showing his aptitude for what he called "the study of Mars."[4]

Lee's fascination with soldiering did not mean that he gave no thought to questions of principle in the Revolutionary War. In his gift for partisan fighting, Lee found a form of service that combined technical skill with revolutionary virtue. His professional ambition and competence promoted the liberty and independence of his country. This union of enthusiasm and patriotism became the central theme of his life. During the Revolution, Lee found in warfare a purposefulness that surpassed any other activity. Repeatedly he took gratification from substituting order for disorder, information for ignorance, action for inaction, boldness for fear, and escape for imprisonment or death. Lee gravitated toward tests of this disciplined exercise of wits on the margin of survival. In none of his later efforts to perpetuate the Revolution would he unite his gifts and his compulsion so fully as in war.

One of the main gifts of Lee's fighting and one of the crucial compulsions of his character was mobility. He took special precautions to be able to escape capture or death because he sought the kind of service that risked them more often. To defy the enemy repeatedly and yet escape, he would need speed, and this became his most conspicuous skill. He did not get the name Light-Horse Harry until 1779, when he took command of his Legion; but his first commission in 1776 made him a captain of dragoons, and thereafter he and his men owed many of their military successes partly to their horses. Lee shared with George Washington an attraction to fine horses; five years after the war, he traded Washington five thousand acres of Kentucky land for the thoroughbred Magnolia. During the war, Lee needed a critical eye for horses because his troopers defeated or outran the enemy by riding superior mounts. Lee himself looked more impressive in the saddle. He was of middle height but thin. Those who knew him said that he was "light and agile," or, "a man of light and weakly form, and not qualified, in personal strength, to make a heavy charge in battle." When General George Weedon praised Lee's courage in combat, he called Lee "that little Hero."[5] Lee relied less on his physical strength than on calculation, which could select horses that enhanced the speed and impact of his corps. Well-chosen and well-tended mounts enabled his troopers to gall a stronger enemy whom they could not beat, then flee to safety. Throughout Lee's life, speed, activity, mobility remained his first recourses. Political office, military ambitions, speculative ventures, and finally the search for restored health kept him moving and planning movement, as if he could forever outflank or outrun enemies, losses, and death.

Among Lee's military gifts, however, his judgment of horses was not the most valuable. More important, he succeeded—perhaps better than any other Continental Army officer of his rank—in fostering discipline among the men he commanded. A variety of witnesses agreed at different times in their praise of the discipline in Lee's units, and especially, after 1779, his Legion. He could be harsh: he threatened instant death for misconduct in combat, and he believed that executing deserters deterred other soldiers by example. But courts-martial and floggings and other uses of force played a far smaller role among Lee's men than did training, action, and glory. The soldiers of the Legion had volunteered to serve for the duration of the war, unlike most Continentals, who were three-year men, one-year men, nine-month men, conscripts, or hired substitutes. In 1780, the Continental Board of War authorized the expansion of the Legion because "its reputation would induce men to enlist, who would not probably enter into other corps."[6] Lee sustained this reputation by ensuring that his men sought action, which gave them opportunities to distinguish themselves. In contrast with the army at large, desertion from the Legion was rare.

Lee buttressed the soldiers' voluntarism by careful attention to details. His was one of the few Continental Army units that usually had full uniforms, sometimes at his personal expense, sometimes by virtue of his aggressiveness in getting a share of captured enemy stores. The well-clothed men and well-kept horses were healthy; in this fact—easy to understand but hard to achieve—lay one of the main sources of the Legion's confidence. "Lieut. Col. Henry Lee was distinguished in our Revolutionary army, for the health and vigor of his corps," an army surgeon recalled. *"I never saw one of his men in the general hospital; and it was proverbial in camp, that Lee's men and horses were always ready for action."*[7] Painstaking attention to the men's hygiene, the camp's sanitation, the unit's equipment and weapons underlay the Legion's survival in the conspicuous service its soldiers sought.

Lee's successful discipline depended, then, more on the soldiers' spirit than on coercion, though Lee and his officers remained ready to use force. Lee called this spirit "veteranship."[8] It included experience in combat, perseverance through hardship, diligence in camp, and the glory of distinctiveness. A man who had known members of the Legion during the Revolutionary War wrote of them: "Both cavalry and infantry were like a band of brothers, having entire confidence in each other, and all having equal confidence in, and personal esteem for, their commander, Lee."[9] Such solidarity manifested itself in a concern for the reputation of the Legion. Lee and his men knew that their conduct would stand out as the deeds not just of the army but of Lee's dragoons or Lee's light cavalry or Lee's Legion. In return for the fame of their more visible risks and accomplishments, they must, to avoid defeat or the disgrace of being ordinary, sustain a high level of veteranship. Lee took pride in the popularity of the Legion wherever it camped apart from the army. His soldiers' uncommon degree of self-restraint in the presence of civilians and civilians' property maintained discipline and reputation while inviting the populace's help—often very important to the Legion's operations. Even when Lee came to seize farmers' wagons and teams for the army, the chief executive of Pennsylvania assured him: "I know of no Officer or corps in whose prudence and discretion more dependance could be placed."[10]

Sergeant Major John Champe—a Virginian in his early twenties whom Lee, on Washington's orders, sent behind

British lines to kidnap the defector Benedict Arnold—had exceptional maturity and poise, as well as a unique assignment. But the reaction of an exceptional man to an unprecedented project comported with the spirit that prevailed in the whole Legion. Although Champe welcomed the offer of a hazardous mission that would help General Washington, would punish treason, and would provide "powerful and delicious personal excitements," Lee had to play several of his oratorical chords to get the sergeant major to volunteer. Champe would accept neither the ignominy of deserting to the British nor the hypocrisy of enlisting in Arnold's new loyalist regiment. Both actions, he said, would shame him, and the dishonor would keep him from being promoted. Lee argued that such scruples need not apply to actions taken on secret orders, and he promised Champe promotion; but Lee's clinching appeal spoke of the pride of the Legion. What would Champe's comrades say about him if some other soldier won for another regiment the glory of having seized Arnold and then the Legion learned that Champe had first been offered the task? "The esprit du corps could not be resisted," Lee recalled, "and united to his inclination, it subdued his prejudices." Champe escaped the pursuit of his own dragoons—who thought they were chasing a real deserter—reached New York, lied his way up the British chain of command, answered Sir Henry Clinton's questions for an hour and received two guineas from him, communicated with American spies in New York, met Arnold, narrowly missed taking the traitor, shipped out with the loyalist unit to invade Virginia, deserted from the British at Petersburg, crossed North and South Carolina, and rejoined the Legion eight months after his departure.[11]

Champe's undertaking epitomized one of Lee's favorite tactics in war: the daring stratagem. Lee took part in such major battles as Brandywine, Germantown, Guilford Court House, and Eutaw Springs. But his most widely praised accomplishments did not occur in battle. Rather, he specialized in the carefully calculated coup, the surprise, the raid that damaged a stronger enemy who then had too little time to strike back before Lee was gone. While he served in Bland's regiment early in the war, he won recurring notice for rustling British livestock and riding back into camp with British prisoners. In January 1778, the *New Jersey Gazette* reported that Lee and his twenty-five dragoons had, since August of 1777, "taken one hundred and twenty-four British and Hessian privates, besides four commissioned officers, with the loss of only one horse."[12] Three months later, Washington wrote Congress to commend Lee's "exemplary zeal, prudence and bravery," and to propose the establishment of "an independent partisan Corps," commanded by Lee, who would be promoted to major. "Capt. Lee's genius particularly adapts him to a command of this nature."[13]

Washington chose his words carefully when describing Lee's genius, and he rightly included the word "prudence." For Lee's exploits, audacious as they might seem, were never so foolhardy as to get him caught. The daring of Lee and his men was brave and risky, but it was also planned, disciplined, and prudent. His most famous stroke in the northern campaigns—the raid on the British fort at Paulus Hook, New Jersey, in August 1779—would never have been tried without reliable intelligence that the post's defenders had grown negligent. Lee had to calculate marching time, tides, the hours of darkness, and the routes of access and escape. Despite several mix-ups and mistakes, he and most of his men made it into the fort on the strength of bayonets and brought off 158 prisoners. For this action Lee became the only soldier below the rank of general to receive a gold medal from the Continental Congress. And the glory of the raid on Paulus Hook was instrumental in elevating him to the command of infantry as well as cavalry, combined in a Legion led by Light-Horse Harry Lee.

"Conduct yourself with perfect caution or you meet with

sure loss & disgrace."[14] Lee's orders to Captain Allen McLane expressed his own rule. "Perfect caution" did not mean no risk; it meant no risk that could be reduced or removed by care. Caution and daring might seem to conflict, and yet they could intensify each other. Together they focused the mind on calculable risks. Operating on a small scale with tested men and reliable intelligence, the veteran partisan could hold more of the threads of the outcome in his hand than most soldiers usually did, thereby leaving fewer threads with the enemy and with chance. The enterprises then would be dangerous but not suicidal or even improbable. Success would lie more with wits, less with force, and seldom with rashness. Discipline, even more than mobility, enabled Lee and the Legion to serve and survive. Mad charges or mad flights would not win the war. To dare carefully was to avoid madness by outsmarting the enemy with esprit de corps, discipline, speed, surprise, and the judicious selection of what to try.

This last quality was the heart of perfect caution. There the officer revealed the scope of his mastery by weighing achievements against the need to survive. Lee's men were attached to him and accepted his strict discipline in large part because he led them to repeated successes which usually got few if any of them killed. "He possessed this peculiar characteristic as a military commander, of being always careful of the health and lives of his soldiers, never exposing them to unnecessary toils or fruitless hazards, always keeping them in readiness for useful and important enterprizes."[15] When Lee later judged the competence that various officers had shown during the Revolutionary War, he praised or censured them according to their approximation of "that happy mixture of caution and ardor" which he attributed to George Washington.[16]

The mixture depended on expertise in combat; it also depended on self-control. The commander had to know both how to fight and when not to fight. Soon after his arrival in the South, Lee had to explain to Nathanael Greene why he had tried a complicated surprise attack on Georgetown, South Carolina, that had failed to take the British garrison or their fort: "my force was inadequate to the assault of the Enemy's enclosed works, nor was the possession equivalent to the certain loss to be expected from such a measure. I therefore determined to pursue my principal objects by means more certain & less destructive to my troops."[17] The "more certain" surprise penetration of the town still left the enemy garrison barricaded against him. In looking back on his and Francis Marion's decision to withdraw the Legion and the militia from the town, Lee believed that for once he had carried caution too far. Even so, he reaffirmed the principle that underlay his other, more successful engagements: "Marion and Lee were singularly tender of the lives of their soldiers; and preferred moderate success, with little loss, to the most brilliant enterprise, with the destruction of many of their troops."[18]

The core of Lee's combat experience was not the lighthorse cavalry charge in battle or the promiscuously destructive mounted raid across the countryside or the foot soldier's attempt to reconcile somebody else's plans and orders with the changing flux of battle. Rather, he enjoyed independent action: the raid, the ambush, the skirmish, the rapid march, the surprise attack, the siege of an isolated enemy outpost and an ultimatum to the enemy commander. Having received a general assignment, he had the tactical command of his troops, usually distant from the control of any superior. To an uncommon extent, Lee's men and their actions were an extension of his will. Commanding a select unit of long-term volunteers, he could develop and then rely on their training, their discipline, and their spirit. The unit's behavior in its distinctive style of combat would depend on his mental discipline—his capacity to devise a stratagem that reconciled daring and caution. To attain such mental discipline required different gifts from those that tried to make unreliable men conform to maneuvers by rote or those that gave a bold cavalryman like Casimir Pulaski posthumous fame. Instead of relying so heavily on rehearsed responses or ill-calculated risks, Lee would have to be more fully conscious of his own responsibility for the survival of his men and for their effectiveness in winning American independence.

Lee met this responsibility by trying to impose an even greater degree of order on combat than armies ordinarily imposed on the process of killing people. He even took pride in limiting the harm done to a defeated enemy. Once the victory was won, Lee could boast—as he did after the raid on Paulus Hook—that his men had refrained from the indiscriminate violence within their power. The great achievement of discipline, of imagination, of intellect, was to engage in a potentially irrational conflict and to impose on at least one sphere of it an order that combined combat and survival. In war there lay a threat even more forbidding to Lee than victories by the enemy: the chaos of undisciplined, unplanned violence, when civil war invited reciprocal murders and when the flight of unready militiamen caused armies to disintegrate into men fleeing alone. The cohesion and effectiveness of the Legion seemed to give war a purposeful order that originated in Lee's mind.

In his written orders to his command before the assault on Paulus Hook, Lee promised to honor instances of conspicuous service in the engagement. He said that his men could count on such notice from him because they had seen "the heart felt satisfaction he feels in observing military merit" and "the love he has uniformly possessed for arms."[19] But his love for arms did not connote an equal enthusiasm for all aspects of war. Rather, he felt a special enthusiasm for the refined style of combat in which he excelled. In March 1778, during the

winter at Valley Forge, the twenty-two-year-old Captain Lee
made a decision whose potential significance for his future he
may hardly have realized. George Washington sent Lieutenant Colonel Alexander Hamilton to invite Lee to join the
Commander in Chief's staff as an aide de camp. In reply, Lee
wrote to Washington that he was ready to serve wherever he
was ordered, but he preferred to command dragoons: "I am
wedded to my sword." Lee knew many of the advantages of
the post he was declining. In addition to keeping him near
Washington, it would provide "a field for military instruction"
and "would lead me into an intimate acquaintance with the
politics of the States." Indeed, after the war a disproportionately large number of Washington's former aides—most conspicuously, Hamilton himself—rose to prominence and power
as businessmen, attorneys, and Federalist Party officeholders.
In saying no to Washington, Lee disclosed the specialized
meaning war held for him—the more focused enthusiasm that
turned him away from concerns of logistical planning, large-
scale strategy, or civil affairs and toward the calculations of the
partisan. To Washington, Lee gave as his reasons "a most affectionate friendship for my soldiers, a fraternal love for the
two officers who have served with me, a zeal for the honor of
the Cavalry, and [an?] opinion, that I should render m[ore?]
real service to your Excellency's arms."[20] Washington was
not offended; a few days later he recommended that Congress
create the "independent partisan Corps" that would enhance
Lee's ability to fight the kind of war he loved best.[21]

Many young officers, eager, as Lee was, to build a military reputation, would have agreed that they could serve the
cause better in a field command than on the staff. Lee, however, was wedded to a special branch of warfare. And when he
called such service more "real," he may have meant, in part,
the heightened clarity and order that he imposed on violence.
Although the Legion was effective in battle, Lee's claim to

have served the cause rested less on killing the enemy than on outthinking him. Raids on a dozen Paulus Hooks might have done less harm to the British than one major battlefield defeat. Thus, he did not seek the positions in the army from which he might do the enemy the most damage—as a line commander—or himself the most good—as an aide to Washington. He wanted to fight in the way that gave combat the fullest union of excitement and rationality. Lee's wartime career suggests that, above all, this purposefulness in defying the enemy with stratagem and discipline gave him his "love" for arms.

The character of such combat appeared dramatically in the incident that gave him his earliest fame. Years before the British army's chief satirist Major John André put "Major Lee with Horses rare" into verse in 1780, the British had been galled by the successful raids and reconnoitering of the youngster and his few dragoons.[22] Sir William Erskine, the British cavalry commander, decided to stop Lee once and for all. At dawn on January 20, 1778, a large party of British cavalry tried to take Lee by surprise at his advance post six miles from Valley Forge. Lee, two officers, and five dragoons barricaded themselves in a house and defended it for twenty-five minutes against the attacks of a force variously estimated at 70 or 130 or 200 of the enemy. After killing three and wounding five of the British, Lee and his party, by shouting, made the British believe that the American infantry was coming. The attackers returned to occupied Philadelphia, taking as prisoners four sentries and a sergeant caught in the open. In his report, Lee magnanimously complimented the British on their "daring" in attacking him, but he could say with pride that the outcome had been "ignominious" for them, due to "the bravery of my men" and the "well directed" resistance. With well-aimed fire, "we drove them from the stables & saved every horse," even though "I had not a soldier for each window."[23] Twelve days later General George Weedon wrote back to Virginia about Lee, "his hidden impulses for military achievements are daily transpiring."[24]

The British foray, aimed specifically at Lee, gave him the occasion to demonstrate the mastery of warfare as he later praised it in the conduct of another officer: "Cool and discriminating amidst surrounding dangers, he held safe the great stake committed to his skill and valor."[25] For Lee the stake was greater than the survival of his unit or the outcome of a battle; on his skill and valor, in part, depended the future of his country. Lee, like many of his fellow officers, believed that the Revolution relied for its success on the Continental Army. If the British could crush the American army, they could kill the American cause as surely as British dragoons might cut down Harry Lee. The greatest stake, then, was life itself—the future of both the revolutionary and the Revolution. The Americans appealed not just to self-defense but also to a vision that the continent would attain through its new freedom. The fulfillment and final justification of the Revolution lay in the future, which, in Lee's eyes, only the army could assure. To Lee, living for this cause meant activity. And physical movement—so characteristic of him that it became a part of his name—reflected and carried out the activity of his mind. The active mind was the life of the revolutionary. The inventiveness of the partisan, the perseverance of the soldier, the ideals of the patriot were all manifestations and safeguards of the central vitality of the mind. Only by holding this stake safe amid surrounding dangers could Lee hope to equal his ambitions as a victorious revolutionary.

Lee's intellect turned more to the control of events than to the interplay of ideas. He studied character more closely than abstractions. Although he kept and used his Princeton Latin and Greek until his death and he read a great deal, he was not an original or profound thinker. His public mental life was devoted to politics, to business enterprises, and to war. But the activity of mental life held no less importance for him by reason of taking these forms than it did for Thomas Jefferson, in whom it took different forms. The word "mind" repeatedly appears in Lee's discussion of himself and his fellow revolutionaries. The word summarized the purposefulness with which the imaginative patriot could, by keeping his own genius alive, ensure the republic's survival. The more intensely one felt the citizen's responsibility to win the Revolution, the more urgently he would devote his mind to the cause. For Lee, that purposefulness was threatened by enemies who would, if victorious, confine or destroy the ability of his mind to attain his ambitions. In peacetime these enemies would appear amid business enterprise, partisan politics, and international alliances. But compared with combat, those later conflicts seemed latent or twisted or subtle or slow. In war the threats to the life of the soldier and the state were most intense and pervasive. To foil them, escape them, or defeat them by the vitality of the mind made survival an achievement of creativity.

Late in life, when Lee recalled the Revolution, he likened it to earlier wars in which "the mind was always on the stretch." War, he believed, stimulated the growth of "heroes, statesmen, orators, and poets. . . . Even our own country never exhibited such a display of genius before or since as she did during her eight years' war. . . . A continuous and ardent excitement of the mind, especially in regaining lost or defending menaced rights, places man in that train of mind and body which brings forth the greatest display of genius."[26] From this excitement of the mind among political leaders came a memorable body of political literature, as well as new governmental institutions designed to prevent subjection to tyranny. The urgency of danger helped make those who understood it prolific in their inventions for self-protection and in their hopeful visions of future safety. So great was the Americans' fear of subjugation that the revolutionaries were willing to resort to prolonged violence to prevent it. In this Lee excelled. His genius expressed itself less in constitutions than in combat. Warfare became for him the most nearly complete way to serve his country and to fulfill his ambition. But expressing the revolutionary ideal through violence entailed a risk as great as any Lee took in the field—a risk that any defeat could be final, even fatal, both for the ideal and for the mind that served it. Lee's imagination, instead of playing over parliaments and factions and kings and committees, more often played over killing. His mind's eye pictured defeat not in votes and laws and taxes and officials but in blood. Survival demanded that he be the best of warriors. More than by any other work of literature Lee was moved by Sophocles' tragedy *Ajax*. In it he saw the hero who, defeated in his ambition to inherit the armor of Achilles, went mad, then tortured and slaughtered livestock, in the deluded belief that he was killing his fellow soldiers—finally regaining his mental power only to see his own shame and kill himself.

Lee committed himself to the Revolutionary War in part because it was not just war for war's sake or the kind of European war he wrote about in 1790 that was fought "for straws or for what is commonly called the ballance of power."[27] The Revolution endowed war with principle. Political ideas held much less of Lee's attention during the war than they later did; but even though his definition of liberty remained inchoate, he felt no less ardent in its defense and certain that American independence was the means to its survival. Such motives, he believed, must strengthen and justify the soldier's striving for rank and glory. The war was being fought to protect "the libertys of America," and the fighters were "a virtuous soldiery." Unlike some of his contemporaries, Lee did not believe that patriotism alone could either make a man a soldier or make an army victorious. However, "love of Country" and defense of "real liberty" gave American war-making a disinterested, self-sacrificing purpose that surpassed the exercise of military professionalism.[28]

Lee's outlook shared many elements of a state of mind that was widespread among Continental Army officers. They, especially the younger ones, felt highly self-conscious about their distinction as officers and patriots; they were preoccupied with the dramatic momentousness of their wartime careers. They cultivated a keen sense of social and military status, and they hotly resented any hint that their rank or honor might be impugned. Many of the officers' civilian countrymen, who set greater store by the libertarian, egalitarian potential of the Revolution, accused such officers of forsaking their country's ideals for the discredited social hierarchy, corrupt authoritarianism, and military professionalism of Europe. The officers, however, did not think themselves betrayers of the Revolution. On the contrary, they regarded army service as the most virtuous and most effective contribution to American independence, and they considered themselves the brains and nerve of the army. Nor were the officers modest or subtle when they portrayed themselves as the pre-eminent patriots of the Revolution. They successfully demanded that Congress recognize the country's dependence on and gratitude for their sacrifices by voting them postwar pensions. Service in the Continental Army officer corps encouraged in many men a self-centered, belligerent arrogance that expressed itself in a conviction of their own importance. This importance, in their minds, united their military careers with the revolutionary cause which they led and most fully exemplified.

Lee, like other officers, contrasted the army's virtue with the wartime delinquencies of the civilian populace. The re-

peated failure of decentralized state and continental governments and of the electorates they represented to supply or re-
cruit the army embittered many officers. The widespread eagerness to make more money from the sale of foodstuffs, the
reluctance to vote taxes or pay them, the trafficking in a
swelling and depreciating paper currency, the expenditures on
manufactured goods imported from allies or the enemy, the
obliviousness to the army's impotence and desperation—these
popular lapses in the middle years of the war led to the ignominious summer of defeat, defection, and paralysis in 1780.
When Lee looked for the cause of America's "calamitys," he
found that "it originates with the people." He and other officers agreed that "the patriotism of the people," which had at
first sustained the war effort, was now "done away."

The experience of first trusting popular virtue to help
win and hold independence, then losing faith in its constancy,
lastingly shaped Lee's view of the Revolution, as well as the
political lessons he took from it. In his eyes, American independence was vulnerable. The European powers stood ready
to divide America into "tributary disunited provinces" and
make it the scene of their continual conflict: "our country will
be to the world, what Germany has been for centurys past to
Europe." Dependence, disunion, and disorder would be the irreversible consequences of allowing Americans' chaotic wartime selfishness to continue unchecked. Instead of securing
the survival of the nation and its liberty through purposeful,
disciplined conflict, the deranged Revolution would give way
to "perpetual war."

Neither the winning of independence nor the future security of the country could safely be left in the unguarded
hands of so heedless a people. In the absence of sufficient voluntary virtue and discipline, government must acquire the
power to defend America with the help of coercion. The evil
effects of a lapse in public virtue were "naturally produced by

the modes of governing established thro' out the United States." Both state governments and the Continental Congress had erred in diffusing their executive authority and subjecting officials too closely to the unreliable will of their constituents. Congress, especially, left too much power in the hands of the states, thereby incapacitating itself to sustain the army that was securing its existence. Now the "perilous" situation demanded "wisdom & vigor in a supreme power"—a smaller, better-paid Congress, "augmented in authority," which could create a well-paid army of soldiers enlisted for the duration of the war.[29]

Lee's analysis of the distresses of 1780 echoed the opinion of Washington, Hamilton, many other Continental officers, and influential political leaders. At this low point of the public's contribution to winning independence, Hamilton first described several features of the governmental policies with which he would later seek to strengthen national authority after he became Secretary of the Treasury. In the years after 1780, public disorder would usually not strike these men as only domestic disobedience to the law; it would also seem a potential threat to America's survival as an independent nation. As they would remember the Revolutionary War, only the army had stood between America and subjugation at a time when most of their countrymen had thrown off all sense of subordination to the public welfare in order to pursue self-interest. That the people realized their peril and their own responsibility for it only dimly if at all made such disorder even more alarming. Blind anarchy no less than purposeful conspiracy could sabotage the revolutionary cause. The government would always need the authority to preserve itself by disciplining its citizens into a civic responsibility they would not voluntarily maintain. The crisis of 1780 must not be allowed to recur.

According to the Marquis de Lafayette, Lee in the au-

tumn of 1780 was "out of joke," sometimes making suggestions "diametrically opposed" to "republican principles."[30]
However, Lee was not seriously beginning to repudiate republicanism as he understood it. Rather, with other officers he
concluded that the survival of liberty depended on the superior
virtue of a few men who, because of their patriotism, had
paramount claim to wield authority for the public good. The
Revolution had shown the need for stronger government and
had at the same time identified a body of patriots in the officer
corps who had proven their fitness to direct public affairs. The
supremacy of civil government would continue; but officers
were especially well qualified to judge the form of government
and influence it when necessary. On April 6, 1780, the Continental Army officers who were in Philadelphia assembled at
the New Tavern and issued a manifesto over the signatures of
General Anthony Wayne, Colonel Walter Stewart, Lieutenant Colonel John Stewart, and Major Henry Lee. They announced their intention "to curb the spirit of insolence and audacity" that they saw among lukewarm patriots as well as the
disaffected. They wanted to break "a spirit of resistance,
which . . . receives encouragement from the lenity of Governments, founded on principles of univérsal liberty and benevo-
lence." To this end, they would "give energy . . . to the future
operations of Government." Their main tactic would be to
censure and ostracize anyone who opposed them, especially
any officer: "We will with alacrity seize every opportunity of
evidencing to the World, our abhorrence of a conduct so *derogatory* to the *dignity* of the *Army.*"[31] This declaration epitomized the growing conviction among many officers that the
esprit de corps of persevering military service was a superior
embodiment of revolutionary virtue, making its possessors
first among patriots. As Lee later expressed the conclusion he
had reached during the Revolution, "Next to our duty to God,
is our duty to our Country, which we only completely dis-

charge when to the character of a citizen faithful and obedient to the Constitution and the Law, we unite the character of a soldier, ready and determined to vindicate and maintain the dignity and rights of our society."[32] No civilian could be a complete patriot. The highest virtue required the greatest risk—the willingness to sacrifice one's life, voluntarily, for the public good. Although civilians might also risk or lose their lives in the cause, Lee always regarded military service as the fullest manifestation of courage. And because courage and dedication during the Revolutionary War had assured America's survival, the officers' wartime virtue should establish their pre-eminence for life.

War—even war fought by patriots on behalf of principle—had another side: cruelty. Lee learned, both as a witness and as a participant, how vicious war could become. He inculcated discipline and praised professionalism partly because he hoped that men could fight in pursuit of calculated purposes rather than shed blood for its own sake. Yet the economy, regularity, and predictability that Lee strove for in war could not always channel or suppress malevolence. He later called the Revolution "this unnatural war," mainly because it was a civil conflict. Neither Lee's eagerness to commence "the study of Mars" nor his devotion to American liberty and independence had prepared him for the prolonged vengeful bloodshed among civilians, especially in the Carolinas and Georgia after 1780. The conflict between loyalists and revolutionaries, embittered by long-standing divisions and widened by ties of kinship, afflicted much of the South with theft, destruction, torture, and killings that perpetuated themselves in vendettas. Unlike "the art of war" that Lee had aspired to master or the discipline that he cultivated in his Legion, this face of war turned toward disorder. It appalled Lee, and in his later recollections of intestine violence, he tried to think of ways by which it could have been avoided. Still, though he might wish to believe that such violence had not been an inevitable part of the war, he could not forget having seen South Carolina "thrown into those deadly feuds, engendering that sanguinary warfare, in some sections of the country, which, with the fury of pestilence, destroyed without discrimination." In Georgia, "it often sunk into barbarity."[33] This sight caused Lee greater alarm than British regiments did. It showed him not a foreign enemy's threat but Americans' turning patriotism into murder. Against such a danger, military professionalism might look like a civilizing influence. Lee wanted to use military authority to hold South Carolina back from anarchy. In June 1781, he urged General Nathanael Greene "to govern this state until civil government can be introduced," lest the army lose all of the state's resources. Lee said of the citizens, "They [exc]eed the Goths & Vandals in their schemes of plunder murder & iniqu[it]y. All this under pretence of supporting the virtuous cause of America."[34]

However, the Continental Army existed in order to amass force against the enemy, not in order to govern a state. And violence, once begun, sometimes proved harder to control than Lee had first supposed. The European ideal of warfare in the eighteenth century sought to entrust combat to small professional armies and to win wars more through technical skill and limited engagement than through attrition and destruction. This attempt at regulation still allowed great sway to havoc; and regulation could not always prevail. The farther from restraint war ranged, the more anxious Lee grew. Even a disciplined army, like Cornwallis's, left its line of march open to the "dreadful" visitation of "that devastating flight of human vultures . . . whose appetite for plunder is insatiate." The war had created lawless bands of brutal men who roamed regions disrupted by the armies and used the conflict as a cover to steal, destroy, and kill. They remained so vivid in Lee's memory when he later described them that he called them "vulture bipeds." They were "the precursor of famine & of plague." To convey their effect, the first word that came to his mind was "inundating."[35] Nor were the armies themselves free from such lapses into uncontrolled violence. After the Revolution, Lee wrote that "the indulgence of the angry passions in war tends to arrest rather [than] to advance victory the great desideratum of all who fight."[36] He had seen the angry passions overcome civilians. The Legion and its commander had also sometimes sought more blood than victory demanded. The eighteen British dragoons killed on the morning of Lee's narrow escape toward the Dan River were casualties of Lee's order to give no quarter to prisoners. This was revenge for the dragoons' killing of an unarmed boy, the Legion's bugler. Later Lee also welcomed retaliatory executions of British officers in reprisal for the execution of American militia Colonel Isaac Hayne—a policy that, if prolonged, would probably have led, as Lee later acknowledged, to "a war of extermination."[37]

The Legion's discipline and purposefulness could usually restrain but could not eliminate the desire to kill men who had hurt the Legion, who might have destroyed it, but who now lay powerless in its hands. Despite their professionalism, soldiers shared some of the violent fear felt by their civilian countrymen fighting a civil war, for whom the drive to kill expressed the drive to survive. Such bloodletting blurred the distinction between policy in war and cruelty for its own sake. The connection between the killing of individuals and the victory of principles was fragile enough in the most disciplined of conflicts. In the viciousness of arbitrary violence, this connection could be forgotten.

Several incidents that involved Lee's command suggest that he knew this danger at first hand—that it had touched both his soldiers and Lee himself. After the surrender of the enemy garrison fortified in the Motte house on May 12, 1781, Lee's men summarily hanged three loyalist prisoners.[38] Earlier, Lee had already set the example of maiming and murder that, when explained, would sound like calculation but, when witnessed, looked like vengeance. Before the Battle of Guilford Court House in March 1781, Lee and his men tortured a loyalist prisoner by tying him down and putting a red-hot shovel against the bottom of his feet and between his toes, but failed to "extort intelligence" from him.[39] Two years earlier, with the main army near Stony Point, New York, Lee commanded the patrols along the army's lines and obtained Washington's permission to execute a deserter immediately after capture. Without authorization, Lee told his patrols to cut off the head of one summarily executed deserter and send it back to camp to be set up as an object of fear that would deter others. His orders were carried out before Washington had time to countermand them.[40] Each of those occurrences might have been rationalized as severity designed to protect the army; yet they revealed the difficulty, perhaps the impossibility, of consistently directing violence toward victory without letting the angry passions become their own end.

This danger was most apparent on one of the Legion's bloodiest days, February 25, 1781, when it perpetrated what came to be known in the North Carolina countryside as "Pyle's Hacking Match."[41] In fact, it was no match. Colonel John Pyle's three hundred loyalist militiamen believed Lee's lie that the Legion troops were Tarleton's British dragoons and so allowed the cavalry to come alongside them on the road where they met. Without Lee's direct order, the Legion turned on the loyalists and, suffering no casualties of its own, sabred, bayoneted, and shot to death about one hundred men and wounded most of the other two hundred, who thought that their friend Tarleton was making a horrible mistake. The account that Lee wrote after the war acknowledged the extent to which he had foreseen and planned this outcome; nevertheless, he tried to portray the conflict as an "unintentional" one begun by the loyalists, whom, he said, he had hoped only to disband.[42] However, one of the American militiamen with the Legion, in his subsequent account of "the deception," recalled that "Colonel Lee knew what he was about." The historian Christopher Ward rightly reasons that "the bloody results of the attack are, in themselves, sufficient proof of its relentless ferocity." And the effectiveness of the massacre argues that it was "a piece of strategy fully matured and intentionally executed, whose outcome shocked its author."[43]

In Lee's later attempt to claim that "humanity" influenced the Legion that day, he contended that his men could not heed the cries for mercy because the Legion was in danger from the loyalists.[44] Somewhat self-contradictorily he also argued that, had he intended a massacre, he would not have allowed so many of the loyalists to escape death. In fact, the Legion had succumbed to something like the murderous passion that so disturbed Lee in civilians who debased a virtuous cause by using it to cloak their private barbarity. Such conduct was not characteristic of Lee's unit; he more often attempted to prevent reprisals by revolutionaries against loyalist prisoners. However, by the end of 1781 he had seen and sometimes joined a more vicious war than he had expected. Neither revolutionary virtue nor military discipline could assure that the enemy could be defeated without chaotic violence. Lee had passed, at least for a short while, some of the weak boundaries that divided the calculating war of wits from the sacrifice of wits to war.

Although Lee sought or held several kinds of military commissions in later years and retained his interest in the techniques of combat, he never again so wholeheartedly endorsed armed conflict as he had done on behalf of the Revolution when he was young. His later writings stressed ways to avoid war and to ameliorate its effects by the exercise of humanity. At the same time, he often glorified the Revolutionary War in retrospect and called it, with some exaggeration, "the mildest of all civil wars known to man."[45] In deploring the effects of war while celebrating the Revolution, Lee tried to establish a distinction that his wartime experience had occasionally obscured—a distinction between virtue and violence, between patriotism and murder. At critical times the populace, the Legion, and Lee had faltered in their ability to discipline their conduct so as not to confuse combat with crime. Perhaps by the end of the war Lee had begun to fear that the distinction could not be maintained.

Lee left the Continental Army before the war ended. He said that ill health obliged him to go home, but Nathanael Greene came closer to the truth when he wrote: "your complaints originated more in the distresses of the mind than in the ruins of your constitution." Before sending the letter, Greene softened it by alluding only to "distress."[46] However, his original words remained accurate. Late in 1781 and early in 1782, discontent and self-pity overcame Lee in a way that even he found hard to explain. He referred to his own behavior as "my stupid conduct."[47] His friends told him that he was making a mistake. In December 1782, the men of the Legion marched in the place of honor at the head of Greene's army when it entered Charleston. But for more than ten months Lee had not been with them. He ended his wartime soldiering not in triumph but in resentful isolation.

The clearest reason that Lee gave for his resignation was that Greene had slighted the Legion and Lee himself in battle reports, thereby giving grounds for others to criticize Lee's conduct. The source of this distress, however, lay not in

Greene's reports—which, as Greene rightly protested, had done him justice—but in the criticism of Lee that originated elsewhere. The fame of Lee's exploits was marred for him by a strain of resentment and censure that came from some fellow officers, Virginians at home, and civilian South Carolinians in the militia. Before he attained command of a legion, Lee was court-martialed twice—once in a minor dispute of the malicious kind that often arose from constant squabbling among junior officers and once at the instigation of Virginia officers who accused him of incompetence in the storming of Paulus Hook. He was acquitted with honor in both trials, but the charges brought into the open some officers' belief that Lee neither deserved nor exploited the special opportunities for combat command given to him. After Paulus Hook, General Anthony Wayne warned Lee: "be well guarded my friend . . . there are not a few, who would not feel much pain on a small Disaster happening to either you or me."[48]

Throughout Lee's wartime career, other officers complained about the favoritism shown him by Washington and Greene. It seemed easy for him to be flamboyant and conspicuously successful because he enjoyed unique autonomy and frequent occasions to be in action. Lieutenant Colonel John Eager Howard, who commanded a line regiment, later recalled: "I always admired Lee as a partizan but he was considered as priviledged to act as he thought proper."[49] Before sending Lee south, Washington told a member of Congress that other cavalry officers were "already extremely jealous of the superior advantages and priviledges which Major Lee has somehow or other obtained."[50] Lee, however, tended to treat his special status less as a privilege granted him than as a rightful claim that could be steadily increased. As Lee was leaving the army, Greene admonished him, "other officers as well as you my dear Sir have their feelings, and are not without their claims. One officer cannot carry on the service alone however meritorious; and jealousies and discontents have not been wanting in the Army at the opportunities afforded you to the prejudice of others."[51]

Many officers who, given a legion of their own, could not have rivaled Lee's mastery of discipline and tactical command probably preferred to impute his greater fame to the commanders' favoritism rather than to Lee's superior ability. Lee, however, compounded their envy by his arrogance. He was not one of the belligerent officers who tried to prove their distinction by frequent duels and fits of temper. Rather, he took his position and his glory as his due; he treated less meritorious patriots with the condescension they deserved.

Such a demeanor especially irked the Carolina militiamen. Some of them later recalled their resentment at having to support "well fed, well dressed, well mounted mercenaries, who looked down upon them as inferiors." They saw Lee acting like "the higher orders of Virginia gentlemen"; this behavior included a "habitual indifference to please those considered by Colonel Lee his inferiors." He treated militia privates and officers as he would have treated his plantation overseers. "It was a common remark among the Carolinians, that Lee would rather a dozen militia men should be killed, than one of his government horses."[52]

The twenty-five-year-old lieutenant colonel had not cultivated tact. He believed that the Continental Army was winning American independence and that his Legion surpassed all rivals in merit. He did not try to hide these beliefs by feigning a humility that he did not possess. Consequently, his claim to superior patriotism, which gave the war much of its purpose for Lee, provoked hostility from officers and citizens, who impugned the competence in which he took most pride. He could not understand such critics; at the time of his court-martial over the Paulus Hook engagement, he called them "those gentlemen who hate me for reasons unknown to me."[53]

Other Virginians, in addition to the officers who preferred charges against him, held grudges. They believed that his arrogance fitted a larger pattern. As Nathanael Greene tried to explain it in 1782, "if your reputation has felt any violence, it has been owing to your being a Lee."[54] One family was trying to monopolize too much of the glory of the Revolution. Even Edmund Pendleton, who admired Lee and welcomed his acquittal in the Paulus Hook court-martial, said that the young major "has been too highly puff'd by some Family Partizans."[55] The family itself understandably took a different view. Lee's father believed that Lee's fame was rising to equal his superior merit: "it will not be in the Power of his Enemys to Pluck from him those Laure[l]s they Cannot Acquire."[56] In the years after Paulus Hook, Lee became Light-Horse Harry, won command of his own Legion, and executed a series of operations in the South that led Greene to call him "one of the first Officers in the world" and to tell him, "No man in the progress of the Campaign had equal merit with you."[57] But his increasing fame did not win over all Virginians; instead, it excited more criticism. One of Greene's officers found on a trip to Virginia that many people were willing to believe "idle reports" spread by officers who questioned Lee's ability and accused Greene of partiality. "The people of Virginia are very jealous of your merit and growing consequence," Greene concluded. "Your family and name must be very obnoxious that the people should refuse you the glory due to your merit and exertions."[58]

That Light-Horse Harry's distinction as first among soldiers should coincide with the distinction of the Lees as first among Virginians caused no wonder for him and his family but failed to win the universal assent of those who would thereby find themselves ranked among the lesser patriots. Beyond resenting the arrogance of this commanders' pet and his puffed-up family, Lee's critics found fault with him as a soldier. South Carolinians accused him of letting the enemy off too lightly and hogging the glory of victory by giving overly generous terms in return for the quick surrender of British forts. Lee and his Legion lorded over enterprises that the militia already had well in hand. Then he added damage to offense by confiscating captured enemy stores for the use of the army—stores that the enemy had seized from citizens serving in the militia. Citizens lost their property even in victory, while the Legion turned out in new uniforms.

These accusations of haste, leniency, and inequity troubled Lee less than the rumors that he had misbehaved in battle. A court-martial had acquitted him of the charges that he had bungled the assault on Paulus Hook, but in the southern campaign there were no official charges—only talk. Accounts of the battles of Guilford Court House and Eutaw Springs spread by letter and word of mouth. They said that Lee had been absent from his assigned posts at critical times when the support of the Legion could have altered the course of the battles. During the battle at Guilford Court House, the Legion cavalry had already moved away from the American left flank when William Campbell's riflemen needed their support against a counterattack by Tarleton's dragoons. Campbell later censured Lee's premature departure. And Lee was charged with having come too tardily to the support of Greene after the Legion had succeeded on the left flank while the rest of the army was suffering reverses. In the Battle of Eutaw Springs, as the Americans began to push the British back, Lee's cavalry was unavailable to oppose the British dragoons and complete the rout of the enemy infantry; Lee was in another part of the field with the Legion infantry, while his cavalry awaited orders. Later in the battle, when Greene hoped to defeat the British cavalry in the open, his aide could not find Lee to give the order for attack; so the Legion's charge was led by a subordinate, whom the British dragoons drove back. Lee's separation from his cavalry attracted special notice because the army narrowly lost its chance for victory in that hard-fought battle. Lee's own account, written a few weeks afterward, blamed the missed opportunity on a variety of vicissitudes but took pains to prove the activity of his unit: "The Legion lost every fourth man engaged, which is the proportion of loss in the army."[59] In later years he argued that the battle would have been won if his cavalry had joined him instead of being ordered on the unsuccessful charge that he had not led.

Lee's most recent biographer convincingly refutes the contemporary censure of Lee's conduct; Nathanael Greene soon compensated for his reticent official report of the battle by subsequent praise.[60] However, both the Battle of Eutaw Springs and the criticism troubled Lee in ways that vindication could not assuage. He had seen more of his men die in one day than in months of partisan operations. He had lost "the bright prospect of personal glory," and after the battle he had, for the first recorded time during the war, fallen "exceeding ill of a fever," which he blamed on "the heat of the weather, & the exertions in the field of Eutaw."[61] He was carried with the army on a litter. One of the most vehement postwar defenders of Lee's actions at Eutaw Springs acknowledged that "Lee had every requisite for his command and station, except personal strength, in which he was very defective."[62] His physical weakness handicapped him more in head-on battle than in partisan warfare. Despite his creditable exercise of command on the battlefield, that was not the kind of combat in which he most fully excelled. Like other sick soldiers that summer, Lee soon recovered from his fever after the army reached the High Hills of Santee; but he could not change his physique. He would never be able to rely primarily on bodily strength. His mind, his discipline, and his good horses had won him pre-eminence as a partisan. He had used them to good effect at Eutaw Springs. Still, he had come away not wearing new laurels but lying flat on his back.

Though Lee might know or even prove that his critics

erred in their accounts, the hostile talk touched still more sensitive spots. Did not Lee's well-known caution and preference for stratagem over the precipitant charge betray "a shyness" in him?[63] After the war, a former officer of the Legion indignantly wrote of the accusations, "Even personal courage has been denied him."[64] This latent innuendo recurred in the censure of Lee. Why the haste to get out of Paulus Hook before doing more damage? Why so quick to reach terms with doomed enemy garrisons in South Carolina? Why had he been somewhere else when needed at crucial points on the battlefield?

This strain of criticism attacked what might seem to have been one of Lee's least exposed points. Hardly anyone had more often braved the enemy, struck, and survived. After all, the frequency and success of Lee's conspicuous exploits had stimulated much of the resentment over favoritism shown to him. But no one could oblige the critics to be consistent, and no refutation of specific complaints could fully rebut the tenor of such questions because they tacitly challenged the worth of the whole method of warfare to which Lee had given most energy. In doing so they questioned both his willingness to face death and his pre-eminence as a patriot.

Lee himself stressed the importance of brave service in battle. A special assignment kept him away from the army during the Battle of Monmouth in June of 1778, and his absence led him to write afterward to Anthony Wayne: "The name of Monmouth reproaches me to the very soul."[65] The fullest service lay in combat. The revolutionaries' call for courage in the fight against Britain did not measure the patriot's worth solely by the effectiveness of his efforts. The survival of independence, Americans believed, would depend on the moral strength of the men who defended it. Discipline and skill, while useful, could not alone demonstrate this strength or substitute for it. In the eyes of revolutionaries, courage could not be proven by retreat, and for most of Lee's exploits retreat was as important as assault. The partisan fighter often risked death and did valuable duty for the cause. But as long as he could flee, he left unanswered the question, How strong was his will to defeat the enemies of liberty? The revolutionaries based their Revolution on their claim to superior moral strength, which during war seemed fundamentally embodied in physical courage. Since first embracing the art of war, Lee had taken special pains to establish this strength above all. Yet, even more than his light physique, it proved to be the point at which he felt most vulnerable to censure—not because he had achieved less than others but because his anxiety surpassed his achievements. In later years, when he wanted to question the revolutionary dedication of his political rival Thomas Jefferson, he would impugn Jefferson's courage in war. It was the most damning accusation Lee knew.

A still greater disappointment awaited Lee: the failure of the last and in some respects most audacious of his cunning raids on the enemy. In December 1781, he found the weak point in the defenses of the British garrison on Johns Island, South Carolina. On one or two nights a month the tide was low enough to allow the Legion, reinforced by other Continental units, to wade from the mainland to the island undetected and trap the enemy garrison. Lee spent weeks gathering intelligence and devising intricate plans for "an enterprise more brilliant than all the past exploits in the course of the Southern war." Nathanael Greene approved the assault, though he felt anxious about sending troops across water controlled by the enemy. He wrote Lee: "I am afraid you are to[o] confident of your strength." Lee's enthusiasm, however, was shared by Lieutenant Colonel John Laurens, who, after several years as an aide to George Washington, had taken a field command. The two young men collaborated in the enterprise, with

Laurens as the senior lieutenant colonel. Lee recalled that they "were willing to stake their reputation and lives on the correctness of the estimate they had formed" of their soldiers' discipline and valor. The troops shared this confidence. On the night of the attack, December 28, 1781, the commanders told the men the details of the plan. When Lee and Laurens said they believed that no enemy, even of equal numbers, could resist the Continentals without being destroyed, "a burst of applause ensued from the ranks."

But the soldiers never got the chance to execute the elaborate plan. The rear column, in its march from camp toward the point of crossing the water, took a wrong turn and got lost. While the column was wandering through the fields of a plantation, the tide began to rise in the river. The vanguard of the forward column, which had already crossed to the enemy island undetected, could no longer expect sufficient support and had to return to the mainland through the rising chest-high water. Lee had enjoyed the "exhilarating" experience, as his men first waded toward the island in the darkness, of hearing the sentries on the nearby British boats cry: *"All is safe."* Now, forced to recall his men "when every heart glowed with anticipations of splendid glory," he experienced "irremediable disappointment." He blamed himself for failing to post a guide at the place where the rear column had missed the route. "This omission," he later wrote, "cannot be excused." What seemed to be unaccountable accidents in military operations, he believed, "generally spring from negligence or misconduct; and, therefore, might be considerably diminished, if not entirely arrested, by unceasing attention." The next day Lee was writing to Greene with plans for new operations, partly because "Laurens & myself both hope for opportunitys . . . to repay us for our present mortification." But these could not fully replace "an enterprise surpassed by none throughout our war in grandeur of design."[66]

In the autumn of 1781, Greene had sent Lee to Virginia

to seek the help of the French Navy in combined operations against the British in Charleston. Lee had watched the surrender of Cornwallis's army at Yorktown and knew that the war would soon end. He had planned the raid on Johns Island to be the pivotal victory in the liberation of the southernmost states, as well as the climax of his wartime achievements. Before the attack he had secured from Greene the promise of a leave of absence "if the affair succeeds."[67] Now Lee could not go back to Virginia with a new triumph that would refute the criticisms of his privileged status and his behavior in battle.

Lee would still go back to Virginia, though. His decision to leave the Legion while it was still on active duty is one of the most fully documented episodes in his career, yet none of the correspondence makes his motives fully explicit. He claimed too many motives. By itself, any one of them might have seemed sufficient cause to resign. Yet he would not take direct responsibility for choosing to quit. Instead, he portrayed himself as a reluctant victim of circumstance and, even as he left the army, assured Greene: "Whenever you think me necessary to you, I will come at the risk of every thing in this world."[68] This at a time when Greene was trying to convince him not to leave. Lee's stated reasons included his ill health, his intent to get married, his belief that Greene had shamed him by slighting public praise of the Legion, his suspicion that Greene was preferring John Laurens in order to please General Washington, his "distress" over "ill natured insinuations" about his conduct.[69] Each of these motives could have been traced to specific events or times; yet none of them had produced a clear decision to resign. Lee, in his discontent, referred first to one, then to another, then to several.

Lee was not receptive to similar pleas from the mouths of other officers. When General Daniel Morgan decided to go home and nurse his health after his victory at Cowpens, Lee tried to persuade him to stay with the army, warning him that resignation might lead people to believe "that his reputation had been accidentally acquired, and could not survive the vicissitudes of war." Nevertheless, "he left us," Lee later wrote, "and left impressions with many not very favorable to that purity of patriotism essential to round the character of a great soldier."[70] Similarly, when some Legion officers took offense at Greene's orders after Lee had gone home and submitted their resignations, Lee told them that he had always considered protest by resignations to be "ineffectual, as they are injurious to the discipline of armys."[71] Reputation, patriotism, and discipline were the cardinal points of pride that Lee felt in his own military career; he could hardly have abandoned it without taking to heart scme of his own admonitions.

However, he seemed not to regard his own departure as a willed decision in the manner of Morgan or the Legion officers. Instead, he moved under the influence of what his friends called "distress," "delicate sensibility," "anxiety," and "melancholy."[72] Shortly before heading back to Virginia in February 1782, he referred to "my grief" and "misery," saying, "if I may judge from my feelings for months past, I ought to dispond."[73] In his own mind, Lee did not choose to leave the army but felt that he had to do so. He could not even face saying goodbye to Greene: "The ceremony of parting from you & my friends in the army is so affecting, that I wish to decline it personally."[74]

Neither Lee's disappointments in combat nor his reiterated motives for leaving the army can alone account for his behavior. His fellow officers repeatedly assured him that he gravely misjudged his own position. He had their love, an unequaled military reputation in America and Europe, and the grateful admiration of all but "the envious and illnatured part of society."[75] In quitting the cause before the war was fully won, Lee may have responded to an even deeper distress than he could explain—a distress of which his public disappointments were only symptoms.

The Revolutionary War had caught Lee up in a more

deeply flawed experience than the successful union of reputation, patriotism, and discipline to which he aspired. Although in later years he retained an active military ambition, a keen interest in armed conflict, and a dedication to increasing America's military strength, he never again spoke of war with the enthusiasm characteristic of his early years. When, in 1792, he sought the command of the Western Army partly in order to be distracted from grief over the death of his wife and son, he wrote: "I am very indifferent as to my destiny & therefore war suits me as well as peace."[76] Combat and command could still preoccupy him and engage his mind, but they no longer promised the unalloyed triumph he had sought and not found in the Revolution. Twenty years later, Lee's objections to the War of 1812 originated not only in the partisan politics and diplomacy of the Early National Period but also in his memory of the war he had seen. The achievements of Lee and his Legion had been tainted—by a selfish populace that ignored its own cause and its own army, by an impotent government that could not mobilize its own resources, by a civil war that threatened to overwhelm discipline with anarchic blood lust, by some fellow soldiers' petty envy that would cheat Lee of his standing as a commander and a patriot. Perhaps even more distressing, Lee and his Legion had sometimes failed themselves and the cause—in lost battles, aborted raids, heedless cruelty. By comparative standards they could claim first place in the army, but Lee's ambition as an officer and a patriot had not appealed to comparative standards. He had obtained unique status and special privileges through striving to subject the vicissitudes of war to the control of his mind. By this criterion he had experienced some disheartening failures and tainted successes. Nor had his accomplishments won him the degree of gratitude from less brilliant officers and less conspicuously patriotic civilians that he claimed as his due. Nothing within the power of the Legion or its commander could make the end of the war as glorious as the beginning had promised.

Throughout his later life, Lee praised the American triumph in the Revolutionary War. He made its history the text by which to judge the orthodoxy of Americans' peacetime conduct. At the same time, the heresies he later deplored—the crimes that betrayed the Revolution—had first come to his notice when they had arisen within the Revolution itself during the war years. His memory of the Revolutionary War was divided against itself. He could write that America's eight years' war brought forth "a display of genius"; he could also write about it, "The consequence of war is a state of mental ire."[77] Genius and ire might rise together, but one held out inspiration, the other fear. For thirty years Lee tried to fulfill the inspirations of the war and to quell its fears. By the time he had become a politician, a general, and a historian, he had extracted from the Revolution a set of principles, heroes, exemplary deeds, and remembered emotions that thereafter embodied for him the true legacy of the war. These he glorified in order to combat the false legacy of failures and crimes which, although prominent in wartime, could not claim to represent the Revolution. However, in 1781 and 1782, Lee had not yet attained the clarity of this distinction. His pride and his shame merged in confused conflict. He claimed a pride in leadership that he felt unable to persevere in; he felt shame over disgrace which most others could not see. The mind that had gloried in being imaginative, purposeful, and decisive fell into a melancholy that caused him to abandon the war. He pleaded ill health, probably with good reason. Repeatedly in the years to come, defeat of his ideals would coincide with sickness. But his distress had deeper symptoms than physical ailments. As he left the army, he tried to forswear his most characteristic trait: "My ambition might have been very great once, it is not so now, & I rest contented with my cross fortune."[78]

The circumstances of Lee's departure gave him little consolation for leaving the Legion. In his last days with the army, he worried about increased desertion—an "extraordinary spirit" affected the Legion—and about "the state of the horses" due to scarcity of forage.[79] Some of Lee's fellow officers spread exaggerated accounts of his resentment and thereby worsened his relations with Greene and Laurens. The tale-bearers said that Lee was leaving because Greene would give Laurens a senior command, that Lee had accused Greene of duplicity and meanness.

Although Laurens's joining the Southern Army did not cause Lee's departure, Lee evidently resented the seniority of the young man who had become a senior lieutenant colonel by joining Washington's staff while his father, Henry Laurens, was president of the Continental Congress. John Laurens's demeanor in combat differed sharply from Lee's. He sought danger and bloodshed without carefully weighing the potential gains or using the caution that could save lives. Before Laurens's rashness made him one of the last and least necessary casualties of the war, Greene said that Laurens "wishes to fight much more than I wish he should."[80] As Lee left for home, he warned Greene against choosing an incautious officer to command the Legion: "If he is an experimenter, he will waste the troops very fast."[81]

But not even this prospect could keep Lee with his men, and sure enough Greene separated the Legion infantry from the cavalry and incorporated the infantry into a larger unit under Laurens's command. The Legion officers tried to force Greene to rescind these orders. When they resigned in protest, he called their bluff by accepting their resignations. Most of them reconsidered and stayed in the army, though Laurens never won their full loyalty. While the Legion's special status, its internal harmony, and its standing with the southern commander deteriorated, Lee was at home in Virginia, receiving the story piecemeal. A friend wrote, "Your absence from the Corps has been too evident to escape even the unobserving."[82] Lee kept saying, evidently with imperfect conviction, "I am ... out of the way of public affairs"; "I have a disgust with all such important topics"; "I wish to become truely obscure."[83] Greene perceptively wrote to him, "I am sorry to hear you continue so melancholy. I was in hopes a change of scenes and new society would have restored you to your former good humour and chearfulness."[84] Instead, Lee continued to worry about the Legion he had left and to complain that Greene was forgetting him.

"You are going home; and you will get married; but you cannot cease to be a Soldier."[85] Nathanael Greene's prophecy was confirmed many times in Lee's life. But Lee was more than a soldier out of place in peacetime. He had also become a soldier out of place in war. His life's theme was his attempt to unite personal achievement and national glory through the purposeful activity of the mind. Warfare remained for him a proven approximation of this goal, and he returned to its patriotic professionalism both in his memories of the Revolution and in his postwar career. Nevertheless, these recurring reminders of his special military talents should not obscure his turn away from war before the end of the Revolution or his lifelong feelings of aversion to the combat at which he excelled.

At the time of his departure from the army, Lee likened his fate to the court-martial, suspension, and dismissal from the American army of the Englishman General Charles Lee. Harry had written his first enthusiastic letter about the study of Mars to the general, who a few years later had called him a born soldier. Now Charles Lee had been forced out of the army after insulting first George Washington and then Congress. Nathanael Greene wrote to Harry, "You say no Officer has been treated so cruelly as you have except General Lee.

This is strange indeed."[86] Greene did not understand the ways in which Harry could see his own disappointment in the war reflected in the fall of the veteran officer he had first admired. To outward appearances, Harry Lee, far from being court-martialed, was leaving despite repeated pleas to stay and effusive praise of his achievements—leaving, at a time of adversity, the Legion he had once called "a command I most sincerely love."[87] He did not yet know that in other fields still greater disappointments awaited him. But he could no longer find a sufficiently worthy purpose for himself in war. He aspired to higher distinction and more satisfactory accomplishments than he had yet attained. His friends knew how difficult it was for him to change fronts while the enemy still threatened. Crazy Jack Stewart, another flamboyant young lieutenant colonel who would be dead before peace came, wrote to Lee: "I hope you are in good Health and enjoy a great Deal of Happiness—you have made a Violent effort to procure it."[88]

THE QUEEN
OF STRATFORD

In the spring of 1781, Light-Horse Harry Lee wrote his brother to brag about the achievements of the Southern Army in the months since the Legion had joined it, promising him that "if fortu[ne] honor us, we shall make our country happy." In closing he asked, "how is the Queen of Stratford?"[1] In earlier years Harry had gotten to know his younger cousin Matilda Lee, the granddaughter of one of his uncles. She inherited the Westmoreland County mansion called Stratford Hall that Thomas Lee had built on the Potomac. By 1782 she was nineteen years old, had "a fine figure" and a bantering sense of humor, could look "strikingly picturesque," and played Scarlatti, Corelli, Campioni, and Tartini on the harpsichord. She was called "a fine lady with a fine fortune," and soon after Harry's return to Virginia they got married. Matilda did not like the deep tan that Harry had acquired in the Carolinas, but she learned that the skin he had not exposed to the sun was "as fair as a lily," in the best style of eighteenth-century beauty.[2]

Lee had left the army primarily because combat no longer seemed to offer him the degree of personal glory or patriotic accomplishment that his ambition demanded. But Lee's ambition had not grown more modest by reason of the disappointment and shock he had experienced in war. On the contrary, these blows to his ideal of conspicuous virtue in the nation's service gave him greater urgency in his approach to peace. He was determined to achieve the union of individual and national happiness that the Revolution had promised but that the course of fighting had marred. For Lee, marriage was a swift and fitting contrast to his life as a soldier. Major Ichabod Burnett wrote from the Southern Army, "I am sure you will find in the happiness of domestick life a pleasing balm for every wound your feelings may receive from the changes in military affairs."[3] But Matilda Lee would learn, and in part symbolize after her early death, the ways in which Harry Lee's love for his family and for the benefits of peace contained public aspirations as bold as any in war. The Revolution was never far from his thoughts. When Matilda bore their first child, in 1783, Harry departed from family tradition and named the boy Nathanael Greene Lee.

Although Lee remembered his fellow soldiers and spoke often of the Revolutionary War, he did not spend all his time looking backward. Instead, he tried to use his genius to shape peace. This attempt was supposed to efface his disappointments as a soldier through the enjoyment of prosperity and love. Lee's grand vision of peace had his family at its center, but he could not long reconcile himself to leading a stable private life. He briefly considered returning to a military career; he held public office; most important, he pursued complex, widespread investments and commercial plans. Eventually, Lee the revolutionary sabotaged the peace of Stratford as surely as if war had come to it. He often held up the family as the saddest victim of war and the greatest blessing of peace. Yet the story of his dedication to peace is also the story of his separation from his family, whose prosperity he ruined. Emotionally, if not militarily, his genius, his activity, and his ambition brought the Revolutionary War home.

When Harry Lee thought about war in the years after he left the army, one of its main cruelties seemed to be its twist-

ing of dedication away from the nurturing of families and toward combat. If the country attained its true destiny, the ideal
American would be "a stout muscular ploughman full of
health full of comfort with his eight or ten blooming children."[4] When Lee described soldiers, he paid special attention
to war's demand that they sacrifice this comfort. He vividly
recalled the emotions of Captain Wahab of the North Carolina militia after troop movements had brought Wahab back
to his own farm, where a loyalist unit had made camp and had
been taken by surprise. While the militia gathered enemy
horses, arms, and equipment, Wahab "spent the few minutes
halt in delicious converse with his wife and children, who ran
out as soon as the fire ceased. . . . Sweetly passed these moments; but they were succeeded by the most bitter." The militia had to flee the pursuing British, and from a distance
Wahab watched the enemy burn his house and leave his family
without shelter. Lee chose this point in his memoirs to para-
phrase one of the most frequently quoted lines of the Revolutionary War: "These were times which tried men's souls."[5]
Loving his family, Wahab had to abandon them so that he
could fight. In Wahab's willingness to choose combat, Lee
dramatized the profound redirection of emotion demanded
by war.

When Lee left the army before the war's end, distressed
by the misconduct he had seen and by his own failure to obtain
a fuller glory, he wanted to end the war's constraint on familial
love. He had observed and enforced this constraint. Neither
Lee nor his favorite colleague among militia commanders,
Francis Marion, got married until after the Revolution. They
had experienced the dedication demanded by combat. In
Marion, Lee saw the total, purposeful self-control of the con-
summate soldier. "The procurement of subsistence for his
men, and the contrivance of annoyance to his enemy, engrossed his entire mind." Marion thought much, spoke sel-

dom, dressed plainly, ate little, drank water, and scorned wealth. "Even the charms of the fair . . . seemed to be lost upon him." They were not lost on Lee: one of the most welcome features of liberating the South Carolina low country was the hospitality its women showed the army. To "the ripest and most symmetrical beauty" they added a combination of sympathy for soldiers' hardships and "the dawning smile of hope; the arrival of their new guests opening to them the prospect of happier times."[6] Yet even in looking at women more closely than Marion seemed to do, Lee could not forget the discipline with which the soldier had to sacrifice feelings to war. When he ordered Captain Allen McLane's troopers to join the Legion in New Jersey in 1780, he told McLane to "manifest your zeal for the public, & your love for your cavalry brethren" by making top speed. "Touch not at Annapolis, Baltimore or Philada. Sensual gratification must be sacrificed."[7] In turning toward peace sooner than his fellow soldiers, Lee sought "the charms of the fair" in a marriage that he would not allow war to delay. When he left the army and became a husband, he believed that he was moving from melancholy to happiness—happiness that war alone had impeded and that peace now would guarantee. Late in life he opposed the policies that led to the War of 1812 partly because they threatened this ideal: "for 50 years we ought to cultivate peace with zeal, that our girls & lads surrounded with the comfort of the plenty & bliss of our country may think first of love & next of its fruits."[8] As he looked forward in the 1780s to the almost limitless growth and happiness of America, he saw in peace a source of dedication and glory far worthier than the deprivations and cruelties of fighting the British.

However, Lee's temperament would not consistently accommodate itself to the domestic life he claimed to want. The opportunities of peacetime gave him a new arena in which to defy death by the inventiveness of stratagems even more grandiose than those he had executed in war. He redirected his ambition toward betterment for his family and his country, but he still equated ambition with life. As an entrepreneur, Lee tried to promote himself from regimental army officer to field marshal of continental enterprises. Although he no longer staked lives in combat, the risks manipulated by Lee's active mind grew larger. Failure could seem no less fatal. Part of the fertility of his genius originated in desperation. For decades after the British had stopped chasing him, he remained preoccupied with mobility. By enterprise rather than with horses he would evade captivity—this time the captivity of an inactive, unproductive country. After the storming of Paulus Hook in 1779, he acknowledged, "Had I been unsuccessful, I was determined to leave my corpse within the enemys lines."[9] Lee would not become a prisoner. Many of his fellow officers uttered similarly melodramatic declarations during the war. But Lee also carried this fervor into his peacetime campaigns. His penchant for the schemes of a fertile imagination would last as long as he lived.

Indeed, he could not altogether abandon his affinity for fighting. Most of Lee's enterprises after the Revolutionary War sought the improvement of peace. At the same time, despite his attachment to his family and his enthusiasm for its well-being, he never fully forsook his earliest love. The intensity of combat could attract a devotion that went beyond military duty or delight in expertise. Proficiency in war demanded unique dedication and abilities that Lee's other, later ambitions would barely tap. He spoke of himself as "wedded to my sword," and "affectionately wedded to my officers & troops."[10] These figures of speech expressed the gratification that Lee derived from his own skill and from effectively employing the skill in collaboration with men he could trust. No amount of prudence, discipline, or experience could alone ensure that a soldier would possess the genius for war that enabled one to excel as a commander. The secret had more in common with inspiration than with professionalism. Lee's word of highest praise for an officer was "aetherial." Washington was uniquely gifted because his mind had received from heaven "an uncommon share of its aetherial spirit."[11] Sir Henry Clinton, by contrast, was not a great soldier: "Heaven had not touched his mind with its aetherial spark. He could not soar above the ordinary level."[12] Lee could know the difference because he had been able to "soar" with the Legion. In fact, the idea that his genius might be questioned or circumscribed proved intolerable to him, so essential was this feeling of inspiration. "Your temper is warm and your heart affectionate," Nathanael Greene wrote to him soon after Lee left the army.[13] In later years Lee's immoderate, wholehearted enthusiasms could not fully recreate the genius of violence. Despite his oft-repeated preference for peace and his energetic efforts to improve it, Lee did not develop a comparable devotion to the new skills it demanded. The noise of business sounded like a muffled echo of the call of combat.

Even the central blessing of peace, the love of his family, became for Lee a reflection of his glory reminiscent of his military career. The *Virginia Gazette,* in its report of the wedding of Ann Hill Carter and the widower Governor Henry Lee, called him "Virginia's favorite Young Souldier."[14] Lee's self-dramatizing flamboyance endeared him to his wife and children. In their eyes he always remained the grand patriot he aspired to be. Ann saved a copy of Charles Stedman's *History of the American War* for Harry from the liquidation of his estate in his insolvency—he needed it for writing his memoirs; his daughter, Lucy Grymes Lee Carter, recommended that her cousin read "the Memoirs of the War written by my dear Father"; his sons listened to him lecture them on the best way to defend Virginia from an attack by sea; three of the boys spent substantial amounts of time in their adult years defending their father's reputation as a soldier and perpetuating the memory of his public services.[15] When he resigned from the army, Lee said that he wanted to become "obscure," but such a wish did not determine his stature within his family. There, even after he had left them, he was "the departed hero."[16]

As a professional soldier, Lee was devoted to violence, no matter with how much skill and order he might grace killing. As a husband, he was devoted to his family and its increase. Beginning the year after he left the army, Lee, like most American husbands of his era, kept fathering children over a period of twenty-four years. During his last years he was preoccupied with trying to imagine and to influence the future lives of his sons and daughters. However, this change from taking life to giving it did not fully expel the temperament of war from Lee's peacetime years. War had also meant movement: not only did his revolutionary service range from New York to Georgia but the Legion was especially valuable for the speed with which it could travel long distances and surprise the enemy. "For rapid marches," Nathanael Greene told Lee, "you exceed Lord Cornwallis and everybody else."[17] Peace would not require such movement; Lee sought a stationary family life at Stratford, where he lived for twenty-eight years after the war. Yet, judging from the large number of his letters dated from other places, he was often away from Stratford. Business deals and political office kept his fondness for movement alive. Other, longer absences usually indicated disruption in his life: Matilda Lee's illness, Indian war, civil insurrection, bankruptcy, exile. The continuing attraction of war, which defied Lee's efforts to replace it, had a counterpart in the intrusion of his combative temperament into his ideal of peace. Even when he was not trying to be a soldier again, his constant activity left him preoccupied with struggle. These disruptions, like his final restless, haphazard wanderings in search of health in the West Indies, meant the gradual ruin of the stability Lee had sought at Stratford. Although he often lapsed and eventually failed, he nevertheless tried to give up a partisan's mobile struggles and live where the household outnumbered the strangers and the mind's eye saw descendants rather than enemies.

The tension between Lee's love of his family and his enthusiasm for war grew more pressing during the three years when he had no wife. The years 1790 to 1793, the time between the death of Matilda Lee and the marriage of Harry Lee to Ann Hill Carter, were important ones for Lee: he became governor of Virginia; he redefined his views and alliances in national partisan politics; he made extensive investments. And, although he could not know that one phase of his career was ending, he sought for the last time the field command of an army in combat. The command Lee most wanted—the Western Army, fighting Indians—went to Anthony Wayne; the command Lee also sought and was offered—a major general's commission in the army of Revolutionary France—he finally declined. These military ambitions no longer expressed the ingenuous enthusiasm with which Lee had first approached "the study of Mars" almost twenty years earlier. Now he wanted to recapture a purposefulness he had found in neither politics nor finance since his first wife's death had broken the family. His turn to army life was a qualified one, a recourse despite misgivings, perhaps—judging from his plaintive letter to Washington after the appointment of Wayne—an expression of desperation.[18] Lee seems to have sought military life again not as the first of his ambitions but as the only remaining activity that offered him the sure prospect of accomplishment. However, that choice no longer lay open to him. He did not disavow his skill in combat or his readiness to fight; he said that an army command instead of the governorship would have taken him to "scenes more congenial to my genius & to my habits"; he could still have spoken, as he had in 1779, of "the love he has uniformly possessed for arms."[19] But war had become for him an unhappy form of love. When he gave it up in 1793, he was committed to peace.

After only a few years of married life at Stratford, Matilda Lee contracted a lingering illness. In 1790 she died, at the age of twenty-seven, and she was followed in 1792 by her oldest son. Harry wrote in September 1792: "I am still depressed in my mind & continue to be subject to unavailing woe."[20] The two deaths "removed me from the happy enjoyment of life." In his "misery," he turned toward combat "as the best resort to my mind in its affliction." In April 1793, when he wrote Washington that he was "bred to arms" and now wanted to "return to my profession," he meant not just military life but war. In late March he had been "almost in the act of embarkation" to join the French army. By May, however, he decided that this year-old plan was "madness"; yet even then, he gave it up "with extreme reluctance."[21] Love for his wife and son had been the heart of peace for him. Reft of them, he sought war. In it lay an equivalent, though converse, intensity of devotion and activity of mind.

But Lee could not recapture the dedication that he had brought to the Revolution and then lost before its end. Confronted with these later opportunities, he was not thoroughgoing enough to embrace a war that revived evils he had seen before. When, in January 1792, he expressed his willingness to command the Western Army, he stipulated: "Of course I could not engage in a fruitless effort, & I should consider the effort vain, unless the composition of the army was fitted for the war, the officers suitable, & the supplys abundant."[22] After his failure to receive that command, he also hoped in vain that European conflict might avoid some of the flaws that had marred the American Revolution. He said that he wanted "fair war on terms of honor," with reliable supplies and united public support. Without assurance of these—that is, with the

likelihood of reliving his earlier wartime disappointments—
"to go would be completion of my lot of misery."[23] In that
case, Lee would not be leading a small, well-trained, well-sup-
plied, élite unit that spurred while the army plodded. Instead,
all the complexities of command, supply, civil politics, and domestic dissension or obstruction would confound his "genius."
These impediments would mock his ambitious imagination by
denying him the control of events. Failing in his futile attempt
to find a more orderly war, he would be caught up in a violence that betrayed his "profession" and made war as purpose-
less as peace seemed now that he was alone. By the time he
asked for advice, Lee can hardly have doubted that Washington would warn him against enlisting with a cause that was "in
the highest paroxysm of disorder."[24] His relative William Lee
refused to believe that Harry would join "the savage Canabals
of Paris."[25] When Light-Horse Harry Lee saw that war
would still be as chaotic as he remembered it, he decided not
to return to the profession he said he loved. He told Alexander
Hamilton, "I mean now to become a farmer & get a wife
as soon as possible."[26] A month later he married Ann Hill
Carter.

Lee's revolutionary ambition could now flourish only in civilian life. In peacetime he becomes a particularly useful figure
for studying the American Revolution as it changes from resistance to postwar independence because he strove con-
sciously to incorporate into his own life some of the public aspirations of his country. After the war, he did not fully
transform himself from an active, inventive partisan to a man
of seasonal routine and domestic concerns on the plantation.
He became as eager to promote and exemplify peacetime
prosperity as he had been to lead the defeat of the invader.
    The vision of independence that permeated the public

appeals and celebrations of the Revolution eloquently evoked the promise of an unprecedentedly prosperous nation that would eventually include all of North America. In confident, detailed descriptions Americans foresaw spreading agricultural bounty, enriched by international commerce and crowned by a creative culture new to the world because it would rest on the well-being of the whole populace. One of the most ominous threats in Britain's attempt to tighten imperial rule seemed to be a design on the part of the king and his ministers to cheat Americans out of their continent's opportunities for ever-expanding wealth. Instead of opening new lands, new enterprises, and sure riches for many people, the British would confine the colonies to serve as a backward auxiliary to the prosperity of the empire. Only a few favorites then would enjoy the wealth that lay waiting for all who could get at it.

After the British had been defeated, this vision of a flourishing continent remained crucial to Americans' definition of their country's future. The United States, by trying to survive as a republic, was defying one of the most certain laws of history. As thinkers then interpreted the past, republics seemed sure to die because self-government could last only as long as the populace possessed enough virtue to voluntarily sacrifice private interest for the public good. The example of previous republics showed that a free people would eventually grow selfish and prefer their own ease to vigilance on behalf of liberty. Thus the people would become corrupt, and economic dependence would lead to political subjugation and to tyranny. Republics, like individuals, had an ineluctable life progression, and, with the onset of corruption, liberty began to die.

Americans had no guarantee that their new republic would not repeat this familiar cycle. But the possession of a vast and bountiful continent offered hope. If a growing populace could continue to open new land as a basis for economic independence and to enjoy prosperity arising from productivity rather than from artificial concentrations of wealth, perhaps Americans could postpone indefinitely the normal fate of republics. As long as the nation's resources did not confine its citizens so that some must subject themselves to others in order to live, perhaps widespread prosperity would sustain virtue and self-government. Not intimidated by poverty, not tempted by bribes, Americans need not lapse into dependence on men who could control the narrowed avenues to advancement. By this reasoning, the expansion of enterprise and wealth that would accompany independence might not be just the brief flowering that preceded decay. Instead, the republic's capacity to reward its citizens' enterprise might thereby safeguard their, virtue and give liberty long life or even immortality.

Although Lee's skepticism about the reliability of virtue in the populace during the Revolutionary War eventually was followed by a deeper pessimism that came over him late in life, in the 1780s and early 1790s he shared optimistic assumptions about the survival of American independence based on burgeoning prosperity. The confidence with which he linked his own and the country's future to expanding wealth revealed his ideal for America. His love for his wife and children was reflected in his plans for their thriving life in peacetime. Trusting the ability of his intellect to foresee and shape the future, he predicated the family's well-being on the nation's rapid rise to continental grandeur promised by the Revolution.

Lee ended his narrative of the Revolutionary War: "the din of arms yielded to the innocent and pleasing occupations of peace."[27] He extended his expectations of harmony and happiness in private life to the whole country. He saw in peace more than freedom from combat: "Peace to America is in one word, our all," he wrote in 1793.[28] One part of this dedication came from Lee's political opinions and his fear of involving the United States in Europe's wars. Beyond these purposes, he also endowed peace with the great promise of a flourishing country. He seemed to assume that the absence of foreign war and internal discord would permit the fruition of inevitably spreading well-being. The statesman's duty was to secure independence and order so that this process could work unimpeded. The citizen's opportunity was to benefit from the constant growth.

The word "prosperity" regularly recurs in Lee's peacetime writings. It expressed his confident vision of the future at the end of the Revolution, whether he was striving to promote it in the early years or later blaming his political opponents for its failure. After Lee's financial reverses had begun, he said of his investments, "I calculated greatly on the advancing prosperity of the country, in this I have been disappointed."[29] His expectations resembled the eloquent evocations of America's future growth, wealth, and culture that pervaded the rhetoric of the Revolution. The sacrifices and destructiveness of the war would be redeemed by an era of national happiness. When Lee invited James Madison to join him in his investments, he assured Madison: "prosperity to our nation & judicious management of the property would ensure us both a very independant fortune."[30] Lee may not have expected all Americans to get rich, but he hardly doubted that the knowledgeable ones who tried would succeed and enjoy "the solid rewards of public prosperity and individual felicity."[31]

But if peace and independence promised such happiness, what could Lee say to the needy veterans who visited him and wrote to him in the years after the war? Why had victory so often failed to reward the men who had won it? Their misfortunes troubled him. He was one of them; he felt that he still had with the men of the Legion "a relation whose ties cannot be impaired even by the hand of time."[32] In his eyes this relation perpetuated his responsibility for his troops. When the young Captain Lee and a few of his men had been surrounded by the British cavalry in the dawn attack near Valley Forge, he had promised the soldiers barricaded with him, "Henceforth, I consider the fortune of every individual present, as inseparably connected with my own! if we fall, we will fall like brothers! If successful in repelling the enemy . . . my fortune and my interest shall be uniformly employed to increase your comforts, and secure your promotion."[33] In the postwar years, Lee acted almost as if he had made this bond with every Continental soldier. Beginning soon after his return to Virginia in 1782 and continuing until late in his life, he wrote to public officials to find out what provisions Congress and the states had made for veterans and to encourage efforts for those in hardship. He took several of his former soldiers to Stratford as employees or tenants; twenty-five years after the war, men still wrote to him when they needed help. His concern did not stop with men of the Legion but extended to all veterans—"this gallant, friendless and ill treated class of our fellow citizens." The poverty of many of them, sometimes worsened by the denial of pensions due them, mocked the Revolution's promise to sustain virtue with well-being. Yet Lee was building his plans for himself and his country on his ability to make that promise come true. If patriots continued to suffer in peacetime, might Lee's confidence in impending prosperity be misguided? He said that he saw in the forgotten veterans "those spectacles which always fill my mind with Anguish."[34]

Despite the presence of such ghosts at the feast, Lee's mind in the 1780s and the early 1790s was more often filled with anticipation and calculation of the joint success he would share with his country. These plans centered on the river which Lee could see from the windows of Stratford—the Potomac. Inside Stratford Hall, Lee could see reminders of his family's long-standing interest in the great river. The portraits of three generations of Lees looked down on their descendants Harry and Matilda: Richard the Emigrant, one of Virginia's greatest landholders at his death in 1664; the second Richard, who had helped the Fairfax family establish proprietary lordship over the Northern Neck; Matilda's grandfather and Harry's granduncle Thomas—president of the Virginia Council, land agent for the Fairfaxes, president of the Ohio Company of Virginia, promoter of westward migration, builder of Stratford Hall and owner of sixteen thousand acres at the falls of the Potomac, where he hoped to control the commerce that the western population and the Ohio Company's fur trade would send down the river. In the fourth generation, Matilda's father, Philip Ludwell Lee, had planned a town near the falls, to be named Philee. Matilda's uncles had joined the Washington brothers in the Mississippi Company, seeking royal grants of two and a half million acres near the confluence of the Ohio and Mississippi rivers. Light-Horse Harry Lee was in the fifth generation of a family that for one hundred-fifty years had looked at the Potomac and seen wealth.

The western land companies and the plans for the falls of the river had shown more vision than results. The British government had tried to circumscribe the ambitious colonial entrepreneurs and to discourage westward expansion in the years before the American Revolution. Now, American independence had freed the West from this constraint, and Lee joined the men who led the new and even more elaborate development of the Potomac. Before the Revolutionary War began, George Washington and other Virginians had planned to open the river to navigation above the fall line by building canals around the falls of the Potomac and improving the river bed. After the war these plans were revived and expanded. Virginia and Maryland incorporated a company that could raise money by subscription, manage the engineering, and administer the canal. Despite the slow progress of the work, compounded by the company's financial difficulties, the project's admirers remained optimistic. In 1793, a writer in *The Virginia Herald, and Fredericksburg Advertiser* said of the company: "every art which the ingenuity of man could suggest is here displayed. . . . They have surmounted difficulties which were called insuperable, and wealth in abundance ebbs and flows along the channel. . . . The neat profits of the soil are greater, and every thing prognosticates wealth and prosperity."[35] Some of this praise was premature, since the canal had not yet by-passed the Great Falls and thus could not operate as designed. Nevertheless, in the same year George Washington's secretary, Tobias Lear, looked forward with optimism to the shareholders' imminent profits from tolls: "they have a certainty of receiving, on the first opening of the river a handsome percentage on their capital . . . and the increase will be almost incredible." Knowledgeable, conservative men "have no doubt of the capital's producing fifty per cent annually, in less than ten years from the time of the toll's commencing."[36] Henry Lee was one of the early investors. He believed that "if the potomac navigation succeeds . . . it is another strong evidence that difficultys vanish as they are approached."[37]

Difficulties vanish as they are approached. That line, written in 1786, could stand as the motto of Lee's expectations for the nation's future and the financial ventures in which he embodied them. Shares in the Potomac Company were only one of the ways by which he planned to tap the prosperity of the river. He also bought land. He joined a widespread enthusiasm in postwar America for get-rich-quick investments in undeveloped land. He purchased property in Virginia, Kentucky, Pennsylvania, North Carolina, and Georgia. His correspondence is dotted with phrases like these: "a great property"; "well calculated for improvement"; "entitled to as much consideration as any property I ever saw"; "the advantages infinitely exceed that of any spot of ground in the U.S."; "the value of the spot is above present calculation"; "a million or two of acres may be contracted for . . . as easy as so many thousands."[38] In addition to his own purchases, Lee loaned money to others, including $40,000 to the former Superintendent of Finance Robert Morris, who was investing in real estate on a still grander scale.

Two of Lee's principal holdings had close ties to the fortunes of the Potomac. Immediately adjacent to the Great Falls he bought five hundred acres where the canal would pass. To take possession he would have to pay Bryan Fairfax both the £4,000 purchase price and the outstanding unpaid quitrents at the rate of £150 per year. He hoped to raise the money by first contracting to sell at a profit some of this land which he did not yet possess. Seven years after this 1788 purchase, he and others contracted for 200,000 acres farther up the Potomac at a price of three shillings per acre. Not foreseeing that the year 1795 would begin the downturn of land speculation, he believed that between 1795 and 1800 the value of this land would rise 667 percent to twenty shillings per acre. He sought partners in these ventures, assuring his old college friend James Madison that "I consider myself bound to let you have a part of the bargain with me." Stretching the facts a bit, he told Madison that the Potomac was open to navigation and that the Great Falls property would yield money at once: "The spot is magnificent & the canal complete—the advantages for water works beyond my expression." There was "no difficulty but want of cash."[39] When Lee's dreams outran his capital, he regretted that he was losing other opportunities. He told one seller, "I very much want your land"; but, without the necessary money, "I must submit to a relinquishment of a scheme which I had much at heart."[40] Lee's energy might almost have become an end in itself—an activity that sought outlet even at the expense of effectiveness. His old friend recognized this long-standing trait in Lee's character. Even before Lee's financial reverses set in, Madison refrained from

joining his investments, "knowing that the fervor with which
he pursues his objects sometimes affects the estimate he forms
of them."[41]

Lee felt confident of making profits on land because it
would quickly grow more valuable through settlement and improvement, as well as through new investors' anticipation of
future development. At peace and free from Britain, Americans would more rapidly increase in number, open new terri-
tory, then expand their production of agricultural commodi-
ties and their consumption of European manufactured goods.
In the eyes of Lee, Washington, and other promoters of the
Potomac Company, canals at the falls were only the beginning
of a vast, interlocking system of transport that would channel
the trade of the West to the Potomac. After all, Detroit was
348 miles closer to Alexandria, Virginia, than to Montreal; no
Erie Canal yet ran eastward through New York; if a canal
were constructed southward from Lake Erie to Cumberland,
Maryland, all the trade from north of the Ohio River could go
through the Potomac. The company could realize a vision of
harmony, unity, and prosperity on the continental scale that
independence now made possible. When Madison asked
Washington for advice about taking a share in Lee's Great
Falls property, Washington said that Lee's purchase had been
"unexpected" but that, if trade from the Blue Ridge, from
upper Maryland, from parts of Pennsylvania, and from the
western waters were funneled in one direction, "it opens a
field almost too extensive for imagination."[42] Lee assured
Madison that "the views of thousands are pointed to establish-
ments over the mountains for the support of numerous fami-
lys. . . . The potomack river will strengthen our connexion by
the easy exchange it affords of those things mutually
wanted."[43] Lee would even have preferred that Americans
negotiating a treaty with Spain forgo their demand that the
Mississippi River be open to American trade. In the Continen-

tal Congress, Lee, obeying state instructions, voted for this demand; but privately he wanted to let the closed Mississippi force western trade through the Potomac until the population of the West grew much larger. To others this preference for the prosperity of the river might look like private greed. To Lee, the river's wealth, the nation's wealth, and his own had almost become identical. In the Virginia constitutional ratifying convention, Lee defended his preference for an open Potomac and a closed Mississippi by saying: "I united private interest to public interest, not of the whole people of Virginia, but of the United States. I thought I was promoting the real interest of the people."[44]

An open Potomac and the land on its banks would become the apex of America's prosperity. At this apex Lee planned a city on his property at Great Falls. It would grow from nothing in response to limitless opportunities. Along the canals through which would pass the bounty of the West and the productions of Europe, Lee mapped out a complex of wharves, warehouses, mercantile firms, and town residences on streets named after the promoters of the Potomac Company. Converging in one area, on land he had possessed the foresight to buy, the continent's expanding wealth would simultaneously enrich his country, his region, and his family. By improving the future, he could thus aspire to perpetuate independence and prosperity—to give the republic hope for immortality. Memorializing these concentric promises of peace, Lee named his city for the Queen of Stratford: Matildaville.

Even this was not all. In the same year that Matildaville was founded, Lee joined other Virginians in working to bring the national capital to the Potomac. A central location, he believed, would reassure southerners that the federal government had not become a sectional weapon in the hands of the northern states. Lee, perhaps thinking of the urgency of his own plans, warned that failure to move the capital south would "fill every mind with passions," threatening "our peace unity & harmony."[45] From the perspective of Lee and other promoters of the river's development, the relocation of the capital would serve larger purposes than political or sectional compromise. Since the Potomac was destined to become the great channel to the West, no other location for the government could so effectively tie the West's volatile expansion to the original states. By uniting his fortunes with the commercial entrepot and the political center of the continental republic, Lee's genius would fix him at the axis of America's imminent happiness.

Peace brought Lee to Stratford, but it could not keep his mind there. He did not content himself with becoming a farmer or caring for a family or being obscure. He left Stratford to serve as a delegate in Congress, as a delegate in the Virginia General Assembly, and as governor of Virginia. But even while he was at home, his imagination peopled the continent, developed transportation, promoted commerce, and built cities. He could visualize the rising value of faraway lands long before that rise began. Looking out the windows of Stratford, he would see the wealth of two continents flowing up and down the Potomac. All these manifestations of happiness attracted his well-known "zeal" and "fervor." As his congratulations to a newly married friend suggest, the love of a wife and children could enhance the excitement of bold economic ventures: "Happy man, who has . . . so quickly & so permanently fixed his bliss. Anxious before for your success in your extensive schemes, I am doubly so now, as the charming Eliza is to share in all your good."[46] Lee must not simply enjoy peace with his own wife and children; nor must he satisfy himself only with private profits arising from routine opportunities. All who loved peace must benefit from his creativity—a creativity that promised to make his zeal more productive than disordered combat ever could. He said of the opening of the Potomac: "the undertaking is among the most useful which could have occupied the human mind."[47]

Lee's euphoric vision of peace did not become reality. Matildaville was officially founded in 1790, the year that Matilda Lee died. The town never grew to be a worthy monument to the Queen of Stratford: no more than twenty-five lots were ever sold; at its zenith the town had six buildings. Although commerce did use the Potomac, problems of engineering and finance kept the Potomac Company from making its river and canals the avenue for continent-spanning trade. The District of Columbia came to the Potomac, but by 1797, Robert Morris was lamenting to one of his fellow investors in the real estate of the new capital and of Matildaville, "Alas! poor Washington, how much we overrated thy square feet when marching over thy avenues and streets."[48] Meanwhile, the extent and value of Lee's far-flung property—even his title to it—grew less clear. In the second half of the 1790s, his fortunes, like those of other visionaries and speculators, turned downward; instead of optimistically expanding, he was contracting toward bankruptcy.

Even before his ruin, Lee's conduct in peacetime revealed some of the problems that undermined his ideal. When Washington's cabinet reviewed the men available to command the Western Army in 1792, the President said of Lee, "A better head and more resource than any of them, but no economy."[49] Those who knew Lee best seemed to agree with this assessment. Both Matilda Lee's father and Ann Hill Carter Lee's father made bequests to their daughters that excluded Lee from control over the inheritance. Lee's own father excluded him from acting as an executor of the will in which he was the principal heir. One who had seen Lee only during the Revolutionary War might have found these attitudes toward him surprising. For, although he had freely spent his own money to keep the Legion equipped, his trademark as a commander had been the disciplined preservation of his resources—economy of energy and lives, yielding the greatest results from the least loss. Yet in peacetime Lee indulged risk without discipline and ambition without economy. The gift of careful calculation based on accurate intelligence seemed to forsake him. After his death, an obituary said of him: "Too ardent in the pursuit of his objects—too confident in others, he wanted that prudence which is necessary to guard against imposition and pecuniary losses, and accumulate wealth."[50] How could Lee seek prosperity so energetically and yet forget the lessons of self-protection he had learned so well? He seemed to assume that in peacetime his resourcefulness would not be risking "losses" or struggling against "imposition," but would help to create sure wealth.

Lee's optimism clouded his perception of the ways in which he brought about his own ruin by undertaking enterprises that surpassed his power to accomplish. Although he often spoke of vast, quick, easy profits and he surely wanted to get rich, greed was not the only motive that drove him—perhaps not even the strongest. He also wanted to play a central role in the flourishing of an independent America. He wanted to be among the first in peace as he had tried to be among the first in war. In Lee's vision, America would wax prosperous in peace without succumbing to the vices that had marred the war. Yet Lee proved even more susceptible to the excesses of prosperity than to those of combat. He deplored Hamilton's plan for funding the national and state debts and for encouraging manufacturing; yet he asked Hamilton for advance information by which to profit on redemption of the debt. Lee criticized speculation in public securities; yet he advised Madison to purchase public securities in order to use the profits to buy land at Great Falls. Lee finally sought investors at Great

Falls from among the rich men who had profited on the public debt. His self-contradictions arose not only from his eagerness to make money but also from his failure to more fully understand the complexity, the risk, and the competitive selfishness of the economic growth he longed for. He wanted a prosperity that flowed inevitably from the agricultural and commercial plenty of peace, not from the corrupt mysteries of financiers. Even though he explored those mysteries, he approached prosperity as if it were a natural and wholesome fruit of peace, hardly requiring caution and economy. Writing about his overvalued District of Columbia property, he acknowledged: "I am very apt to give liberal sums for any thing I buy, & I suppose I may have done it in the city lots as in many other instances."[51] Rather than profit artificially to the disadvantage of his countrymen, he hoped to promote and share wealth for all. Instead, his limitless ambition corrupted his ideal. Perhaps he was slow to see this connection because, after his escape from the abuses of war, his new vision was his last hope.

If anything, Lee's impetus to achieve great effects with his venturous genius was stronger in peace than in war, since he risked not only himself but also his family. Some of his bad investments and unrepaid loans to other speculators were made with money that came from his wife, his children, and other relatives. He of course intended that they should benefit from his success. In fact, however, he had sacrificed their welfare and finally large pieces of the Stratford estate itself to his energetic, misguided enterprise. When Lee's brother recommended Lee's oldest son for a government job in 1816, he reminded President James Madison that Harry Lee's "errors & misfortunes have placed his son in a situation very different from that which his early expectations gave him a just right to hope."[52] Lee believed that his family was his first love, yet instead of protecting it, he had made it more vulnerable. The continental designs of generations of Lees had crumbled in his hands. His pursuit of the rewards of a newly free country left his family the victims of his ambition, as other families had in wartime been the victims of combat.

Peace played Lee false. If a stable life as a farmer and a husband could have assuaged his disappointments in war, he could have found it at Stratford with much greater ease than did many other veterans who, as he had seen, lacked even that much. But the American Revolution seemed to promise him a more glorious victory that would make his genius the instrument of his country's immortality. Finding this promise crippled by violence, selfishness, and innuendo in wartime, he strove in the following years to make the happiness of peace more nearly perfect than the glory of fighting had been. Victory in this struggle would discharge the duty that the Revolution imposed on those who had sought an independent America: to secure the nation's future by perpetuating virtuous patriotism. Lee could not rest content with his private well-being any more than he could settle for routinely executing military orders or handling Washington's paperwork as an aide de camp. The ideal of revolutionary virtue made the patriot responsible for creating as well as enjoying the prosperity on which America's survival depended. Lee tried to demonstrate in postwar enterprise a creativity that would fulfill the purposes of independence free from the taints of war.

A future as bountiful, virtuous, and secure as the revolutionary generation envisioned was as improbable as a war that avoided viciousness, greed, and civil conflict. The Revolution's most visionary promises could never be fully won, and this unattainability left other patriots besides Lee looking back at lives marred by failure. With some of Lee's contemporaries, this perversion of the Revolution was dramatic, even lurid: Robert Morris's grandiose investment plans ending in a debtor's cell; Charles Thomson's intimate knowledge of the Revolution's political secrets ending in his disgruntled destruction of his manuscripts; Aaron Burr's rise to the vice presidency ending in political defeat, a duel, and a trial for treason. Others, though not so fully isolated from their former successes, nevertheless ended their careers distressed by their country's betrayal of their revolutionary efforts: John Adams, defeated for re-election to the presidency, spent part of his retirement trying to make sure that historians would accurately report his many revolutionary services, which had been scorned by the partisans who called him a monarchist; Patrick Henry, who had built an unmatched popular reputation as a guardian of liberty against governmental power, ended his days damning French infidels, supporting the Alien and Sedition Acts, and winning election to Congress as a Federalist. Even those Americans whose political careers seemed singularly successful—Washington, Jefferson, Samuel Adams— found cause for bitterness in their later years. They deplored partisan malice and the corruption of America's independence by luxury or by foreign influence; and they feared that their visions of the country's future would die with them. Although Federalists were losing their claim to guide the country and although land speculators were losing their visionary empires, the end of the eighteenth century and the early years of the nineteenth created other losers as well. No matter what their politics or their investments, dreamers were losers. The prospect of American independence had stimulated dreams of harmony, liberty, and prosperity which—however diversely interpreted—had in common their partial defeat by events after independence. In the experience of this disappointment, Henry Lee's career carried a familiar pattern to an extreme degree. Lee's ruin was more spectacular than most, partly because he tried more single-mindedly to make his unrealistic version of the Revolution's promise come true.

Lee's oldest son, who inherited a depleted Stratford and did not manage to keep it in the family, later wrote of his father: "Gen. Lee entered into a course of sanguine and vi-sionary speculations, endeavouring to acquire wealth, not by rational and productive industry, but by a combination of bar-gains which could scarcely benefit one party without injury to the other, and which were often mutually detrimental. To the task of extending and diversifying these transactions so as to make the success of one compensate if possible for the failure of others, he devoted no little amount of misapplied talent and activity."[53] "Activity" remained Lee's watchword in peace as in war. His ambition obliged him to defy the forces that might confine him—tyranny from abroad, corruption and loss of virtue in America, the constraint of a plantation or a region which did not prosper. Such confinement, in its own way, seemed as fatal to Lee as capture by the enemy in war. When one of his friends was jailed for debt in 1797, Lee said, "I think it would have been comparative humanity to have put him to death rather than thus detained."[54] The paralysis of ge-nius frightened Lee as did few other fates. Against this threat he tried to mobilize the resources of a continent. He hoped that peace could turn his activity toward the betterment of his family. But nothing—not even his family's peril—could still his striving. He could defy this danger only by guaranteeing the survival of the Revolution that he had helped to win.

No military enemy but rather Lee's own schemes first put him in prison. By the time he declared himself insolvent, mistrust of him and of his vision of the future had gone deeper than defeat at the hands of political opponents, deeper than demands by his creditors—it had penetrated the home that for almost thirty years he had equated with peace. While Light-Horse Harry was in jail in 1809, he repeatedly asked Ann to wait for him at Stratford. "Mr. Lee constantly assures me," she wrote, "his intention is, to live with his family, after his release from his present situation." But, for her, Stratford was no longer "the part of the world I wished to fix in." "I gave

him a positive promise" that "I should not take any step towards fixing myself elsewhere" until he got out of jail, "re-
serving to myself the right of choosing my place of residence
afterwards."[55]

UNION

WHILE HE WAS STILL A YOUNG CAPTAIN, HARRY LEE assured his regimental commander that he wanted to avoid being "accused of local partiality, which I conceive improper in any officer."[1] This desire to place professionalism above regional ties gave an early example of the dedication to national union that Lee took from the Revolutionary War. Although he wavered in this commitment while he was opposing Hamilton's revenue program, the rest of Lee's career, from the war years until his death, demonstrated his anxious concern that Americans remain united. Unlike most of his contemporaries, Lee could not regard the federal union as a provisional compact, subject to dissolution if it seemed to conflict with liberty. Liberty and independence could not survive without the federal union; in fact, Lee believed, they were threatened even by the erosion of domestic unity through political antagonism. Division would destroy the central guarantor of the country's future: "peace, that blessing so inestimable to America." Together, peace and union secured America's prosperity, "which can only grow out of national identity."[2]

The Revolutionary War showed Lee what happened when union was weakened or lost. These lessons impressed him, and he often repeated them for the benefit of those Americans who seemed not to understand the dangers he had seen. The Revolution had been that worst of conflicts, a civil war. Soon after arriving with his Legion in the South in 1781, Lee wrote Anthony Wayne that "tories . . . are taken and killed daily."[3] Lee never got used to this kind of war. Neither the atrocities committed by the loyalists nor his own role in killing Americans who served the king reconciled him to convulsive, vindictive violence among people who had long shared the same land. Memories stayed with him. After the loyalist post at Augusta, Georgia, surrendered in May 1781, Lee recalled thirty years later, "the militia of Georgia . . . were so exasperated by the cruelties mutually inflicted in the course of the war in this state, that they were disposed to have sacrificed every man taken." Lee and Andrew Pickens stopped them "with great difficulty."[4]

Civil conflict surpassed war between nations in its disorder partly because it deprived people of an assured loyalty and cohesion. Neither side could claim an unqualified allegiance based on the birth, kinship, and history that both sides shared. Such a war left men in isolation to choose between rival sides in "a domestic difference," while neither side possessed all the sanctions of nationality. Lee came away from the Revolutionary War eager to establish that nationality beyond question. In later years he hoped that it would spare America "those bloody convulsive struggles made by the minority, in opposition to the majority." And, if the country had to go to war again, it might then "be exempted from the ills which inevitably follow the want of unanimity." The Revolution was the first among several experiences that made Lee anxious to avoid settling the question of allegiance by armed conflict among partisans. Warring citizens might have sincere devotion to principles, but Lee had learned that principles did not necessarily restrain bloodshed—in fact, might be lost in it. The surest restraint was indissoluble union. He wanted that union in order to secure liberty and self-government, but no appeal to conflicting interpretations of these ideals could justify disruption of the nation. As he had seen, and as the history of republics taught him, disruption invited violence. He could not "believe America so elevated above the ordinary lot of humanity, as to be exempt from all danger of this afflicting calamity."[5]

The bitterness of civil war was only one of the wartime failures of union that distressed Lee. Even the people who professed to be united on the American side proved unreliable in their active effort for their own cause. The trouble, which grew most alarming in the summer and autumn of 1780, was not loyalism but the revolutionaries' selfish preoccupation with profits and trade. "Confusion and disorder had reached its height," Lee later recalled.[6] Independence could not safely rest only on the virtue of the populace. During that summer, Lee decided that "this union cannot be preserved much longer, unless a power equal to the support of it is established." The union was essential to independence because without it the American states would become "tributary disunited provinces" of warring European nations.[7] In July he predicted that three or four states would be subjugated by the British in the absence of drastic measures to mobilize the public. In addition to the people's loyalty, the union needed the sanction of coercion.

The Revolutionary War helped establish in Lee's mind a political distinction that his later partisan opponents did not share. He discriminated between "Wise politicians," "our rulers," "our great men," on the one hand, and "the people" or "the country" on the other. Because the United States was a republic, the people would choose their leaders. But Lee counted on the leaders rather than the public to remain consistently responsible, with the help of governmental authority, for the survival of sufficient virtue to sustain the union. If the populace had a "fit of patriotism"—as it did when alarmed by the reverses of 1780—this was a temporary boon, to be improved by those who had the foresight to anticipate inevitable future lapses.[8] In later years, when Lee saw threats to the nation's survival in popular selfishness or disorder, he put most of the blame on the form of government or on the men in power. Since the public's susceptibility to discord had been proven, little else could be expected from them if their government did not guide them. Only through permanent national unity could America maintain the authority of patriots over an unstable people—authority that the Revolutionary War had shown to be essential to American independence.

When Lee was writing his memoirs and came to the spring of 1781, he described the reaction of the populace to Cornwallis's movement. from North Carolina into Virginia. He first wrote: "A stupid torpor prevailed throughout the country thro which his Lordship took his course ascribable not to the inhabitants, but to the incapacity & impotency of govt." In revising the sentence, he crossed out "incapacity." He intended to blame the torpor on the weakness of the government. He also crossed out "stupid" and substituted the word "general."[9] The prevalence of stupidity might seem to transfer to the public some of the blame for a weak government's inability to resist the invader. Lee probably still believed that the inhabitants' "torpor" was "stupid" as well as "general," but he wanted the enemy's unopposed march to dramatize the consequences of giving government too little power. He thus implied that if the state or Continental governments had been stronger, they could have obstructed the invasion by preventing or overcoming the general torpor. Only if the Continental government could tax, spend, mobilize, and command could it maintain the country's independence.

The Articles of Confederation gave the central government no autonomous source of revenue, no authority or agents to enforce its enactments. After the Articles were ratified in 1781, no less than before, states failed to comply with

Congress's directions for support of the war. Disapproval or inattention by a few states could stop Congress from even giving directions, and the opposition of any one state could prevent Congress from expanding its authority. In describing the original system of government, Lee emphasized the absence of union: "The congress was composed of deputies from the several states, and resembled more a diplomatic corps executing the will of the sovereign, than the sovereign commanding the execution of its will. It cannot excite surprise to the reflecting reader that our finances, under such auspices, soon sunk." During the Revolutionary War, the United States had experimented with state sovereignty and voluntary union, and the experiment, in Lee's view, had bankrupted the country. By 1780, "the credit of the United States had become the general topic of derision."[10] During that year Lee urged drastic remedial measures: "prove that bonum publicum calls for it & you might alter constitutions & turn finance as you pleased."[11] Although permanent alterations did not occur then, the war years had gone far to link in Lee's mind the idea of union with the idea of a strong sovereign central government.

The collapse of the government's credit was the central proof of this connection because of the grave consequences of the country's insolvency. To it Lee could trace the immobilization and suffering of the army, with the accompanying danger that organized resistance to the British might dissolve for lack of resources. Since Lee was convinced that the army alone sustained effective defense, he concluded that its disbandment would quickly lead to the loss of American independence. In later years, when Lee saw threats to the authority of the central government, he knew what they portended—ruined finances, willful disorder, lost armies, and foreign subjugation. Others might trust the sovereignty and judgment of the state governments, while expecting to stop short of these wartime evils. In such trust, Lee detected a "retrograde step . . . towards the antient confederation." The step could be fatal because "that system has been demonstrated by experience, to be incapable of holding the states together."[12]

When Lee thought about the nature of union and the prospect of disunion, he could not free his political imagination from the images left by the Revolutionary War. So vivid were the effects of disunity that they came to mind in any discussion of public issues or forms of government. The danger of division heightened the urgency with which Lee tried to promote America's continental prosperity. Peace must not be entrusted to a government so weak that it would be unable to keep a volatile people from fragmenting and fighting each other. Responsible patriots had the duty to ensure peace by maintaining the union, leaving the public to devote itself to the nation's growth, undistracted by internal conflict. Lee had used military discipline to make his Legion both effective in striking the enemy and long-lived. Now he advocated political discipline to preserve the country's life. An appeal to the electorate or to the states against the authority of the national government would usually not mean for Lee the protection of civil liberties and constitutional balance. Rather, it would seem an invitation to the return of discord.

Henry Lee served as one of Virginia's delegates to the Continental Congress from 1785 until 1789. His observation of Congress and the states left him convinced that the government established by the Articles of Confederation could not preserve the union and thus could not maintain American independence. Because the states had sometimes ignored Congress's requisitions of money and because Congress could not get the necessary unanimous consent to an independent source of revenue, the collapse of the nation's credit seemed imminent. The country had foreign and domestic debts but too little income. Lee wrote to his father from New York in the spring of 1786, "We have very gloomy prospects with respect to national faith dignity & importance. Indeed unless matters soon alter, the United States must inevitably become more insignificant than words can express."[13] Lee had been elected to a body that, he later recalled, "was expiring from absolute debility."[14]

More dangers than the weakness of Congress alarmed Lee. The public's selfish irresponsibility in wartime, left unchecked, had grown worse in peace. Not content with neglecting the nation's solvency, some states pandered to the public's desire to cheat on private as well as public debts. By making depreciated paper money legal tender, a state like Rhode Island "so rebelled against justice, and so knocked down the bulwarks of probity, rectitude, and truth, that nothing rational or just can be expected from her."[15] In Massachusetts, insurgents who opposed the state's rigorous taxation to redeem its public debt in hard money took up arms and kept the courts closed. Lee was certain that their ostensible complaints masked their true goals: the "subversion" of government, "abolition of debt & division of lands."[16] This spirit, he believed, was "not confined to one state or to one part of a state, but pervades the whole" of New England. In fact, Americans as a people suffered from "evils which menace their natural life." The uncertainty of the public credit fostered speculation and neglect of productive enterprise in favor of "vice and prodigality." By September of 1786, Lee had concluded that "the period seems to be fast approaching when the people of these U. States must determine to establish a permanent capable government or submit to the horrors of anarchy and licentiousness."

The ancient cycle for the decay of republics seemed close to completion almost as soon as it had begun. Lee believed that his countrymen could found an enterprising, prosperous, expanding nation. But such an achievement required a cohesion and a degree of self-sacrifice that too few Americans would voluntarily attain. "It is high time," he wrote in April 1786, "that our people be coerced to habits of industry."[17] Lee's attention focused not on the many examples of stable productivity, public solvency, and orderly self-government that have attracted the notice of recent historians of the Confederation period but on the omens of disorder that warned of dissolution.

The magnitude of his plan for America's future intensified his distress when he saw proof of its vulnerability. Only a national government could use American trade as a commercial makeweight in Europe; only a national government could keep the trans-Appalachian West united to the East; only a national government, by maintaining the soundness of contract and credit, could turn Americans toward their productive future and away from short-sighted scrambling for selfish, divisive advantage to individuals, states, or regions. Lee adopted the most alarmist interpretation of the postwar economic depression and of the difficulties with public credit partly because they threatened his vision of America's coming continental grandeur. Even if the states could have pacified insurgents, collected taxes, and employed their citizens in agriculture, such a weak and stagnant republic would not last long. "Temporary and disunited exertions" would leave the country prey to "the evils which menace our existence." If Americans wanted to "enjoy that happiness which we so arduously contended for," they would need a government that could ensure their unity, their industriousness, and their growth—in short, their survival. When Lee arrived in Congress, he did not take long to conclude that in the absence of support from the states, "so circumstanced is the federal government, that its death cannot be very far distant."[18]

Lee, like other members of Congress, felt "particularly

zealous to amend & strengthen" the power of the central government.[19] When that strengthening took the form of a new
constitution, Lee quickly became one of its strongest advocates, soliciting support from prominent Virginians and serving in the state ratifying convention. There he outlined the
arguments for permanent national union and autonomous federal sovereignty to which he would grow even more attached
in later years.

The need for a strong national government seemed
especially clear, Lee believed, to the men who had done the
most to win independence. Years before the disorders and financial difficulties of the mid-1780s, the officers of the Continental Army had learned the fatal effects of giving the government no security other than the disposition of citizens and
states to make voluntary efforts. In founding the Society of
the Cincinnati in 1783, the members intended, Lee and others
wrote, "to use our collective influence in support of that government, and confirmation of that union, the establishment of
which had engaged so considerable a part of our lives."[20]
Even after public hostility toward the Society convinced its
members to keep it out of politics, Lee trusted veterans to remember that independence required a reliable national authority. Although one of the Massachusetts insurgent leaders,
Daniel Shays, was a former Continental Army captain, and
former Continental soldiers formed the backbone of the insurrection, Lee still wanted to believe that "the late officers &
soldiers are on the side of government unanimously."[21] Since
Lee's own wartime experience had committed him to strong
government, he felt sure that the war had affected others similarly.

A recent study of Virginia's ratification of the constitution finds a high correlation between senior rank in the Continental Army and support for the constitution in the state convention.[22] The officers' wartime experience had enhanced

their emphasis on Continental unity and central authority. However, their primary influence as proponents of strengthened government lay not in their numbers, the degree of their unanimity, or even their motives, but in their unique credentials as revolutionaries. For Lee, the importance of the war experience went beyond the lessons it had taught veterans about government; above all, it had shown their trustworthiness. When they endorsed a government that was the product of many hands and many motives, the officers' past defense of independence on the battlefield gave special weight to their opinion.

The most eloquent spokesman for the opposition to ratification in the Virginia convention was Patrick Henry, whose standing among the first of patriots could hardly have been impugned in the eyes of most Virginians. Lee, in debating Henry, reminded the convention that Henry had not served in the army: "It was my fortune," Lee said, "to be a soldier of my country. . . . I saw what the honorable gentleman did not see—our men fighting. . . . I have seen proofs of the wisdom of that paper on your table." No Anti-Federalist, particularly no civilian like Henry, could justly charge Lee with endangering liberty or betraying the Revolution; he believed that he had done more than his critics to keep the republic alive. "I trust that, young as I am, I shall be trusted, in the support of freedom, as far as the honorable gentleman." At the same time that it had attached him to liberty, the experience of fighting the British had convinced Lee that liberty depended on national union. Like other veterans who favored the new government, he would reject the assumption that "love for an American" conflicted with "affection for a Virginian." The war had established that "the people of America . . . are one people. I love the people of the north, not because they have adopted the Constitution, but because I fought with them as my countrymen, and because I consider them as such."[23] Support of the constitution would be only the first of several causes in which Lee appealed to his wartime service as a vindication of his fidelity to revolutionary principles in peacetime politics. Having risked his life to defeat a tyrant, he seemed to assume that this risk guaranteed that he would always thereafter place the survival of the republic first. This reasoning might look faulty to his opponents; it convinced Lee not so much by logic as by emotion. Even in private correspondence he exaggerated the number of veterans who agreed with him politically. Perhaps out of civilian ignorance or selfish motives, men could risk the death of the union by opposing the constitution, but he and his fellow officers had run that risk before and were uniquely qualified to prevent its recurrence.

Lee's faith in superior patriots underlay his confidence in the constitution. He linked the union and its flourishing with the stature of the delegates to the constitutional convention— "citizens selected by the people, from knowledge of their wisdom and confidence in their virtue."[24] In fact, only indirectly had the drafters of the constitution been "selected by the people," and this connection was not the main source of Lee's confidence in them. Rather, the success of the constitution showed the ability of government to offset a lapse of virtue among the populace. Instead of "weak and feeble governments," the United States needed to have "the officers of the nation possessing that power which is indispensably necessary to chastise vice and reward virtue."[25] The nation could not survive without public spirit, but its survival need not depend only on voluntarism. Giving authority to leading patriots enabled them, where necessary, to enforce good conduct. Lee knew that such authority might itself threaten liberty. However, he told the Virginia ratifying convention, "I dread more from the licentiousness of the people than from the bad government of rulers."[26]

After Virginia ratified the constitution, Lee's reliance on the strength of leaders turned him toward George Washing-

ton. Even before an election could be held, Lee joined others
in urging Washington to accept the presidency: "Without
you, the govt can have but little chance of success, & the people of that happiness which its prosperity must yield." Lee
worried most about "the various minoritys" who would persevere in their hostility to the new government. He wanted to
get James Madison into the Virginia legislature to thwart Patrick Henry and keep Virginia from joining New York to sabotage the constitution. Only Washington, supported by such
able men, could defeat those who "continue to inflame the
passions & to systemize the measures of opposition." He, like
Lee, recognized that America's survival depended on "an indissoluble Union of the States under one Federal Head,"
which he had advocated in 1783. Now the success of this
cause seemed to depend on him. Without Washington in the
presidency and Virginia among his supporters, "confusion &
anarchy may be the substitute of order & good govt."[27] Lee's
sharp contrast between reliable leaders and political confusion
arose from his fear of leaving the public with insufficient guid-
ance in the political demands of virtue. Having seen the populace choose selfishness and disorder even in the midst of a war
for their own liberty, Lee thereafter took this danger for
granted. In the 1780s and 1790s he did not doubt Americans'
capacity for virtue, but he did doubt their inclination toward
it—an inclination that patriots in government must bolster.

The leaders of the Revolution, however, were mortal.
The republic would not be able to depend on their wisdom
forever. What would sustain independence after the men who
had won it were dead? Lee's answer was a permanent union.
The constitution was a compact among the people, not the
states, creating a national government that would govern in
direct contact with the public. For this reason, Lee argued in
the ratifying convention, the phrase "We, the people" began
the document "with great propriety." Eleven years later, Lee

expressed a conviction that had grown stronger in the time since the adoption of the constitution: "our national independence, and consequently our individual liberty . . . our peace and our happiness depend entirely on maintaining our union." All of these rested on the constitution: "our union cannot survive our existing government." The United States must never again risk the dissolution and subjugation to which it had come so close during the Revolutionary War and the following years. By denying subsequent generations the opportunity to reconsider their allegiance to the constitution, Lee would come as close as he could to securing virtue in perpetuity. By 1799, European war and American partisan controversy had encouraged him to state his views boldly: "In point of right no state can withdraw itself from the union. In point of policy, no state ought to be permitted to do so. The safety of those which remain would be endangered by the measure, and consequently their whole force would be exerted for its prevention."

These conclusions were implicit in Lee's original enthusiasm for the constitution as a safeguard against domestic discord. From the beginning he had been eager to suppress the irrational impulse to civil conflict. In the Virginia convention, when George Mason warned that armed resistance might oppose the implementation of the constitution, Lee denounced him for encouraging violence. By predicting such "horrors," Mason's speeches might "easily progress into overt acts, among the less thinking and the vicious," arising from "the madness of some and the vice of others." The thought of "these impious scenes . . . which I execrate" moved Lee to oratorical prayer: "God of heaven avert from my country the dreadful curse!" Denouncing Virginia's resolutions in opposition to the Alien and Sedition Acts eleven years later, Lee still equated a willingness to risk the union with a loss of reason. He again hoped that "good sense . . . will resume its empire, and turn us from the precipice to which our passions are so rapidly hurrying us."[28]

In a recent study of the concept of a perpetual union, Kenneth M. Stampp has found no one in the Federalist period except Henry Lee who, by asserting that the union was permanent, explicitly denied state sovereignty and the right of secession.[29] Lee's readiness to take the implications of the constitution farther than his contemporaries originated partly in his keener awareness of the derangement that could overtake a people who defied or dissolved their government. This emotional defense of order, more than a rigorous intellectual consistency, put Lee in the forefront of the advocates of national consolidation. He announced to the Virginia convention that, if the opponents of the constitution "should risk the awful appeal" to violence, the supporters would "encounter every difficulty and danger" in its defense. But when he imagined such a conflict, he said, "my feelings are so oppressed."[30] The permanence of the American union became linked in Lee's mind with the preservation of peace, order, and sanity.

The constitution seemed to be the main guarantor of the peaceful prosperity Lee sought after the Revolutionary War. That the movement for a constitutional convention began with interstate meetings by promoters of the Potomac Company was not a coincidence. The wealth of the West would enrich the whole country only if the union had a government strong enough to promote and maintain the connection. Speaking of the Potomac region, Lee assured Washington in 1786 that "no event comprehends more fully the strength and future consequence of our particular country than the cementing to the interest of Virginia by the strong tie of commerce the western world."[31] Such development of the opportunities of peace was arrested by "the imbecility of the

Confederation . . . that defective system which can never make us happy at home nor respectable abroad." By 1788, Lee knew that a decentralized government based on voluntarism would never mobilize the nation's potential for agricultural productivity and commercial enterprise. Under proper leadership, the populace would be capable of great expansion. Left to themselves, the people would pursue local, selfish, dead-end interests. Under the Confederation, Lee said, commerce was languishing, the price of produce and land was "very low," and the country was suffering a "decrease of population and industry." Such exaggerations and inaccuracies make Lee's description even more interesting because, in blaming the Confederation for cramping peace, he sketched a reverse image of the vision he cherished: flourishing commerce, industrious farming, rising land prices, and growing families.

After Lee's own plans had begun to go sour, he looked back at the constitutional convention and Washington's administration as the fullest embodiment of the connection between wise leaders and national prosperity. Their success in establishing America's strength and wealth seemed to confirm the expectations with which Lee had originally supported them. In 1788 the opponents of the constitution looked like enemies to America's future. Replying to Lee's criticisms of the Confederation, Patrick Henry told the Virginia convention, "You are not to inquire how your trade may be increased, nor how you are to become a great and powerful people, but how your liberties can be secured."[32] In Lee's mind this was a false distinction. The nation's growth and the security of liberty depended on each other. As soon as the constitution had been ratified by nine states, Lee was eager for Washington to become President and begin to foster the development of the country's resources so long delayed by governmental paralysis and so vulnerable to the agents of disunion. Lee believed "that our peace & prosperity depends on the proper improvement of the present period." Now that the constitution had won an opportunity to prove its usefulness for these purposes, "my anxiety is extreme that the new govt. may have an auspicious beginning."[33]

During the summer of 1788, Lee's plans for the future seemed especially vulnerable. Matilda Lee had fallen ill of an unnamed disorder that began with "much burning and tingling" and progressed to "difficulty of breathing & great debility of body," worsened by "fevers every now & then."[34] Harry, at the age of thirty-one, had been "severely afflicted" with rheumatism in the winter and spring of 1787. Matilda's illness, however, was more serious, and it troubled Harry deeply. He delayed congratulating George Washington "on the auspicious prospect which the adoption of the new constitution presents to our country" because he felt "inadequate from my temper of mind." Matilda's "continued ill health" left him in "misery."[35] Her sickness, however, did not dampen her own political opinions, and she expressed "in all company" her dissatisfaction with the Virginia legislature's failure to send James Madison to the United States Senate. She called it "a dreadful blow."[36]

At the same time that Matilda Lee's illness undermined the happy future Harry Lee had planned for his family, he increased his efforts to make his vision come true for the Potomac. Within weeks of the ratification of the constitution he was in New York for the last session of the Continental Congress, reporting to his relatives on the probable location of the national capital: "I think that the ten miles square may be to the south of the susquehannah which will assist in its consequences very much the trade of the chesapeake."[37] By the spring of 1789, Lee was diligently promoting his plans to take advantage of that trade through his town at Great Falls. He persuaded James Madison to write promotional literature, George Washington to recommend the location as a sound investment, and Thomas Jefferson to solicit buyers in Europe. Lee anticipated an imminent rise in the value of the property near the Potomac Company's canal and announced the receipt of "many applications from respectable people for lots." He heard that "the desire of fixing at the great falls is very general among the commercial people here & above on both sides of the river." On a trip for Matilda to visit western Virginia for treatment at medicinal springs, he continued to work on the affairs of the Potomac Company. He said that he had found a widespread "persuasion that we shall continue long to be one people & that the potomack river will strengthen our connexion" with the West. The security of union and trade had "seized the minds" of "men respectable in character family & fortune," who would now head west. Lee was anxious that his site at Great Falls be ready for the boom. Late in 1788 he had offered Bryan Fairfax wood rights on the land in exchange for the rents outstanding—"such is my zeal to possess the property." By March 1790, he said that warehouses were under construction, but £3,000 of back quitrents remained due to Fairfax. If this "small" sum could be raised to clear the title, sales and construction could begin, and then in Lee's town "the lots might be rented on moderate ground rents to the amount of six hundred pr. annum." Trade, growth, and profits would begin almost immediately. "The object is great," Lee wrote, "very great indeed."[38]

Lee's efforts to build Matildaville seemed to grow more frenetic as his wife's health deteriorated. In May 1789, she was "very low"; in March 1790, he said, "Mrs. Lees health is worse & worse, I begin to fear the worst"; in June he told Washington, "My long afflicted Mrs. Lee is now very ill & I fear cannot be preserved."[39] Meanwhile, Lee became so eager to take possession of the Great Falls land by paying off Fairfax that in the spring of 1790 he planned to take out a five-year mortgage on 4,200 acres of his property in Virginia. Matilda Lee stopped this plan in August, days before her death, by persuading her husband to join her in a deed of trust that committed some of these lands, as well as the Stratford estate, to their children—beyond Harry's power to alienate.

In August Matilda died, evidently in childbirth. Her baby died, too. President Washington sent condolences, and Lee wrote on Washington's letter: "The deaths of my wife & son."[40] In eight years of marriage the Lees had five children, only two of whom lived to maturity. One of the most time-consuming consolations Lee found for the disruption of his family by illness and death was his work for the permanence of American union on a continental scale—governmentally secured by the constitution, commercially connected from the Chesapeake to the Great Lakes. When he turned away from the causes of private distress, Lee trusted that "Our nation may be made happy & respectable" by Washington's administration. He told Washington: "I anticipate with delight our approaching felicity."[41] Unable to prevent the inroads of death at Stratford, Lee had devoted his energy to the nation's survival. Union would promise to America a strength that surpassed the ruin of private dreams. Lee sought for the United States the perpetuity that no man could attain for himself. Lees were mortal; their country was not. Among Light-Horse Harry's reasons for supporting the constitution, he later recalled, was that its authors had drafted the fundamental law in such a way that it "promised immortality to the work of their hands." To preside over its implementation there could have been no fitter patriot than Washington, who, Lee imagined, would have charged those who came after him to "give immortality to that union, which was the constant object of my terrestrial labours."[42]

Henry Lee's devotion to the union and to a strong national government underwent a period of what James Madison called "despondency" during Washington's first administration.[43] For three or four years between 1789 and 1793, Lee became an outspoken opponent of Alexander Hamilton's program as Secretary of the Treasury—a program he denounced as a "base perversion of the constitution."[44] Lee's views, which survive primarily in letters to Madison, shared opinions prevalent among Virginians. Although the letters were not published, they served as a political manifesto, and Lee's attitudes were "loudly propagated" and "much talked of."[45] His criticism of the administration's policies coincided with his prominence in the Virginia legislature in 1789 and 1790, as well as with the early part of his three one-year terms as governor of Virginia, beginning in 1791.

Lee censured Hamilton's plans for the federal government to fund the national debt at face value for its current holders, to assume the states' Revolutionary War debts, to promote manufacturing in America, and to charter a national bank. Lee's strictures drew on attitudes that historians now call Jeffersonian. He wanted agriculture to "reign triumphantly" in the United States because it fostered "bodys & minds" that were healthy, productive, and independent—free from "submission & adulation." Hamilton's program threatened to introduce the "decaying blighted fruit" of "base principles & wicked measures adopted thro necessity in corrupt monarchys." Using the public debt to attach a "money interest" to the administration was a technique for "arbitrary governments," by which "a change may be worked in our national character which will debase us as men, & destroy us as a people."[46]

In 1786, under the Confederation government, Lee had begun to deplore "jobbing in paper securitys." He complained that "agriculture commerce and every other proper ground to render a people wealthy & respectable yields to the allurements of this vice."[47] Hamilton's measures would worsen the destruction. Lee called the speculation in public securities "buying & selling in the funds," "stock-jobbing," "stock gambling," and "Tontine days." He warned that the political manipulation of a national debt could make a people selfish and dependent, subjecting them to "oppression" as the government contracted new debts through "wanton expeditions, wars & useless expences." He wanted to pay all original holders of the public debt at face value, while paying subsequent assignees at a depreciated value. He feared that the federal government's assumption of state debts would work to Virginia's disadvantage by costing the state more in taxes than the redemption of its own share of the debt. Lee reported to Madison that during the 1789 session of the Virginia General Assembly the feelings of enmity toward the federal government were "rather encreasing, than otherwise."[48] In the 1790 session, Lee voted for a resolution that denounced the assumption of state debts as an unconstitutional exercise of power. His colleague John Marshall later recalled Lee's "eloquence and earnest speeches on the subject."[49]

The governorship of Virginia, to which the legislature elected Lee in November 1791, did not wield much power and had not usually been an object of partisan or factional rivalry. Even after Lee's political views began to change, he was returned to office for the customary third term in 1793. Nevertheless, Lee's articulate hostility to nationalist measures probably was an important reason—if not, as his critics later claimed, "the prime incitement"—for his election to the office.[50] Lee became a spokesman for Virginians' growing opposition to the policies of the Washington administration. However, Lee did not play this part for long. In the first years of the administration, he was distressed to discover conflicts between his plan for the federal government's role in America's future development and the program of his friends in office. He told Hamilton, "I never did nor never can admire the funding system of which you confessedly was the father." But Lee did not want to be a partisan. He wanted the conflict to go away. "Why do not these virulent partys coalesce? Is there no middle ground on which a union might be formed."[51] Only gradually did he see that his ideal of a flourishing continental union whose productivity was fostered by a strong national government contained in practice contradictions that he could not reconcile. The years of Lee's governorship mark the erosion of that ideal and the beginning of a partisan commitment to the Federalist administration. The political controversies over the French Revolution, American foreign policy, and domestic disorder in 1793 and 1794 fixed Lee's new orientation. But in the preceding years he had to make choices that moved him toward that decision.

In 1793, Lee explained his positions on public issues by telling Hamilton, "our countrys prosperity will ever be with me the first object."[52] Lee saw in Hamilton's program a threat to the growth he had envisioned. Speculation would distract people from productive labor toward profitable schemes. The perpetuation of an interest-paying national debt would encourage wars and thereby sacrifice the stability needed for the country to prosper. Concentrating wealth in fewer hands might promote manufacturing or mercantile enterprise; but, in the process, it would undermine the country's future by making citizens weak dependents rather than adventurous, prolific developers of new lands. Lee would have preferred to combine a commitment to national solvency with reliance on expanding agricultural prosperity by paying the public creditors through the sale of federal land in the West. Such a policy would both promote the expansion he counted on and avoid the evil effects of Hamilton's program. That Lee thought it feasible further reveals his optimism about the rapid growth of the West.

When Lee, in 1792, thought about Hamilton's policies,

he felt bitter because the federal government, after three years, had not produced the results he had anticipated. "We owe our prosperity such as it is, for it is nothing extraordinary to our own native vigor as a people & to a continuation of peace, not to the wisdom or care of govt." The new government had given the country uniformity in commercial regulation and financing of the national debt, but "the public of the U. States have as yet tasted only the promised felicity and that too very scantily." Before the end of Washington's first term, Lee's dreams of national happiness were beginning to give way to anxiety over maintaining the nation's existence.

Lee turned from opposing to supporting the administration under the influence of his fear of civil war. The vehemence of Virginians' opposition to Hamilton impressed Lee. The policies of the federal government seemed to benefit the North at the expense of the southern states, and Lee began in March 1790 to warn that, without "real taxation" and a centrally located capital, "we southern people must be slaves in effect, or cut the Gordian knot at once."[53] David Stuart wrote to President Washington, "Coll: Lee tells me, that many who were warm Supporters of the government, are changing their sentiments, from a conviction of the impracticability of Union with States, whose interests are so dissimilar to those of Virginia. I fear the Coll: is one of the number."[54] Confronted by unalterable policies that "tend to depress the south & exalt the north," Lee in April felt ready to join those who sought relief through disunion—"To disunite is dreadful to my mind, but dreadful as it is, I consider it a lesser evil than union on the present conditions." Lee took for granted that separation of the states would lead to civil war. Even so, he wrote, "I had rather myself submit to all the hazards of war & risk the loss of everything dear to me in life, than to live under the rule of a fixed insolent northern majority."

After he had become governor, however, Lee no longer

endorsed such extreme opposition to the national administration. He still denounced Hamilton's "execrable" measures, but he had decided by January of 1792 that he could "see no redress, unless the govt. itself be destroyed. This is risking too much because great evils indubitably must flow from discord & the people must suffer greatly whatever may be the event of such an experiment." Lee believed in 1792, as he had in 1780 and as he would in 1799, that the disbandment of the union would lead directly to bloodshed among Americans. Having known such conflict during the Revolutionary War, he would not really revive it after all. "While we deprecate & lament the obnoxious" consequences of Hamilton's program, "we must submit to it, because effectual opposition may beget civil discord & civil war."[55] Lee's anxiety for "the tranquillity of the whole" remained uppermost, and he decided that "the good of the state is entwined with the good of the Union."[56]

Seventy years later, Light-Horse Harry's most famous son, Robert E. Lee, confronted civil war and sided against the union. His gifts as a commander made him a valuable addition to the secessionist cause and enhanced, if not prolonged, the resistance to the union. He fought the war his father had feared. Beginning his thirty-five-year career in the United States Army, the younger Lee had won appointment to the United States Military Academy partly on the grounds that the nation owed a debt to the children of Henry Lee for their father's military services in establishing American independence. When Robert, in 1861, resigned his commission and abandoned his oath to defend the United States, he turned away from his father's political legacy. After the Civil War, Robert acknowledged as much when he wrote of his father's outlook in the 1790s: "Although his correspondence at this time, as well as the course of his life, proves his devotion to the Federal Government, yet he recognized a distinction between his 'native country' and that which he had labored to associate with it in the strictest bonds of union."[57] Robert may have emphasized his father's distinction between Virginia and America because in 1861 Robert had offered his attachment to Virginia as his main reason for supporting secession. Light-Horse Harry had also recognized conflicting loyalties but had chosen the union.

Henry Lee had a deeper aversion to civil war than his son did, and perhaps a deeper understanding of it. Both father and son experienced civil wars. Both fought for the revolutionary side against the established government. But Harry came back from the Carolinas appalled at internecine violence and increasingly dedicated to permanent union, while Robert, during the Civil War, became a defender of the states' right to secede, which he had formerly denied. Throughout his life, Harry would try to separate the Revolution's ideals from the domestic brutality it had provoked—for him the legacy of independence was unity and patriotism. Robert, on the other hand, argued that he had fought for the Confederacy in order to defend "the Constitution and the Union established by our forefathers."[58] In retrospect, he believed that the legacy of the Revolution had inspired secession and civil war. Robert E. Lee took solace from believing that his conduct had the consistency of destiny—guided by traditional attachment to Virginia, by the principles of the American Revolution, and by the will of God. Perhaps this conviction spared him much reflection on his role in making Virginia one of the main victims of the war's devastation. After the Civil War, instead of recording any such reflections, he appealed to his father's revolutionary cause to explain abandoning the military career begun under his father's aegis and to justify abolishing the nation his father had helped to create.

Robert E. Lee did not share all of his father's aspirations; he did not claim to be shaping the future of a continent or making a violent revolution the instrument of bounty, union,

and peace. He referred instead to duty, honor, and divine de-
cree. He would obey Virginia's decision, the Confederacy's
orders, and God's hand in events. After his death Lee was
widely praised for the resolute, healing example he had set in
his last years by accepting defeat. Both his acceptance of defeat and his equanimity in setting such an example after the
war may have owed much to the absence from his life of a revolutionary vision like his father's that made the victory of
ideals essential to happiness and made defeat fatal. Like other
ex-Confederates, Robert E. Lee denied betraying the American Revolution either in seceding or in losing a revolutionary
war to secede. The legacy he drew from the American Revolution neither inspired him to defend the United States nor
blamed him for helping to lead the Confederate States to destruction. Having joined a cause with less visionary ideals than
his father's and having claimed less control over its outcome
than his father had, Robert E. Lee could escape many of his
father's reflections on the corrupting effect of pursuing a
cause by killing. And being less troubled than his father by
this corruption, with its burden of responsibility and evidence
of depravity, he more readily fought and justified civil war.

Light-Horse Harry Lee's anxiety to prevent the renewal
of civil war shaped his political opinions in the 1790s. When
he opposed the policies of the national government that he had
worked to create, he responded partly to the political climate
of Virginia but primarily to his anxiety about American prosperity—especially the growth of the West and the agriculture
and commerce of Virginia. When he turned to the active support of the national government, even of the policies he had
denounced, he was reacting to the threat of disorder and violence. Although the process was spread over several years, this
change marked a reorientation of Lee's political outlook. He
began as a proponent of strong government, then warned of
its abuses, then ended as a proponent of strong government

again. In the process, his motives for supporting the national government shifted in emphasis. From the beginning, public order had concerned him. But his early expectations from a central government had mostly emphasized its preservation of the union as a guarantor of widespread wealth and happiness. He later stressed the importance of union under a strong government primarily for its preservation of internal peace. Lee's opposition to Hamilton's program and his brief toying with the idea of disunion began in the decline of his postwar vision of prosperity and ended in the rise of his alarm over the danger of disorder and civil war.

Even before Lee's personal finances turned sharply downward in the late 1790s he had begun, in politics, to think less often expansively and more often defensively. The hopes that he had derived from the return of peace gave way to a struggle with enemies, with opponents whom Lee regarded as enemies of peace. In this cause he would defend the policies that he had once threatened to resist. He argued in 1799 that the assumption of state debts by the federal government and its method of funding the national debt, while perhaps not accomplished on the wisest plan, were necessary: "What else could an honest government do with a public debt it was unable to pay?" Nor was the bounty that Hamilton's program gave to speculators a valid argument against it: "The public debt however provided for would still, as it approached its nominal value, have settled in the hands of monied men."[59] Measures to maintain the government's credit did not, as the Republicans charged, portend monarchy. By the end of John Adams's administration, Lee was looking back over the Federalist years as an era of stable government, sound policies, and prosperous times—"in contributing to which prosperity," he wrote Hamilton, "no man alive has done more than yr. self."[60] The proliferation of enemies in the 1790s and Jefferson's coming to power in 1801 gave Lee some more dangerous opponents to blame for the fading of his peacetime vision. His friends the Federalists were at least devoted to order and to union. And the more he thought about them, the more clearly he remembered that they had also been devoted to prosperity—had, in fact, achieved it until driven out by the forces of discord.

THE MOB

WHEN LIGHT-HORSE HARRY LEE SPENT PART OF HIS last days detesting "Democrats" and damning a Baltimore mob, he was remaining true to a lifelong skepticism and contempt. His youthful political observations during the Revolutionary War encouraged him to doubt the good judgment and public-spiritedness of his countrymen. This doubt helped make him suspicious of governmental institutions and political leaders who purported to represent the public will closely. Lee never forsook the ideal of republican government; but he believed that its security lay in enabling the electorate to choose officials whose wisdom and authority would foster a patriotism that surpassed most citizens' voluntary attainment.

Lee's strictures on the lapse of public virtue during the war and his anxiety to ensure public order with strong central government in the 1780s foreshadowed his later hostility toward groups that seemed to threaten the survival of peaceful union. This hostility, from the 1790s onward, became more desperate and defensive. Lee's political outlook held less confidence that government and eminent patriots could maintain a prosperous, independent republic. His alarm grew as he found himself confronted by more enemies, as more of the populace and then the government itself fell under their influence, as these enemies seemed to do more harm to the nation. Lee had a smaller part in public affairs; that part spoke less of a continental vision that the people might implement, more of threats to survival posed by the people. Lee's shifting emphases and rising ire resembled the reactions of many of his political allies. In his encounters with the mob, he pursued a career that is distinctive less for his political opinions than for the intensity with which he linked his life to his outlook on the public legacy of the American Revolution. One of Thomas Jefferson's biographers, Merrill D. Peterson, calls Lee's career "political suicide."[1] Lee would have agreed that his public life died a violent death, but he probably would have described it as a casualty of war.

Lee's character and early experiences seemed to predispose him to mistrust citizens who tried to act in concert without proper leaders. The ancestors whose portraits hung in Stratford Hall had been defenders of traditional authority: the first Richard had remained loyal to the House of Stuart during Cromwell's ascendancy; the second Richard had supported Governor William Berkeley against Nathaniel Bacon's rebellion and had waited longer than most Virginians to turn his loyalty from the House of Stuart to King William and Queen Mary. In Virginia, the Lees were accustomed not only to supporting authority but also to wielding it. Harry's great-great-grandfather, great-grandfather, and granduncle had all served on the Virginia Council. When Harry, at the age of three or four, was first taken to the capital at Williamsburg, six Lees sat in the House of Burgesses—his father, two uncles, and three cousins—and a seventh Lee was on the Council. Thirty years later, when the time seemed ripe for Light-Horse Harry to enter the legislature, one of his cousins wrote to another, suggesting that Harry's uncle Richard retire and make room. Henry Lee grew up learning how to ride horses, give orders, and move among powerful politicians. He always conceived of government as the counsel of eminent men for the benefit of lesser ones.

Lee's reliance on pre-eminent patriots to guide the public mirrored his emulation of the great men of antiquity. He read the ancients throughout his life, dropping his occasional allusions and quotations not as phrasebook adornments but as the purest examples of the characterizations that he applied to his contemporaries. His political outlook did not originate primarily in his classical reading; however, he invoked the classical models of conduct to show that the well-being of the state depended in large part on the strength of its heroes. The fort at West Point, New York, was "the American Thermopylae"; Nathanael Greene in the southern campaign had to "imitate the example of Scipio Africanus"; the volunteer corps of the provisional army of 1798 would be "like the sacred band of Thebes."[2] As legislators, Lycurgus, Solon, and Numa "attract universal admiration" for their "promotion of human good; the only way in which man can, however humbly, imitate Almighty God and merit our love."[3] Hannibal, "the prince of war," stood first among soldiers.[4] Historical figures, quasi-mythical leaders, heroes from a legendary, poetic past— Aeneas, Hector, Epaminondas, Xenophon, and again Hannibal—the example of antiquity proved that gifted, virtuous men made a people great. Or if, like Hannibal, they failed to do so, the blame lay with some domestic enemy, like Hanno, for "preferring the gratification of his personal hatred to the prosperity of his country, which in the issue became ruined."[5]

Many Americans who did not develop Lee's kind of contempt for the waywardness of their countrymen would have joined him in praising the great men of antiquity. Emulation of classical heroes did not oblige a person to scorn lesser men. Lee, however, stressed in his praise the singularity of such greatness—the strength of character, the powers of mind that enabled a superior man to command, to make law, to benefit his people. The admirable qualities belonged to the hero. They might not prevail in the populace; they might even

emerge in opposition to the populace. This truth was best expressed by Horace, one of whose odes seemed to describe an
American hero, George Washington:

Justum et tenacem proposti virum
Non civium ardor prava jubentium,
Non vultus instantis tyranni
Mente quatit solida.
[The man who has a just and solid purpose
Is shaken from his firm resolve
Neither by the clamor of fellow citizens urging wrong
Nor by the sight of a threatening tyrant.]

In his funeral oration on Washington, Lee wanted to cel-
ebrate Washington's popularity while clearly establishing that
it came from public respect for unique wisdom and virtue, not
from Washington's representativeness. "Unshaken by domestic turbulence," active in "quelling internal discord," Washington matched or surpassed any model patriot who made his
people greater than they could make themselves. Even before
Lee stood in the pulpit of the German Lutheran Church in
Philadelphia and quoted Horace over Washington's bier, a
Virginian from Petersburg, having heard that Lee would be
the funeral orator, had placed a bet that Lee would use the ode
in the oration. The man had "so often" heard Lee "at tavern
and courthouse" declaim those lines "with theatrical strut and
emphasis" in allusion to Washington that they seemed sure to
flow into the oration "*like an associated idea.*"[6]
    Washington's career proved for Lee the validity of a po-
litical truth that was also taught by antiquity: the great patriot
served the welfare of his country through the workings of his
own superior character and judgment. This fascination with
the hero reinforced Lee's willingness to challenge or to despise
the opinions of his countrymen when they differed from his
own. After the raid on Paulus Hook in 1779, Alexander Ham-

ilton said: "Lee unfolds himself more and more to be an officer of great capacity, and if he had not a little spice of the
Julius Caesar or Cromwell in him, he would be a very clever
fellow."[7] Lee probably did not see himself as a dictator or an
admirer of dictators; rather, he would champion the public interest even in the face of public hostility. Family tradition says
that Lee set great store by a seal ring he owned which had
once belonged to a Roman consul.[8]

Within the wavering mind of a leaderless populace lay the
constant threat of disorder. This danger, more than any other,
encouraged Lee's hostility toward the people who opposed
him, and this concern gradually supplanted his efforts to shape
America's future. Although he continued to judge the decay
of his times by the standard of his earlier vision and did not
give up his dream of prosperity, he found most of his political
energy consumed in resisting the enemies of peace. Among
Americans, disorder wore many faces—militiamen, Indians,
slaves, and rebels against governmental authority. Finally, the
domestic insurgents seemed to be joined and guided by aliens
who first perverted the French Revolution, then came to
America and sought to pervert the legacy of the American
Revolution.

The worst form of disorder was war. Twenty-five years
after leaving the Continental Army, Lee reiterated "what I
have often declared whenever war was expected, that it is a
terrible scourge however amiably conducted or successfully
terminated." Lee's memory of its violence made war seem to
him as much a scourge as an art. Yet while he shrank from
"all its many evils," he believed that war wrought still worse
havoc when it was fought by ill-trained civilians.[9] To rely primarily on militia for combat invited a confusion that killed the
people whom such a policy claimed to respect.

Lee's mistrust of civilians in battle arose from his experi-

ence during the Revolutionary War. His wartime letters repeat remarks like these: "had the militia not given way, we
must have been completely victorious"; "irregulars are completely unfit for the war in this country"; "the Militia . . . have
got dispersed & languish"; "you can have no idea of the conduct of the Militia, which may disappoint again."[10] Like many
Continental Army officers, Lee felt contempt for the conduct
of most militiamen in combat. Historians have shown that the
militia, while not usually effective for major battles, sieges, or
prolonged service, did important work as auxiliaries to the
Continental Army and in maintaining the authority of revolutionary civil government.[11] Lee later praised the wartime militia for its accomplishments. However, he worried most about
sustained combat and the losses caused by the public's reluctance to support a sufficient number of regular soldiers.

Americans were willing to create a standing army of pro-
fessionals in time of war, but most clung to the heritage of
English political thought which warned against maintaining a
peacetime army. Only while citizens remained virtuous
enough to defend themselves could liberty survive. If quies-
cence and ease permitted taxation in order to hire mercenaries, the public would soon lose its ability to resist tyranny.
During the war this argument was sometimes used to justify
reluctance to strengthen the army; in later years it became one
of the bases for opposing the establishment of a permanent
American army. Lee challenged the application of these traditional beliefs to American policy on several grounds. First, he
argued that a virtuous willingness to fight—even when it
brought men to the field—did not suffice for the country's defense. War also required skill. Without training and continuous service, well-meaning citizens could lose both their cause
and their lives. Second, Lee denied that Americans who were
paid to serve in an American army thereby became mercenaries. Their professionalism would not alienate them from

their families or the republic they had volunteered to defend. In the first years of peace after the Revolution, Lee, like other critics of the wartime militia, knew that the public's suspicion of an army and hostility to taxes would prevent the establishment of the regular army he preferred. He supported, as an alternative, a plan for a national militia that would increase professional training and centralize command. Even this compromise had too many opponents; Lee wrote from Congress in 1786, "we lament the indifference which pervades our country on this important subject."[12] In later years, alarmed by European war and related domestic divisions, he joined other Federalists in creating a standing army.

The debates over the nature of America's military force during the years after the Revolutionary War were made more complex by the growing recognition, even among the advocates of peacetime reliance on militia, that modern war required trained soldiers. Politicians' praise of the fighting prowess of the militia helped mislead the electorate with the idea that citizens' virtue could alone overcome an enemy's military professionalism. Putting faith in this belief also spared the public the fear of a large permanent army, as well as the taxes needed to support such a force. Lee, although willing to praise the wartime militia for its accomplishments, would not qualify his belief in the need for professional soldiers in order to accommodate the preferences of the public. As his opponents persisted in celebrating the patriotism and reliability of the militia, Lee grew more skeptical of military policy formed to obey the electorate rather than to guide it.

The picture of militiamen fleeing or dying came often to Lee's mind when he spoke of the Revolutionary War. On occasions twenty-five years apart he recalled the Battle of Guilford Court House during which "the North Carolina militia took to flight" in an "unaccountable panic." "Their abandonment of the regulars," Lee told the Virginia ratifying convention, "occasioned the loss of the field." In his memoirs he added a detail he had not told his fellow delegates while he was still active in politics: "Lieutenant colonel Lee joined in the attempt to rally the fugitives, threatening to fall upon them with his cavalry"; but "these unhappy men" ran on through the woods, throwing away guns, packs, and canteens. Their "base desertion . . . threw the corps of Lee out of combination with the army, and also exposed it to destruction." Lee knew "many instances" of such unreliability—battles, skirmishes, and sieges in which the conduct of armed civilians differed sharply from the conduct of veterans.[13] Yet the militiamen, though Lee criticized them, did not receive the greatest part of his blame. The deeper fault lay in the government that sent such unready men to defend the nation. Lack of discipline not only led to flight and defeat but also sacrificed more men to disease than to battle. "A govt that can & will not place its citizens on an equality with its foe . . . does really commit murder."[14] In thus "throwing away . . . lives," public officials "provoke the vengeance of Heaven."[15] Lee believed that the proponents of defense by state militia could recall as clearly as he did that, during the Revolution, "this same opinion . . . brought into real hazard, and threatened with total destruction, the liberties and independence of our country."[16] Their unwillingness to draw from the war the same lesson that he did smacked of hypocrisy. The men who would praise the militia's courage and then send militiamen to their deaths were "demagogues, who flourish in a representative system of government."[17]

Lee saw a connection between appealing to a popular electorate and advocating such an unsound system of defense. Flattering the voters' innate military prowess while excusing them from conscription, from more rigorous militia service, or from taxes to support regulars would help win office for men who were ignoring the effects of their policy on the conduct of war. Those people who demanded more freedom from gov-

ernmental authority were not necessarily freedom's best defenders. The irresponsibility of leaders who failed to learn and
implement the lessons of war would worsen the scourge when
next it came. "The best blood of America," Lee recalled,
"was prodigally and ineffectually expended during the war, for
want of the aid to be derived from discipline and skill."[18] To
protect the citizens, one must not just appeal to them—one
must discipline them.

As in the debate over militia, threats of disorder claimed
Lee's attention even during the years of his greatest political
popularity. While he was governor, he devoted himself to
winning Indian wars and crushing slave insurrection. He had
some understanding of the origins of the problems he faced.
He knew that unrest among the slaves on Virginia's Eastern
Shore originated partly in "the practice of severing husband,
wife and children in sales."[19] He also objected to calling Indians "savages." Late in life he wrote, "They appear to me to
merit a very different appellation, as we well know they are
not behind their civilized neighbors in the practice of many of
the virtues most dear to human nature."[20] However, such
hints of limited sympathy did not impede his determination to
suppress all unrest. His capacity for sharing the feelings of a
people other than his own was subordinated to his anxiety that
Virginia avoid turmoil.

Although he affected the appropriate reluctance and humility, Lee badly wanted the command of the Western Army
given to Anthony Wayne. As governor, Lee still had to deal
with small-scale conflict in western Virginia. Lee called the
Indians "a gallant desperate people . . . who are fighting pro
aris & focis"—for their altars and hearths.[21] But even when
avoidable combat was provoked by western militiamen who
attacked the Indians in violation of orders, Lee wanted to reduce or end the threat to whites by crushing the Indians. He
worked diligently, touring the area of conflict, obtaining
money for defense from the federal government, and writing

detailed letters of instructions for frontier settlers' self-protection. In gratitude for his labor, the westernmost county of Virginia was named for him. And after Wayne broke the Indians' resistance, Lee could finally refer to them as "the subdued savage."[22]

In his memoirs, Lee, like some other slaveowning Virginians of his era, called slavery a "dreadful evil, which the cruel policy of preceding times had introduced." He "lamented" that the United States Constitution had not provided for "the gradual abolition of slavery"—a view that he did not mention in 1788 when he was working for the ratification of the constitution.[23] Lee owned slaves until they, with his other property, were lost in his bankruptcy. In Congress in 1800, Lee spoke against receiving a petition from free blacks that advocated "such measures as shall in due course emancipate the whole of their brethren from their present situation." He welcomed the closing of the slave trade; but "he hoped the House would never intermeddle with the property of any of the citizens," and he denied its right to do so.[24]

Lee both deplored the existence of slavery and defended its legal security because he feared revolt. The blacks were "an inveterate enemy," ever ready to murder their masters.[25] When he reported that slaves on the Eastern Shore had for six months planned an insurrection in 1792, he ordered officials "to crush the mad attempt." He could picture in vivid detail what would follow the failure of suppression: "whenever the slaves shall proceed to positive hostilities they will begin with firing the town, expecting the inhabitants in their zeal to extinguish the fire will fall an easy prey to men prepared for their slaughter."[26] Lee knew how slaughter worked. His active imagination could draw on bloody scenes within his memory to build from only a few hints a frightening description of madness and chaos.

But he could imagine a still worse terror: insurrection in

the midst of war. Americans could not safely devise their foreign policy without recalling their internal enemies. The presence of slaves made the United States, and especially the
southern states, more vulnerable. In building their military
defense and weighing the cost of war, they must beware of
what war might do to them. To justify the army that had been
legislated during the crisis with France, Lee recalled in Congress, in January 1800, that one motive for creating the army
had been "the proximity of St. Domingo to our Southern
States," which were "weak from their peculiar condition."
France might still rendezvous "invading forces" on that island
to send troops "white and black" against America.[27] Few lis-
teners would need more than Lee's oblique words to visualize
the threat at which he hinted. Ten years later, while he was
hoping that the United States would avoid war with Britain,
Lee paused at the mention of slavery in his memoirs to write a
footnote warning that "a state of war" might give "opportunity and instigation" to a slave revolt. When he thought of the
danger of this doubly "bloody tragedy" he asked, "what can
be more dreadful[?]"[28]

After 1793, Indians and slaves troubled Lee much less
often than did the unruliness of groups which opposed him politically. In his struggles with these opponents, Lee began in
victory and ended in defeat. In 1794, as a major general of
militia in federal service, he commanded the expedition that
silenced or arrested all who had dared defy the federal excise
tax on whiskey. In 1812, he was almost killed by a mob in
Baltimore. Although his strength steadily eroded, Lee refused
to resign from the political battles. They were the struggle to
determine the outcome of the Revolutionary War. He could
not reconcile himself to having lost it.

Lee's enemies played a trick on him. They turned him
into a tory. He never fully understood how this had happened;
it became one of his main preoccupations. He wrote political

pamphlets and military history partly in order to prove his life-long dedication to American liberty. He had tried to protect liberty from a series of his opponents who, unchecked, would lose it to anarchy or to foreign despotism. Yet despite the continuity of his patriotism, he had been transformed, as he saw it, from a defender of the government against a mob to the victim of a mob prompted by the government. Lee's willingness to fight a series of battles with his domestic enemies—battles in which defeat grew ever more likely and more costly—arose in part from his anxiety to maintain public order and defeat political rivals. His conflicts also showed his determination to establish that his was the true legacy of the American Revolutionary War. In conflict with the mob, his version of that legacy would increasingly insist that liberty was secure only in the hands of patriots who had proven their virtue in adversity—not with those who tried to derive liberty and virtue from the strength of numbers and the unchecked will of the many.

In response to the insurrection in western Massachusetts in 1786, Lee could still believe that strengthening of the federal government might suffice to maintain peace. He would have worked for such strengthening had Shays's Rebellion never occurred, but this resistance to expensive courts, rigorous enforcement of stringent taxation, and the payment of debts and taxes in specie, clinched Lee's argument for central authority. Lee attributed extravagant designs to the Shaysites: "the abolition of debts public & private, a division of property & a new government founded on principles of fraud & iniquity, or re-connexion with G.B." Lee feared that the insurrection would grow—through half of Massachusetts, all of New England; "the contagion will spread and may reach Virginia"; "if Massachusetts yields . . . the victors will extend their conquest & very destructive consequences will pervade from that victory the whole empire."[29]

Lee viewed the insurrection under the influence both of

distorted rumors and of a theory of politics that helped his imagination fill the gaps in his information. He could predict more than he knew. From their study of history, the revolutionary generation concluded that republics were especially vulnerable to popular disorder. The onset of such disorder might signal the resumption of a cyclical progression—from popular government to no government to despotism. Not all revolutionaries agreed on which events posed this threat, but Lee and other advocates of strong government could seize the familiar pattern to explain the danger. They shared the fears that they tried to arouse in others. When Lee, in the Virginia ratifying convention, said of the Shaysites that "Nothing was wanting to bring about a revolution but a great man to head the insurgents," he was repeating the alarm that he had expressed privately to his brother eighteen months earlier. He saw no inconsistency in telling Washington in 1786 that "a beginning of anarchy with all its calamitys has approached," then telling the Virginia convention that the Shaysites might have established a monarchy. The one would inevitably have led to the other, and the United States would thus have "a mob government for a time, which will terminate in despotism among ourselves or from abroad." Shays's Rebellion was to Lee "madness" that forced the question "whether we shall conquer this effort or whether it will conquer us." Lee placed his hope for America's survival on government strong enough to crush all insurrection and prevent the kind of "revolution" that the Shaysites threatened—namely, "a civil war."[30] Again, in the uprising of farmers as in the revolt of slaves, he foresaw the overthrow of reason, ending in domestic bloodshed.

The creation of a stronger government under a new constitution did not end this threat. In fact, during the 1790s Lee's defense of the Revolution's heritage grew more complicated. He confronted the beginnings of disorder in its new shape: partisan politics. He saw a direct causal connection between factional opposition to the federal administration's measures and organized defiance of the law. Although he continued to worry about the inherently violent dispositions of ungoverned men, he began to blame public unrest on malicious partisans who duped the wayward and made them cat's paws for the work of subversion.

Like President Washington, Lee applied this interpretation to the Whiskey Insurrection—western Pennsylvanians' resistance to the enforcement of the federal excise laws. The direct tax on whiskey was widely unpopular in the West, but only in four counties of Pennsylvania did concerted defiance obstruct the law. There federal officials were assaulted in the summer of 1794. Eager to establish the national government's authority beyond challenge, Washington called out almost thirteen thousand militiamen from Pennsylvania, New Jersey, Maryland, and Virginia. They marched in the autumn under the command of their state governors, with Lee, the governor of Virginia, doubling as federal Commander in Chief of the force. They met no resistance. They arrested some accused offenders, who were handled roughly but soon let go, and the militia returned home in a few weeks.

Although Lee later called the insurrection "a comedy," he took its warnings seriously.[31] Such disorder, if unchecked, would force Americans "to obey a mob."[32] Lee's view of the insurgents mirrored the report of one of Washington's commissioners: "a frenzy seemed to be diffused thro' the country, the still voice of reason drowned, and the wildest chimeras to have taken possession of men's minds."[33] The passivity with which the western people met the army did not reassure Lee. Without the presence of federal force, he believed, "the reign of violence and anarchy will return."[34] He had seen this specter before, and he knew the inevitable outcome of anarchy—"despotism in some shape or other."[35]

In his proclamation to the inhabitants of the four western counties of Pennsylvania, Lee attributed the whiskey rebels' lawlessness to "the doctrines by which they have been misled." He believed that "the gradual approaches of disorder and anarchy" flowed out of partisan attacks on the federal administration. Lee, Washington, and other Federalists charged or hinted that there were direct connections between the anti-tax violence, the Democratic Societies that criticized Federalist policies, and the members of Congress who opposed Hamilton's financial measures and Washington's foreign policy. The swift slide from faction to chaos was unmistakable and, unless it was stopped, irreversible. The western Pennsylvanians had joined the migration to new lands that dominated Lee's vision of the future. He called them "a people by situation capable of every happiness"; but they had been "duped by artful leaders to sacrifice it." Lee's address sought to discredit the political leaders under whose influence the Pennsylvanians had "vilified & abused" the federal government. These leaders, by accusing the administration of conspiring "against the liberty and happiness of the people," were "sporting with public passions."[36]

Convinced that "the late wicked insurrection . . . may be fairly traced to the principles & sentiments delivered by members of Congress on & off the floor," Lee hoped that the suppression of the rebels would also silence partisan opposition to the administration.[37] Faction and rebellion loomed ever larger in his fears.

In September 1794, shortly after Lee's appointment to the command, Alexander Hamilton said of him, "He is all zeal."[38] Lee's enthusiasm gained urgency from his alarm over the prospect that the insurrection might find support in Virginia. The whiskey rebels had friends in Maryland and Virginia, but none who were willing to imitate them. More important were the Virginians who felt reluctant to help suppress them. Resistance to the militia drafts in Surry County alarmed Lee. When Captain Nathan Jones was about to draft three men from his company for service in Pennsylvania, "a certain Benjamin Billeo stepped out of the ranks and told the Captain if he was done [with] his speech he had something to say to the men, and then told them, all that was for liberty to follow him."[39] Captain Jones was left with only nine or ten men, and the rest of his company would not allow him to draft from among the remaining men or even write down their names unless they wanted to volunteer. The open defiance in Surry County was not typical of the state and did not last long. Lee did not even need men from the south side of the James River to fill his complement of militia. However, he suspected that the Surry malcontents would try to influence men in other counties. "If we permit our laws to be violated with impunity farewel to order farewel to liberty & all the political happiness we enjoy." The resistance was "pregnant with mischief of the blackest dye" because the insurrection in Pennsylvania was a "wicked & daring attempt to destroy our government & with it our liberty."

In Lee's mind, isolated instances of disorder could quickly multiply and overwhelm the nation's fragile tranquillity. As Lee drafted letters against the Surry resistance, his indignation took him too far. His manifestos usually strove to isolate the whiskey rebels by proclaiming that most Americans supported the government. But in reaction to the militiamen's defiance, Lee accused them of being "so cowardly as to fear the rabble who have usurped dominion over the U States."[40] After rereading the sentence, he crossed out the latter clause. Obviously, with Washington as President, the constitution in effect, and its supporters in office, the United States had not yet succumbed to "the rabble," and Lee wanted to help assure that the country never did. For a moment, however, his pen had revealed the greater danger he detected behind some

Americans' willingness to oppose their government. For a moment he had already seen in the Whiskey Insurrection the future that he feared.

Lee won praise for his command of the federal force in western Pennsylvania. Even an extensive contemporary criticism of the administration for suppressing the lawbreakers with troops said, "There are no complaints of governor Lee having been inexorable or inhumane."[41] Five years later, Lee had acquired a reputation as "an exterminator," but this accusation of militarism did not originate in his command of the expedition against the whiskey rebels.[42] Despite the official commendations and public testimonials for Lee, he returned to Virginia and to private life embittered, with his popularity impaired. His offenses, in the eyes of his critics, were political rather than military. His crime was not abusing his command but accepting it in the first place. By doing so, his opponents charged, he had joined the administration's malicious plan to link the Republican opposition with lawless disorder and to use disorder as justification for a standing army.

A newspaper writer expressed the resentment of those who disliked the federal government's overwhelming military enforcement of the excise laws. The writer denounced Lee's proclamation to the western Pennsylvanians for its "party rancour." In it, Lee had blamed the insurrection on Republicans' criticism of the federal administration. Going beyond his commission to enforce the law, he was violating the people's right to their own political opinions by unjustifiably linking those widely shared opinions with an isolated instance of disorder. This was a "bayonet attack" on freedom of thought, since a government official had authority only to correct citizens' illegal behavior, not their political opinions. The writer accused Lee of using the justness of his role as law enforcer to make his partisan defense of the administration's policies seem equally just. This partisanship looked all the more strange because, when Lee had first become governor, "he loudly propagated unfavourable opinions of the operations of the general government" and won office "by condemning the combinations forming under treasury measures." What had happened to the "love of equality" by which he had passed Virginians' test of their officeholders? The writer attributed Lee's change to ambition. Lee's third and last term as governor was ending; perhaps, his critics suggested, he thought that he had missed the appointment to command the Western Army in 1792 by reason of his censure of the national administration; now he had "heightened the zeal" of his efforts to ingratiate himself with the administration by "his encomiums on the federal government." Thus had Lee "risen to the rank of persecution" by taking "the path of separation from his countrymen in general."[43]

Other critics of the administration also accused Lee of partisanship in suppressing the rebels. Rumor said that he commanded under the political "mentorship" of Secretary of the Treasury Alexander Hamilton, who marched with the army in an ill-defined but influential status.[44] While Lee was in Pennsylvania, the Virginia General Assembly invoked a state law forbidding state officials to accept federal appointments, and the Assembly declared the governorship vacant before the end of Lee's term. The majority then elected a Republican to replace him. Historians of Virginia politics agree that the dismissal of Lee marked the change of the governorship to a partisan office.[45] Lee had helped begin the process by his introduction of foreign policy issues into state affairs. As "his disagreement with the public opinion of his country" grew sharper, it led to his expulsion from office.[46]

The General Assembly's formal commendation of Lee's conduct as commander did not assuage his distress over the dismissal. Even the vote of thanks had been adopted only after a resolution of "indirect censure" had been "dextrously warded off."[47] Early in 1795, a Republican who talked with him found that "political hostility immediately ensued." Over wine after dinner, Lee revealed that "his feelings are hurt beyond description from the late political occurrences in this country."[48] He had seen in the Whiskey Insurrection a chance to expose the violent tendencies of opposition to government. Cowing the mob would dramatize the government's widespread support and its secure authority. As Washington's choice for Commander in Chief, Lee had defended the Revolution and the constitution. He had bragged that the army's fortitude proved the American people's determination and ability to preserve their government. Yet Lee had not returned to Virginia in triumph. He received praise but not the united support he claimed; instead, his enemies had grown more numerous and more hostile. Lee reported to Hamilton in January 1795: "I have become an object of the most virulent enmity to a certain political junto." From representing the United States against lawbreakers, Lee's position seemed almost reversed. Now he was "collecting defensive weapons" for use against the "junto who affect to govern the U.S."[49]

About the time he was hearing "that my imagination cannot present to me in true colours their invention & circulation of tales to deprekate me," Lee fell ill.[50] He was "laid up for . . . four weeks with a violent cold."[51] Again, as in the period after the Battle of Eutaw Springs, defeat, censure, and sickness all troubled Lee at once. He had quelled the rebels, but he had not subdued the Republicans; he had only alienated them. At the same time he failed to win the full trust of the administration that he supported. Hamilton had accompanied the army to western Pennsylvania partly because he "thought that even Lee might miss the policy of the case in some particulars &c &c."[52] Later in 1795, Secretary of State Timothy Pickering successfully opposed the appointment of Lee as Secretary of War. Pickering, who had recently held the office, said, "the department comprehends a multitude of details, and demands economy in its numerous expenditures." He did not need to explain how that consideration disqualified Lee. Furthermore, the "appointment would doubtless be extremely unpopular: it would be disapproved by the enemies of the government without acquiring the confidence of its friends."[53] Americans seemed more likely to agree in mistrusting Lee than in relying on him for their defense. He might tell himself that by returning to a military command he had helped perpetuate the Revolution. But the successful national future that would unite his countrymen in prosperity lay still farther from his grasp. Aspiring to be the guarantor of peace, Lee had become the victim of discord.

As partisan alignments became clearer in the mid-1790s, Lee's commitment to the Washington administration, to the Federalists, and to a powerful national government grew stronger. By 1794, the last year of his governorship, Lee had muted or suppressed his public criticisms of Hamiltonian financial policies and had become a firm Federalist. Perhaps he was, as Merrill Peterson says, "a political turncoat still seeking to recover solvency and reputation as a Federalist."[54] Perhaps, as Republicans charged, he had abandoned the proper political views of a Virginian out of ambition for national office. If these assessments fit Lee, they are further evidence of his flawed judgment when seeking his own interest. Except for an inactive military commission, the only offices he held after leaving the governorship and his command of the militia army in 1794 were those given to him by the voters of Westmoreland County and the Northern Neck. Lee soon saw proof that his newly ardent Federalism would not necessarily bring him advancement or popularity. His partisanship of the 1790s had other motives to persevere.

Lee's fear of civil war intensified his hostility toward the Republicans as their organization coalesced in Virginia and in Congress. Like other Federalists, he accused the Republicans of going beyond opposition to the administration or its policies: they attacked the existence of the government. He believed that the political division of the 1790s had begun with the contest over the ratification of the constitution, which "unfortunately excited an irritation which has never yet been assuaged." As Lee had invoked Shays's Rebellion to justify the adoption of the constitution, he now invoked the Whiskey Rebellion to show that Republican opposition would subvert the constitution. Speaking and writing against the Virginia Resolutions that opposed the Alien and Sedition Acts, Lee several times recalled the Whiskey Rebellion. Republicans, by falsely charging federal officials with conspiring to create a monarchy, provoked public hatred of the government and its officers. Nor was the Republican sabotage only "senseless" or "unknowing"; it bore the marks of "a digested system." The authors of the plan wanted to convince Americans, among whom love of liberty was a national trait, "that the government is radically and systematically opposed to that happiness it was instituted to preserve."[55] If the Republicans widely instilled this notion, a liberty-loving people would inevitably defy or destroy their government. Although Lee energetically supported the ostensible purposes of the Alien and Sedition Acts and the Provisional Army, his defense of these measures, once begun, centered on more fundamental questions. At his most fervent, he repeatedly warned that the Republican "system" of attack would lead to disunion and civil war.

Most students of American politics in the Early National Period now credit the Federalists and the Republicans with believing the warnings against monarchy and anarchy that often underlay controversy over immediate issues.[56] The accusations of conspiracy were not hypocritical attempts to inflate partisan differences over governmental policy into maliciously false charges of subversion. Not reconciled to the permanence of rival political parties, not accustomed to the alternation of parties in national office, not confident of the security of independence and republican government, Americans often equated the pursuit of party policies with the survival of the nation and its liberty. Opposition seemed to threaten these goals, and from this threat Americans inferred the existence of an organized plan of subversion, embodied in the rival faction. By 1800 Henry Lee had spent almost twenty years trying to avoid a resurgence of the civil conflict he had first seen during the Revolutionary War. He was especially apt to see a malign plan in Republican criticism of government: his horror of civil war convinced him that no group could invite it as the Republicans did without purposefully seeking to destroy the union.

The consequences of hostility toward government were dramatized to Lee, as to many of his political allies, by the French Revolution and its intrusion into American politics. France suffered some of the worst of the violence that Lee feared for America. The French Revolution, in Lee's mind, threatened to bring to the United States alien instigators who intensified the internal sources of unrest. Lee's harsh reaction to the Whiskey Insurrection derived some of its fervor from his conviction that this foreign influence was at work in Pennsylvania, especially through the Democratic Societies. He knew how appealing a return to revolution could seem; he had come close to taking a commission in the French Army. In the time of grief after the death of his wife and son, he sought in such a command "full employment corresponding with my feelings." At the same time he worried that if the European monarchs defeated France, they might think "the exploit but half accomplished, unless we also be politically changed." Fighting for the French Revolution might help protect republicanism in America. In September 1792, Lee was "wishing to

enter the service of the Republic" but was also asking
"whether the Disunion prevalent there will endanger the Revolution."[57] The growing signs of "Disunion," along with the
advice of his friends and the prospect of remarriage, kept Lee
from going to France.

For this short while, Lee wanted to enlist in the war in
Europe, but he did not want the war to come to America.
This concern helped turn him away from identification with
the French Revolution. Did the Revolutionary War alliance
with the Old Régime in France oblige the United States to aid
the French revolutionaries in fighting Britain? Would American neutrality cause France to treat the United States as an
enemy? Lee wanted his countrymen to "cling close to peace as
the fairest road to their general good."[58] During 1793 and
1794, he moved decidedly toward the opinion of Alexander
Hamilton and other Federalists who believed that the greatest
domestic threat to peace lay in some Americans' manifestations of attachment to France. Division among Americans
would make their continent another arena for constant war
over the European balance of power—"The bloody and the
wicked scenes of Europe will be re-acted on this side the Atlantic."[59] Lee was thinking of this prospect when he warned in
1794 that joining the war in Europe would "entail on posterity irremediable mischiefs & may by one blow pull down the
political edifice which . . . offers most comfortable quarters to
the human race." Within a few months of his first letter, Lee
had abandoned his brief attachment to the French Revolution
and had grown highly critical of other Americans who perse-
vered in theirs. Revolution in Europe no longer seemed to
offer "fair war on terms of honor" to General Lee at the head
of a French legion. It now threatened to destroy the peacetime
legacy of the American Revolution. Believing that his political
opponents were risking this fate, Lee wrote: "Surprise aston-
ishment & indignation alternately agitates my mind."[60]

In addition to the threat of involvement in Europe's

wars, Lee feared that Americans would imitate the French Revolution. Unlike some of the more extreme Federalists, he did not usually talk as if the Terror were imminent or even probable in the United States. However, he saw in opponents of the Federalist administration a "malignant combination" of domestic "conspiritors," whose organization "menaced from its very nature the destruction of the constitution & government under which we live." The new French minister, Citizen Edmond Genêt, found allies "in high employments . . . in state & congressional office" for his attempts to sabotage Washington's policy of neutrality. Lee wanted to dismiss these officials and silence their "noisy clamorous & impudent" followers, who gathered "at taverns . . . gambling & drinking all night & all day abusing men & measures however respectable, however proper." Lee had decided not to fight for France; a few weeks later he had rejected Genêt's argument that America's safety depended on active aid to the republican régime in France; the French Revolution had become, in his eyes, a device with which the enemies of government could first kindle, then "fan the fire" of disorder.[61] In 1800, Lee recalled the machinations of Genêt as proof that "the people of America are liable, like other nations, to all the disasters which spring from factions and factious men."[62] During the partisan conflicts of the 1790s, he was fighting this "unextinguished fire."[63]

As governor, Lee combated the influence of the French Revolution mainly by his efforts to enforce the neutrality proclamation. He markedly advanced the process of making the governorship a partisan office by using the proclamation almost as a platform for re-election in 1793. The mobilization of critics of the proclamation matured party organization in Virginia. In October, Lee introduced this national issue into state politics by pressing the General Assembly to endorse the proclamation—a vote he won despite having started what one historian calls an "uproar."[64] In November, his address accepting re-election dwelt on this victory. He praised himself for his "sense of duty " and his "promotion of the true interest of the commonwealth"; he praised the proclamation "as the result of the most affectionate zeal for the happiness of our common country"; and he praised the national administration for securing "the permanent establishment of the blessings of peace."[65]

During the following spring and summer, before he marched against the whiskey rebels, Lee took the field to maintain strict neutrality in Virginia. The presence of French and British vessels threatened "the harmony and peace" of Norfolk, and Lee anticipated unrest: "the discord between the hostile frigates I fear will be communicated to the inhabitants."[66] Three months later his alarm was borne out when a Norfolk mob tarred and feathered a bystander who spoke against their salute of a French frigate. Of the more than four hundred men in the procession, one hundred-fifty were blacks. "The precedent," Lee said, "is replete with danger."[67] In July, he turned to military force to keep Virginians neutral. He mobilized seven or eight hundred militiamen to stop the outfitting at Smithfield, Virginia, of a vessel intended as a French privateer. The ship's owners had resisted a marshal, but Lee made sure that they would not resist the militia: he ordered the use of cavalry to seize the ship. A newspaper writer called this decision "a novelty of the tacticks," but praised "the prudence of his excellency in undertaking this affair, his coolness in planning, and his judgement in the selection of the troops." The expedition was a reminder that Governor Lee had "experience of the efficacy of cavalry." Sure enough, the "enemy . . . capitulated upon the first charge of the horse marines." Lee had again shown "his wonted decision and activity" in using the techniques of the Revolutionary War against disobedience of the law.[68] Now he was turning his cavalry, his genius, and his activity against the agents, employees, or friends of revolutionary France. By suppressing them, Lee would protect the American Revolution and, in so doing, would help Washington "to save our common country from the scourge of War."[69]

However, the next year Lee learned that the clamors of faction could come dangerously near to sabotaging Washington's work for peace, embodied in the treaty with Great Britain that John Jay negotiated. In June 1795, Lee sent Jay "friendly congratulations" on the treaty.[70] But when the administration offered Americans peace, the Republicans accused the Federalists of partiality toward Britain, of violating the treaty with France, of betraying the American Revolution. Worse yet, the belligerent abuse turned against George Washington and threatened to undermine the previously unquestioned public esteem for the living symbol of patriotism. Even more than the criticisms of the treaty and the hostile "inventions" spread by "the agitators of our country," Lee brooded over the "wicked . . . political influence" of attacks on Washington. If political partisans could discredit Washington, there could hardly be a limit to the possible success of their efforts to betray American independence. Lee was a delegate in the Virginia General Assembly of 1795, and the affront that alarmed him was one of the milder of the contemporary strictures on the President. The Republicans in the Assembly passed a resolution commending Virginia's senators for voting against ratification of the treaty. Then the Republicans amended a Federalist resolution of confidence in Washington's "great abilities, wisdom and integrity" by substituting a commendation only of his "integrity and patriotism." Thus the Republicans had implicitly contended, Lee later wrote, "that Washington was destitute of wisdom." The insistence of Federalists in the Virginia Senate eventually won the General Assembly over to adoption of the original Federalist resolution, by which, Lee said, "virtue has gained a complete victory." Only by intense effort had they "crushed this disgraceful assault upon the reputation of the father of the nation." Even this brief indication of the political vulnerability of the Federalists' most secure leader caused Lee great distress. He fell ill, "afflicted" with "pain in my head," which he attributed not only to exposure in bad weather but also to "the extreme mental agitation I have undergone." The pain had lasted for more than a week when Lee wrote that it "will never cease I fear until I can get relieved from the present agitating theatre."[71] His temporary illness foreshadowed the debilitating effects that he would suffer from defeats in politics and in business enterprise. Each setback, each proof of the strength of his opponents, became a new impediment or confinement working against his ambition to shape the future. Perhaps he was beginning to guess the course of his political future: defense, retreats, and rearguard actions to escape final defeat.

The growing political strength of opposition to the Federalist administrations coincided, in Lee's mind, with the growing danger of disorder. The group that most ominously combined these threats to peace was the foreign-born residents of the United States. Swelling in numbers through immigration, they were also seizing the easy terms of naturalization to become citizens and often to join the Republicans. In response to this increase in the number of his political enemies, Lee's nativism intensified. He confined his welcome for the foreign-born in America primarily to conspicuous and gifted men, especially military officers like Lafayette, Steuben, and Pulaski. He did not trust the loyalty of lesser men. During the Revolutionary War, he gave strict orders to the Legion's recruiters "never to enlist a British soldier, a foreigner, or a drunkard."[72] Lee's hostility did not stop with this widely shared suspicion of mercenary wartime recruits. Late in the 1790s, "the numerous aliens, long fostered by American hospitality," looked worse than opportunists—they were infiltrators working for revolutionary France. If the naval war and diplomatic confrontation with France led to an invasion of the United States, Lee expected these "dangerous aliens" to give "keen and operative aid" to the enemy. For years they had been trying to sabotage religion and government in order to prepare "the American people for the reaction of the French and Saint Domingo tragedies." The federal government must "rid their country of such eventual misery"; defenses of aliens' alleged rights served "only to excite more and more the begun ferment."[73]

Lee worked hard to quell that ferment. More than almost any other partisan controversy in his life, the conflict over the Alien and Sedition Acts of 1798 enlisted his strongest efforts. These federal laws gave the national government broad powers to deport aliens and prosecute citizens for criticism of the government or its officials. The Republican critics of the legislation regarded it as a malicious partisan use of federal authority to suppress the Republican Party. The Federalist sponsors of the laws described them as a defense of constitutional self-government against the attacks of incendiaries and foreign agents. Lee took an active role in defending the legislation against the Republicans. In the Virginia General Assembly, he argued against the Virginia Resolutions, which denounced the acts and proposed concerted opposition to them. He wrote the address to the public that the minority of the legislature published, responding to the criticisms in the Virginia Resolutions. He wrote another, longer pamphlet to present a more fully developed argument on behalf of the acts. He won election to the United States Congress from the Northern Neck of Virginia and defended the legislation in the House of Representatives.

"The CRISIS is indeed an AWFUL one," Lee warned.[74] The struggle over the Alien and Sedition Acts—part of the

RIGHT. Charles Willson Peale, *Henry Lee.* Light-Horse Harry shortly after he left the army. (Courtesy of the Independence National Historical Park Collection, Philadelphia)

BELOW. *The Death of Pulaski at Savannah.* The cavalryman's death in combat, repeatedly recorded by Light-Horse Harry Lee. (Courtesy of the Prints Division, New York Public Library, Astor, Lenox, and Tilden Foundations)

RIGHT. Charles Willson Peale, *Nathanael Greene*. Lee's wartime commander and friend. (Courtesy of the Independence National Historical Park Collection, Philadelphia)

BELOW. Sir Joshua Reynolds, *Banastre Tarleton*. The commander of the British dragoons who fought Lee in the South and chased Jefferson in Virginia. (Courtesy of the National Gallery, London)

Charles Willson Peale, *John Laurens.* After Lee went home, Laurens took Lee's command and then became one of the last casualties of the war. (Courtesy of the Independence National Historical Park Collection, Philadelphia)

Charles Willson Peale, *Henry Lee.* Lee before he had become Light-Horse Harry. (Courtesy of Mr. Nathaniel Burt and the Frick Art Reference Library, New York)

Charles Willson Peale, *Alexander Hamilton.* The future Secretary of the Treasury and Federalist Party leader a young Continental army officer. (Courtesy of Mr. Nathaniel Burt and the Frick Art Reference Library, New York)

OPPOSITE, ABOVE. *Battle of Guilford Courthouse.* An inaccurate rendering of the battle, showing a cavalry charge by Tarleton's British dragoons. (Courtesy of the Anne S.K. Brown Military Collection, Brown University Library)

OPPOSITE, BELOW. Attributed to James Peale, *Washington Reviewing the Western Army at Fort Cumberland, Maryland.* The army that, under Lee's command, crushed the Whiskey Insurrection in 1794. (Courtesy of the Metropolitan Museum of Art, New York, gift of Col. and Mrs. Edgar William Garbisch, 1963)

Artist unknown, *Henry Lee*
(1729–1787). Light-Horse Harry's
father. (Courtesy of the Virginia
Historical Society, Richmond)

Artist unknown, *Ann Hill Carter Lee.* Second wife of Light-Horse Harry Lee and mother of Robert E. Lee. (Washington-Custis-Lee Collection, Courtesy of Washington and Lee University, Virginia)

Charlotte Partain, *Stratford Hall.* (Pen-and-ink drawing © 1980 by Charlotte Partain)

Charles Willson Peale, *Gouverneur Morris and Robert Morris.* Government administrators, Federalist Party leaders, financiers, and promoters of land speculation. (Courtesy of the Pennsylvania Academy of the Fine Arts, Philadelphia, bequest of Richard Ashhurst)

C. Partain ©1980

George Beck, *The Great Falls of the Potomac.* The obstacle
to the Potomac Company's plans for commerce on the river,
seen here in a painting owned by George Washington.
(Courtesy of the Mount Vernon Ladies Association of the Union)

George I. Parkyns, *Washington, D.C.* The Potomac River
and the lands on which Lee hoped to prosper, as they
looked in 1795. (Courtesy of the Prints and Photographs
Division, Library of Congress)

T. Cartwright after George Beck, *Georgetown and Federal City*. The Potomac
River and Washington, D.C., in 1801. (Courtesy of the Prints and Photographs
Division, Library of Congress)

ABOVE. Ruins of a building on the site of Matildaville. (Photograph courtesy of the Virginia State Library, Richmond)

LEFT. Part of the Potomac Company's abandoned Great Falls canal. (Photograph courtesy of the Virginia State Library, Richmond)

RIGHT. Abandoned lock of the Potomac Company's Great Falls canal. (Photograph courtesy of the Virginia State Library, Richmond)

BELOW. George I. Parkyns, *View of the Suburbs of the City of Washington.* Waterfront trade, probably in Georgetown, about 1800. Lee had hoped to see much more commerce on the Potomac River by 1800. (Courtesy of the Prints and Photographs Division, Library of Congress)

Artist unknown, *William Augustine Washington*. One of the many creditors whom Lee could not pay. (Courtesy of the Virginia State Library, Richmond)

Artist unknown, *Charles Simms*. Former Continental Army officer, Federalist Party leader, and Potomac Company director, Simms attacked Thomas Jefferson's war record and helped Lee publish his memoirs. (Courtesy of the Virginia State Library, Richmond)

Artist unknown, *Alexander Contee Hanson*. The Federalist editor whom Lee joined in Baltimore in 1812 and with whom Lee was attacked by a mob. (Courtesy of the Prints and Photographs Division, Library of Congress)

Stratford Hall, the plantation, and the Potomac River.
(Photograph courtesy of the Virginia State Library, Richmond)

Bass Otis, *Thomas Jefferson.*
Jefferson in retirement, when
he disputed Lee's version of
the Revolutionary War.
(Courtesy of the Thomas Jefferson Memorial Foundation;
photograph by Edwin S.
Roseberry)

Rembrandt Peale, *George
Washington.* Washington near
the end of his term as Presi-
dent. (Courtesy of the Detroit
Institute of Arts, gift of Mrs.
James Couzens)

607 Oronoco Street, Alexandria, Virginia.
The house in which the Lees lived after leaving Stratford Hall.
(Photograph courtesy of the Alexandria Library)

ABOVE. Gilbert Stuart, *Henry Lee.* Lee in his fifties, shortly before he went to jail. (Courtesy of Mr. Carter L. Refo)

LEFT. Michael Miley, *Robert E. Lee.* A photograph taken in Lee's last year, after he had edited Light-Horse Harry's memoirs. (Courtesy of the Virginia Historical Society, Richmond) larger crisis over the creation of a standing army and the threat of war with France—became a climactic effort in Lee's resistance to the growing danger of the mob. After Thomas Jefferson became President and Lee left public office for the last time in 1801, he grew increasingly occupied with his own financial problems. He remained a fervent critic of Jefferson's conduct as President, but unlike many other Federalists, gave little sign of believing that Federalism or the virtues of Washington's administration could be restored to their rightful place. Instead, Lee's later writings on public issues dealt primarily with ways to retard or ameliorate the multiplying evils of Jeffersonian ascendancy. His career after 1800 confirmed the fear that seemed to prompt his intense political activity in 1798 and 1799: this crisis would be the last chance for him to defeat the enemies he had been fighting.

The increasing political activity and success of the Republicans, the vocal opposition to the neutrality proclamation, the prevalence of support for revolutionary France, the upsurge of insurrection in Pennsylvania, the political welcome for alien radicals, the censure of the Federalists as pro-British monarchists, the defamation of Washington—all these instances of disorder and bad judgment speeded the erosion of Lee's trust in the public. Unable to see merit in these attacks on peace and harmony, he could only conclude that they were imposed upon the public through the power of delusion. The popular delusions were manipulated by partisans, some of whom—like James Madison—were conscientiously misguided, more of whom—like Thomas Jefferson—were ambitious hypocrites. Lee did not change his belief that American independence and self-government rested on the support of the people. But having concluded that popular political judgment could be so easily and so dangerously misled, he grew increasingly afraid that the necessary allegiance to the constitution and the government would be destroyed. Instead of relying on his countrymen to reject the falsehood and selfishness of the attacks, as he had rejected them, Lee expected the attacks to succeed—to alienate the people from their institutions—unless the lies could be stopped at the source.

This reasoning underlay Lee's defense of the Alien and Sedition Acts. These measures, he argued, gave the government "the means of preserving itself." He felt even greater alarm at the Virginia Resolutions and related protests against the acts than at the offenses which the acts outlawed. The opposition, he charged, arose from a "pernicious system," a "pernicious design," which appealed to "wicked citizens . . . incapable of quiet." The Virginia Resolutions "inspired hostility, and squinted at disunion." Union had become a more nearly absolute good for Lee than for most of his countrymen, and his strongest assertions of the union's worth and permanence came in rebuttal to the protests against the Alien and Sedition Acts. By denying the constitutionality of the acts, by inviting concerted opposition, and by charging the administration with monarchical ambitions, the Republicans were, in effect, "recommending resistance" to the acts. When the state encouraged citizens to disobey the laws, "insurrection would be the consequence."[75]

Insurrection and war would complete the destruction of the vision that had shaped Lee's life after he left the army. He attributed the setbacks of his hopes for peace to the undisciplined mob and to the demagogues who aroused disorder rather than to his own ill-disciplined investments, loans, and extravagant continental schemes. Shortly before Lee went to jail for debt, he was pressing advice on Madison and describing his fears about the country's future if Madison's presidential candidacy were sidetracked by Republican rivals. "The scum of this nation & the outcasts of foreign nations will be the ruling interest & intolerance the most persecuting, will be the daily practice. Geographical partys will in the four years be formed, [the] seat of govt in spite of all the sanctions of law

& use will be removed & the bands of union will be first loosened & then dissolved."[76] Here, in brief, were the concerns that had come to dominate Lee's thinking about public life by the 1790s. The destruction of his plans for the Potomac and for peace, the lapse into mob rule, disunion, and civil war—these public disorders threatened to throw the country back into the barbarity and anarchy of civil bloodshed. Lee's imagination made the scenes more ominous as the years passed, but their basic elements remained familiar: they were the wartime evils he had tried to efface with the love and prosperity of peace.

The grandiose scale of Lee's ideal intensified the danger posed by these evils. So fully had his mind linked the country's happiness with his own fortunes that he most readily explained his private troubles as the effect of sabotage directed against the nation. This reasoning suited his temperament because, instead of admonishing him to curtail his enterprises and alter his notion of peace, it invited him to redouble his activity—not only by investing in his vision but also by combating those who threatened his success. "If we love the Union," Lee wrote, "if we wish peace at home, and safety abroad; let us guard our own bosoms from a flame which threatens to consume all reason, temper and reflection."[77] Pursuing this course, Lee tried to impose on a whole society an order that would also change his own life from the confusion he had created to the harmony he had foreseen.

Lee had shared some of the unruliness that he increasingly opposed: he was distracted from productive labor by visionary speculations and by partisan political agitation; he denounced Hamilton's financial program and promoted opposition by helping to establish and circulate the *National Gazette* under Philip Freneau's editorship; for a while he found disunion preferable to the federal policies for taxation and funding of the national debt; he still sought war—for himself, he said, not for his country; he had sympathized with the French

Revolution enough to come near joining its army. When Lee strove to suppress the mob, he was fighting a confusion, some of which he had joined in public life or still experienced in his private life. Not all the chaos came from the mob; not all the subverters of peace were outside the walls of Stratford. Yet Lee could neither control the enemy without nor outrun the enemy within. To forgo or attenuate his favorite devices—discipline and activity—would have obliged him to acknowledge that he no longer shaped the Revolution, that his own weaknesses had in part betrayed his ideal of independence. Such an admission was a surrender Lee could not make. If he hoped that success in imposing peace and order on America would also create the well-being that he expected for himself and his family, he did not get the chance to find out. The United States was moving away from, not toward, the kind of order that Lee sought. If he ever looked for some other method of bringing order into his private life, he did not find it.

Lee's defense of the federal government as the guarantor of American independence found its fullest development in his arguments on behalf of the military establishment created by the Federalists in 1798. Under the same aegis as the Alien and Sedition Acts—the threat of war with France—this establishment was an unprecedented standing army with auxiliary forces, not intended primarily for frontier Indian fighting. The augmentation of the army provoked much criticism, both for its expense and for its threat to civil liberties. Republicans charged that the new army was another element of a Federalist plot—along with the Alien and Sedition Acts—to pervert republican government with the autocratic instruments of monarchy. They warned that Federalists would use the army to suppress domestic political opposition. In fact, however,

Federalists were divided in their view of the utility and purpose of the army once it had been established; its most enthusiastic proponent and second in command, Alexander Hamilton, as well as some of his followers, seem to have calculated on the intimidating effect or coercive potential of a permanent army in domestic politics. President John Adams, on the other hand, disassociated himself from the new establishment as its high command became the preserve of his opponents within the Federalist Party.

Henry Lee left no record to indicate that he supported the new army for its usefulness in overawing political opposition. From his background and political views, one could plausibly infer that he shared the intentions that the historian Richard Kohn attributes to the army's proponents: buttressing a hierarchical social order with a quasi-aristocratic permanent standing army.[78] However, if Lee shared this predilection, he expressed it in more immediately pressing concerns. He feared war and the destructive effects of war on government and social order. In the new military establishment, he saw a way either to avoid war by demonstrating America's strength or to ameliorate its effects by employing military professionalism.

Soon after George Washington accepted titular command of the new army, Lee offered his services in "this menacing period."[79] After receiving a commission as major general, though not an active duty command, Lee heard from a fellow Virginia Federalist, "I have no doubt . . . that the same patriotism & valour which gained you so much applause in the late revolutionary war, will be crowned in future with ten fold success, & render you victorious over your countries foes, foreign & Domestic."[80] Lee himself liked to cast the crisis in the language of the Revolution: defense of the nation from European conquest, a test of Americans' resolve to fight for the public good. The danger of war again demanded the military skills from which he had derived so much gratification and with which he had achieved more conspicuous successes than in his peacetime life. But a war between France and a factionally divided America also threatened to bring a widespread anarchy that the revolutionaries had only glimpsed fitfully and locally during war with Britain. Lee did not say how deeply or for how long he feared imminent invasion, but his alarm over the consequences of invasion was genuine. He could imagine the scene "had the destination of Buonaparte been America instead of Egypt."[81] In the absence of a trained and ready military force, America would again resort to inconstant militiamen, who would fall victims to their own inexperience and leave their unprotected country open to violence and subjugation. Political antagonisms among Americans made the country even less prepared to resist conquest, especially because the Republicans seemed ready to subordinate America's interests to the policies of France. Disunion would "invite the enemy to our country." To protect the United States from these threats, Lee devoted most of his effort to advocating the military establishment of 1798. The need for such an army seemed so obvious and the consequences of its absence so fatal that Lee found it hard to imagine a patriotic, conscientious opposition to it. The opponents of the army operated under "the pretence of promoting your happiness." But their eagerness to abolish or reduce the army was "so strange that it excites suspicions truly alarming." Republicans would seek "union with the invader, for the purpose of accomplishing a *delectable* reform."[82] Americans who persisted in sabotaging an adequate military defense when opposed by a victorious European professional army might secretly be planning the foreign subjugation that their policy invited.

Both sides in the political conflicts of 1798 to 1801 claimed to embody the legacy of the Revolutionary War. Each promised to defend it from the attacks of the other. The change from Federalist to Republican control of the government, as well as the political eclipse of Henry Lee, marked a shift from one prevailing view of the war's legacy to a different one. Lee, like many other Federalist politicians, appealed to his record of service in the Revolutionary War and especially in the Continental Army as a proof of his patriotic intentions in postwar politics. Lee and his colleagues tended to assume that their political positions twenty years later still deserved the united support of a struggle for the country's existence. Because the political conflicts of the Early National Period were preoccupied with defining the liberty won through independence and with determining America's relation to wartime enemy and ally, such claims to special competence attained in war could sound plausible. Who could be more worthy of public trust than the men who had risked the most to win the Revolution? This certainty helps explain how Lee could condemn the mob—a category that kept swelling in size as he added more of his countrymen to it—while not doubting that he spoke for the Revolution and its heritage of liberty and self-government. As a measure of fidelity to the revolutionary cause, political consistency in extending some of its principles—such as majoritarianism and trust in the public's wisdom—could not override a record of personal service. Lee could confidently invoke the legacy of the Revolution against the mob because his own career of persevering virtue amid popular delusion and delinquency seemed to him to embody that legacy more fully than did an appeal to political abstractions.

The political conflicts of the 1790s and the Republican ascendancy that followed made this belief ever harder to sustain. Lee consoled himself with the argument that Republicans won support by deluding people. But he could not alter his political defeat and isolation. This defeat at the hands of the mob became especially troubling to him when his opponents tried to strip him of his proudest distinction—his status as a revolutionary patriot. The Republicans, like the Federalists, set great store by the example of the Revolutionary War as an index of patriotism. Instead of automatically conceding the superior merit of military veterans, the Republicans refought the war in politics and rhetoric during the 1790s, casting the Federalists as the British or tories and themselves as the patriots in combat. Thus Lee, who believed that his wartime service had proven his devotion to liberty and aversion to tyranny, found himself ranked among the monarchists.

Lee did not understand that the Revolutionary War had become a defining rhetorical pattern for the Republicans' opposition to Federalist measures. He had helped to win the war, but now his critics spoke as if they were winning it again by opposing the very government that, in his view, the war had been fought to establish. Lee's incomprehension came out in indignant questions. The Virginia legislature charged that the volunteer corps of the Provisional Army had been created to promote a political creed. "What," Lee asked, "is that political creed which has rallied them together? Is it any other than this—that it is their duty, and their determination, to defend the soil we tread on, and to fight the battles of their country? Are all who will do this, the instruments of monarchy?" The legislature also denounced the "swarms of officers" appointed to enforce the laws. "Why," Lee asked, "is it to be supposed, that those who discharge faithfully the duties of an office confided to them by their government, must 'inculcate political tenets tending to consolidation and monarchy'?" Lee reminded his readers that "our ancestors . . . in the revolutionary war" raised an army to defend the country. Anyone who had accused them of monarchism in the way that Republicans now accused Federalists would have been scorned or punished. "Where," Lee asked, "is the change in our situation which authorizes condemnation of a measure now, then admitted to be wise and indispensable?"[83]

Lee's questions could not be answered. They wrongly
assumed that the Federalists' wartime patriotism could justify,
in the name of the American Revolution, all of the measures
that they might adopt to defend the government. Not even
the aegis of George Washington could still win united public
acceptance of this assumption. For a growing number of
Americans, the Revolutionary War had not elevated a group
of leaders so much as it had provided a vocabulary and a pattern of political behavior with which to oppose government.
Appealing to the defense of liberty against consolidation, Republicans could win the new political Revolutionary War by
defeating men who had helped to win the original one. Thus,
when Lee listened to his opponents he found himself on the
alien, losing side of a war that he thought had ended and had
proven his patriotism forever. Looking back on this defeat, he
indignantly recalled: "the men who framed, adopted, and gave
practical effect to a government, erected for the very purpose
of insuring to posterity the blessings of civil and religious
freedom, were denounced as anglico-monarchial aristocratical
tools, and abettors of despotism; while these unblushing agitators . . . took to themselves the dignified and alluring title
of protectors of the rights and liberty of our common
country."[84]

Federalists found it hard to formulate an effective rebuttal. If they appealed to the record of the Revolution, Republicans could turn the appeal against them by portraying the
partisan contest as a new revolution in which Republicans
were the truer patriots. And if Federalists abandoned the revolutionary test of patriotism by calling for obedience to government as the postwar guarantor of independence, they played
the very role that Republicans were giving them—tories who
augmented government at the expense of liberty. Unable, in
this changing conception of revolution, to maintain his former
stature as a pre-eminent patriot, Lee could only recall earlier

times when the lines had been clear, when "the men whose wisdom in council and valour in the field, had so greatly contributed to her success in war and to her prosperity in peace, were not yet regarded by their deceived fellow citizens, as conspirators against the rights and liberties of their countrymen."[85]

The ruin of Lee's public stature as a patriot was completed with the coming of the War of 1812. In this second War of Independence, the Republicans could finally refight the Revolutionary War with military, as well as political, belligerence and with themselves rather than the Federalists as the military guardians of the republic. The American concerns that moved the Republicans toward war with Britain—commercial rights, territorial expansion, national honor—embodied a Jeffersonian version of the legacy of the Revolution. By securing a continent into which a growing population could expand without losing its agricultural character, by relying on European industry and trade to provide necessary manufactures and to purchase America's agricultural surplus, the United States could prosper without developing the industrial cities, the concentrations of wealth, or the dependent masses of people that marked the onset of corruption and authoritarianism. America could be spared Europe's poverty, tyranny, and wars without forgoing the fruits of Europe's industrial productivity. This arrangement seemed so essential to America's future that when the belligerents in the Napoleonic Wars interfered with American commerce by obstructing neutral trade or by impressing seamen from American ships, the interference looked like an attack on America's independence. Although both Britain and France violated the neutral rights claimed by the United States, Republicans directed America's resentment toward Britain. They interpreted interference with American trade and violation of American sovereignty as parts of a design to reverse the outcome of the Revolutionary War. Britain sought not just to protect itself from Napoleon but to resubjugate the United States into a colonial status, in fact if not in name. Americans would have to fight another War of Independence. A second war would secure by combat the national grandeur that seemed essential to the survival of liberty and virtue in America—that is, to the perpetuation of the American Revolution.

Although Lee opposed the Republican policies that led to war, he did not resist them. He tried, through military advice, to help the country win the war. Nevertheless, he believed American victory to be unlikely, and he felt a deep aversion to the return of war to America. In 1808 he wrote that "there is every possibility of the most disastrous defeat and scarcely a possibility of the slightest success."[86] He spoke of war, in private correspondence and public political writing, with a newly vehement horror. He warned that liberty would be endangered if Americans and Britons "imbrue their hands in each others blood."[87] Looking back on the Revolution shortly before the second war with Britain, he even wished away the years of combat in which he had achieved his greatest successes. The war should have ended, he now believed, in the autumn of 1777. If the British had seen then that they could not win and had acknowledged American independence, the two countries could have turned "to the renewal of amity, with preferential commercial intercourse." Instead, however, six more years of conflict had followed, and Lee now thought of the lives and money thus lost in the Revolutionary War as a "useless waste."[88]

War in America, as he had seen it, and now in Europe, as he studied it, seemed to offer much less of the virtuous glory and controlled finesse that he once had pursued. Rather, it wrought havoc amid citizen armies and across whole continents. It brought to Lee's mind the most frightening of visions. Transposing and paraphrasing biblical passages, he warned, in 1808, of the coming violence that he felt powerless to prevent—violence of the kind that he had seen in the madness of Ajax and joined on the day of Pyle's Hacking Match: "The period seems fast approaching when we may cry aloud with the prophet Nahum: 'I hear the noise of a whip, and the noise of the rattling of wheels, of the prancing of horses, and of the jumping of chariots; they rage like a tempest in the street; they blaze like torches; they run like lightning. The horsemen lifteth up both the bright sword and the glittering spear. There is a multitude slain, yet no end to the slaughter; they stumble upon the corpses, because of the great number.' "[89]

The most violent conflict over the American decision to fight another war took place in Baltimore soon after the declaration. Lee was in the fight. Why he joined a group of Maryland Federalists in defending a newspaper office against a mob remains open to speculation. Lee later said that he had come to Baltimore to contract for the publication of his memoirs. He told city officials that his presence with the Federalists "was the effect of accident; that he came there by invitation to play a game of whist." But the Federalists had come to town on Sunday, July 26, 1812, looking for a fight. When Lee "called in" on Monday evening, they expected him to join them, and they had judged their man correctly. "He suggested the possibility of our being taken by surprise, and that it was our duty to let no night pass without being fully prepared to resist an attack."[90] For whatever reason Lee had come to Baltimore or to the headquarters of the Federalist newspaper, he was not accidentally caught among the opponents of the mob. Instead, he took command of the defense.

Lee was wary of attack because he knew what provocation the Federalists offered in coming to Baltimore. Their leader, Alexander C. Hanson, had published a newspaper in Baltimore, the *Federal Republican,* in which he had denounced the Madison administration and especially the war with Britain. Two days after the declaration of war in June, he had deplored the conflict as "unnecessary, inexpedient, and entered into from . . . motives . . . of undisguised foreign influence." Announcing his intent to render "odious and suspicious . . . the patrons and contrivers of this highly impolitic and destructive war," he wrote, "we detest and abhor the endeavors of faction to create civil contest through the pretext of a foreign war it has rashly and premeditately commenced."[91] Another two days after this editorial had been published, a mob had torn down the newspaper's office building, and Hanson had fled to Georgetown. There he had continued to publish and to plan for his return.

Baltimore was a Republican city, and its Republicanism attracted volatile support from a large number of recent immigrants. Many of the Irish, Scots-Irish, Germans, and French whose arrival had contributed to the rapid growth of the city's population were connected with the oceangoing commerce that seemed threatened by British restrictions, seizures, and impressments. They were quick to support the declaration of war, and many of them had joined in driving Hanson out of the city in June. There could be little doubt that the most active political partisans in Baltimore set out to close down the *Federal Republican.* The mob that had destroyed the paper's office had included native-born citizens as well as immigrants, men in middle-class dress as well as laborers, mechanics, and sailors. Mayor Edward Johnson, who a month before had helped lead a meeting to express Baltimore's support of war, seemed mainly concerned not with suppressing the mob but with dissuading the rioters from further destruction after they had dispatched Hanson. Even the city's leading Federalists, who were embarrassed by Hanson's extremism, did not act very sorry to see him go.

For a month Hanson planned his return to Baltimore. He believed that with the proper help he could have defended his office from the mob, and he intended to try again. He recruited some belligerent young Federalists from Montgomery County in southern Maryland. They felt eager to help him fight the foreigners and Republicans who were gaining political predominance. Hanson began to express less interest in publishing a newspaper than in "wresting Baltimore from the tyranny of the mob." He believed that for winning the fight, "we should be hailed as the saviours of the city." As evidence that the plan could succeed, he cited an incident in the career of his father's friend General Henry Lee, "who, during the revolutionary war, took possession of a house in which he repelled with only ten men a large body of British Regulars."[92]

The example of the Revolutionary War appealed to Hanson and to his "Spartan band" as they moved into 45 Charles Street with weapons and copies of the *Federal Republican*.[93] Hanson afterward recalled their courage as they prepared to maintain "the Liberty of the Press, the security of property and person . . . the very principles and privileges, for the assertion and defence of which the War of Independence was declared." The Federalists in other cities who later praised the defenders of the Charles Street house often likened them to soldiers of the Revolution, giving special prominence to James Lingan and Harry Lee, the authentic veterans. In June, Hanson had claimed to speak for 90 percent of the people; by the time of his return to Baltimore, he was representing 99 percent against the "pick-pockets, footpads, foreign vagabonds and privateersmen," who were trying "to usurp the government" at the instigation of President James Madison and the Republicans.[94]

On Monday, July 27, Hanson and his friends distributed copies of the *Federal Republican* in Baltimore. The new issue blamed the June riot on "a conspiracy against the editors . . . at the seat of the general government." Hanson described his enemies' plan "that war would be declared before the 4th of July, and . . . that on that day the office would be demolished, and the proprietors thrown into the fangs of a remorseless rabble." He accused the mayor of having "permitted the mob to rage unrestrained," and the governor of having done nothing, due to "his knowledge of the real authors of the riot, and the political motives by which they were actuated."[95]

Word of Hanson's defiant return attracted hostile boys and men to Charles Street by evening. The arrival of other Federalists and of arms and ammunition heightened the anger of the people in the street. Contrary to Hanson's accusation, the mob that opposed him did not need instructions from the Madison administration. The men had a will of their own. Those who had torn down Hanson's office in June had later dismantled merchant ships suspected of trading with Britain and had then turned on Baltimore's blacks. They tore down the house of a free black man who was "charged with the expressions of affection for the British nation." They threatened to tear down the church building where "frequent assemblages" of black people raised the suspicion of insurrection; and blacks suffered "many acts of violence" at the hands of the mob.[96] The men who gathered outside of Hanson's house on the night of July 27 had shown that they were not subject to the orders of anyone.

The mob contained boys, workers, sailors, well-dressed men, native-born Americans, and the Irish, French, and German immigrants who formed a large part of the city's population. They had in common their enthusiasm for war with Britain. Soon after the declaration of war, a Federalist in Baltimore had complained that "Gangs of jacobins parade the streets each night and insult or offer violence to the persons of those who presume to dispute the wisdom of Executive policy."[97] The same men who opposed Hanson "threatened the destruction of all British manufactured goods."[98] One citizen told the mayor on the night of July 27, "our country is at war, and we will shed our blood to put down all opposition to it. The constituted authorities of our country having declared us in a state of war, no virtuous or good citizen will oppose it. The Federal Republican does oppose it, and we will put it down."

Supporting war enabled these men to speak for the American Revolution. After driving Hanson out in June, the mob had threatened to tear down the house of a man named Hutchens, who, rumor said, had drunk to the toast, "Damnation to the memory of Washington, and all who espouse his cause."[99] They, not the Federalists who opposed the war, were the true defenders of Washington's cause and of the symbol of American independence. Hanson and his friends, the *Baltimore Whig* charged, had become "wretches who commit treason, in the name of the revered Washington."[100] By supporting the Republican administration, by fighting Britain, by defeating the Federalists' monarchical conspiracies, the Baltimore mob, as American revolutionaries, would win American independence. The *Maryland Gazette* later described the mob as "boasting an exclusive attachment to our Republican Institutions."[101]

The men in the streets could make this boast because they claimed to represent the public. One newspaper report referred to the two sets of antagonists as "the people" and "the tories."[102] In trying to prevent a riot, the Baltimore authorities found reason to believe this claim. Lee asked Lemuel Taylor where the city fire brigade was, and Taylor "answered they were then in the street"—part of the mob.[103] The militia commander, when asked where his men were, pointed toward the mob and said, "There."[104] Wherever the militiamen were, few of them answered the call to keep the peace. As the gathering outside Hanson's office grew more threatening, Richard K. Heath, a bystander, warned members of the crowd that the mayor would use his authority to quell the mob. They replied, "the mayor was the friend of the people, and would do nothing against them."[105] He could not have done much, even if he had wanted to, because militiamen said "that they never would turn out to protect traitors and disorganizers."[106] Despite his claim to represent 99 percent of the public and his ambition to rescue the city from mob rule, Hanson had almost succeeded in provoking the crisis that Lee had long feared— the deluded populace now joined or condoned lawless violence to assure the dominance of a political faction. The Federalists who gathered at Hanson's house to defend the Revolution from usurpers stood alone against the people.

In this emergency the Federalists turned to Lee. He resorted to the techniques of partisan warfare that Hanson had praised when planning a return to Baltimore. Lee had been outsmarting British dragoons before Hanson was born; now he said "that he could and would defend the house against all the force of Baltimore."[107] The Federalists made Lee their commander; he wrote a plan for the defense of the house and named a commander for each room. The Baltimore City Council later published an unsigned letter, written a week before Hanson's return to the city, which outlined a plan for the defense of the house. They attributed the belligerent letter to Lee. Lee, on the other hand, afterward said that "he knew nothing of Hanson's design to defend his house, when he left Alexandria for Baltimore."[108] No matter what his surprise at the confrontation or his reluctance to shed blood, Lee accepted the commission and revived his partisan skills against the mob. The men in the street had a field piece, which Lee planned to seize if it were brought up to be fired. He told "his comrades" on the first story "that for this purpose he should put himself at their head and rely entirely on the vigorous use of the bayonet," under a covering fire from the house.[109]

But as the gathering in the street grew larger and more threatening after dark, Lee disappointed Hanson. The old general was no longer the eager fighter whose wartime career had inspired Hanson's hopes of quelling the mob. Instead, Lee restrained the young Federalists who wanted to open fire on the men in the streets. "He requested all those in the house to be silent, and keep no unnecessary light that might . . . attract the notice of the mob." While men and boys threw rocks at the house and broke all the windows, Lee insisted on waiting for them to "get ashamed of their own conduct and go away" or for the authorities to disperse them.[110] The young Federalists "illy brooked" Lee's restraint.[111] At last, Hanson insisted on shouting threats at the mob and firing over their heads. This provocation had the effect Lee feared. The mob rushed the house and broke in. The attackers fired into the house. A pistol that was aimed at Lee flashed and misfired. The Federalists fired into the crowd of attackers and drove them back, wounding at least three men, one of whom died. The bloodshed further enraged the mob; Lee tried to prevent still greater violence, which looked imminent. He said that he "wished, above all things, to avoid the effusion of blood."[112] Over the protests of Hanson, he persuaded the Federalists to surrender to the custody of the militia commander, General John Stricker, and go to jail. They were taken there on the morning of July 28 and locked in "the part of the prison appropriated to negroes and rogues."[113]

Hanson, in arguing against the surrender, had warned Lee that "there is no confidence to be placed" in the assurances of protection.[114] He was right. None of the officials—Mayor Johnson, General Stricker, or Judge John Scott—wanted to risk the political unpopularity or mob indignation that would have followed from calling out a large militia force to protect the jail or from releasing the Federalists on bail so that they could escape. On the 28th, the leaders of the mob "publicly and frequently" announced their plans for the Federalists: "we shall take them out of the jail to-night and put them to death."[115] When a friend of the Federalists warned Mayor Johnson that their lives were in danger, the mayor "expressed considerable indignation" over their coming to Baltimore to help Hanson "and called them foreigners; he expressed an opinion that they had no right to come for that purpose."[116] Judge Scott refused bail. General Stricker mobilized a small militia force, then stationed it away from the jail and dismissed it in the evening. A Baltimore newspaper writer later explained that many militiamen "abhorred any attempt to massacre" the Federalists, but "so strongly disapproved their conduct that the very idea of risking their lives in the defense of men who had rashly provoked their fate by such wanton deeds of blood, was revolting to them."[117] Hanson had planned to redeem Baltimore from these Republican officials, whom he called "his bitter enemies." Now Lee, instead of leading a desperate defense to break the mob's power, had surrendered. Hanson "repeated over and over, that . . . they would all be sacrificed."[118]

Sunset on July 28, the disbandment of the militia force, and the mob's storming of the jail followed one another quickly. When Lee heard the mob coming through the outer door, he damned the "base perfidy of General Stricker's unkept promise of protection.[119] Until then, Lee "never could be brought to suspect his fellow soldier of the revolution capable of dishonor." Now he knew that all of the prisoners would be murdered. But Lee did not want to die by "base hands." "Glowingly and with much emphasis" he proposed that the Federalists take the pistols they had brought into jail and kill each other. However, the younger men hoped to have the strength to survive the mob's attack and they rejected this idea. Lee then dissuaded them from using the pistols against the mob.[120]

All the doors were opened, and by the light of candles in the darkened jail the mob worked over the Federalists, beating and knifing them repeatedly, all the while cursing them and calling them tories. The two old Continental Army officers, Lingan and Lee, attracted special notice. Both of them denounced their attackers. Lingan pulled back his clothes and showed the rioters scars from wounds which he said that he had received in the Revolutionary War "while they were in France or among the bogs of Ireland."[121] The mob killed him. Lee tried "resisting and reproaching them." As they knocked him down, he called them "base villains, defied their enmity, and said they disgraced the country in which they had found an asylum." His expressions of "contempt and reprobation" stopped only when he was beaten into speechlessness.[122] While some of the mob struck the Federalists, others poured hot candle wax into their eyes and stabbed them with penknives. Men tried to cut off Lee's nose and gouge out an eye. His cries of pain "only excited new outrages and curses." As the mob grew, Lee was pointed out to new arrivals as "the d——d old tory general," who had "died true game—huzzaing for king George to the last." After the Federalists lay motionless, their attackers joined hands, and one of them sang a song, all repeating in unison after each verse the chorus

> *We'll feather and tar every d——d British tory,*
> *And this is the way for American glory.*

Between verses, the singer "would propose three cheers for Jefferson or Madison, or some such worthy of democracy."[123] Only when the mob was convinced that most of the Federalists were dead did the beatings end and the rioters disband.

Reports of the riot in Baltimore aroused intense partisan reactions throughout the United States. Lingan alone died at the hands of the mob, but early rumors had Lee and other Federalists dead or mortally wounded. The Federalist press, in denouncing the mob at great length, portrayed the victims as patriots defending the Revolution. The rioters were enemies of America. They were immigrants, and immigrants were foreigners, not Americans. They could claim no share in winning independence; now they had betrayed the hospitality that America's freedom offered. The *Connecticut Journal* damned the editor of the *Baltimore Whig* as an Irish Robespierre who had promoted the violence. "The sedition law is dead, but we hope in God there remains some of the good sense of our ancestors—enough to teach this fellow, that instead of patronage for such labours as his, he can meet with nothing but scorn and detestation from every native American."[124] Denunciations of the rioters likened their conduct to that of "the sanguinary mob of Paris."[125] The violence was "a prelude to the dissolution of all free government, and the establishment of a reign of terror."[126] Thus the Federalists, indignantly rejecting the rioters' use of the word "tory," tried to refute the mob's claim that it represented the American cause in war against Britain. Federalists were still the proper guardians of America against "the horrors of anarchy," which portended "destruction to all the principles and institutions which uphold the fabric of our liberties, our national character and existence, as a civilized people."[127]

For the first time in many years, Light-Horse Harry Lee's military and political services received widespread public praise as the Federalist press celebrated the patriotism of the soldier of the Revolution cut down by a mob. The accounts stressed his close ties to George Washington—even contending that he fell "invoking the spirit of WASHINGTON his friend and companion in arms."[128] However, the praise did not mean that Lee had now won the central role in public life he had so long wanted. He became important as a symbol, not as a leader. By the time of the riot Lee had long been out of the public eye, and even his admirers did not always have their reasons for admiring him clear in their minds. The compliments sometimes contained hazy or inaccurate information about his career. Was it Henry Lee or Arthur Lee who had served as governor of Virginia? Of which army had Harry been Commander in Chief? The Federalist accounts primarily wanted to show that the Republican national administration had instigated the riot and had patronized the subversion of the American Revolution typified by a foreign mob. Even among his admirers in 1812, Lee was not so much a hero as a victim. The United States, as well as the legacy of the Revolution on which the country was founded, had fallen into the hands of demagogues. The destruction of veterans and victors of the Revolutionary War confirmed for Federalists that no degree of virtue among patriots could protect the country from the mob in politics.

The riots in Baltimore did not silence Federalists. The violent excesses turned voters away from the Republicans in Maryland, and Federalist denunciations extended the political effect to other states. Newspapers and Federalist admirers urged Lee to write an account of the Baltimore mob. He could turn his "lucid pen" to partisan advantage.[129] No longer victorious as a hero, he could, in defeat, serve as a propagandist. Republican newspapers, in blaming Hanson and his friends for the riot, expressed contempt for Lee as a bankrupt and a *"Captain"* of the Federalists.[130] To give him the rank of captain was to underline with sarcasm the ignominy into which he had fallen. Republican writers would not lament the assault on a revolutionary officer; rather, they would join the attack. Lee's defenders complained that "apologists for MOBOCRACY . . . are, with a diligent malignancy, exerting themselves to traduce the Character of this estimable Gentleman."[131] The published scorn helped Republicans to contend that "the rioters were 'more sinned against than sinning.' " They accused Lee and the Federalists of "hasty and savage firing among the crowd."[132] In calling Lee a failure, a cheat, and a trouble-maker to extenuate the mob's attack on him, Lee's critics, like the mob, repudiated him as a revolutionary hero. No Federalist account of the riot, written by Lee or anyone else, could have restored this stature to him by portraying him as a victim. Through opposition to the war and to Republican primacy, Lee had become a traitor. "There can not be a question," the Philadelphia *Democratic Press* said of Hanson and his allies, "that they are in the pay of the enemy."[133]

As soon as the mob left the jail, friends of the Federalists carried Lee and others a mile to a hospital. Doctors stitched a large wound made by a club on the top of his head; they sewed together his nose, which had been slit by a knife, and they stitched a cut in his upper lip. Lee also had other cuts and many bruises from blows and from attempts to strangle him. His right eye was swollen shut. After the crowd dispersed, he was placed in a carriage and taken to York, Pennsylvania, for safety. A man who saw him the day after his arrival said that "Lee was as black as a negro . . . his clothes torn and covered with blood from tip to toe." A week later he could speak only one or two words with great difficulty and could take only liquids in small amounts. Lee's recovery was slow and incomplete. Back in Alexandria, he appeared with his family in church, wearing white bandages around his forehead, over the crown of his head, and under his chin. He could not see clearly, and he said that his health was "deranged." For months he wore a black cloth on his head to cover his wounds. He complained of a "painful face & weak body." For the rest of his life his face was heavily scarred and he suffered intermittent pain. He would spend most of his time in his remaining years seeking relief from what he called "my mob injuries."[134]

The Baltimore mob ended Light-Horse Harry Lee's career as a revolutionary. He would never regain good health. Nor would he again be flamboyant, defiant, audacious, or victorious. He would abandon most of the activities that had shaped his life: command, politics, investment, family, agriculture. His exile to the Caribbean in search of restored health only confirmed his separation from the society that had taken shape since the Revolutionary War. If he had not left the country, obscurity itself would have been a form of exile. Unable to guide or promote the country's growth, unwanted in its councils, ignored or little heeded for his experience of the revolutionary past, Lee could no longer hope to preserve any share of the public service and private prosperity that had long been his life's main purposes. For one who tried as Lee did to embody the Revolution and its promise, such a defeat left him almost as isolated from his countrymen at large as he was from the rioters in Baltimore.

Beginning at eight o'clock on the morning of August 27, 1812, people in New Haven, Connecticut, could go to a new exhibit in Mix's Museum. Besides the usual artifacts, animals, birds, and snakes, there would be a display depicting the *"Cruelties of the Baltimore MOB"* in "a group of WAX FIGURES as large as life." This "striking and interesting" exhibit had been obtained "at considerable expence" by the proprietor of the museum, who urged the public "to call soon." When they did so, they would see General Lingan baring his breast to show his revolutionary scars to an assassin who was about to stab him. They would see Alexander Hanson prone and bleeding under the uplifted club of another assassin. And they would see General Lee being beaten by "the merciless gang" as he lay "with his mangled head on the breast of Mr. Hanson." The proprietor assured the public that the waxworks had no partisan purpose, "either Federal or Republican, Democratic or Aristocratic, French or English." Rather, they were a public-spirited demonstration of the "pernicious tendency of Mobs." The exhibit should appeal to "every friend to liberty and peace." The price of admission was twenty-five cents.[135]

5

"THE SWINDLING HARRY LEE"

WHEN THE *Baltimore Whig* DENOUNCED THE "MUR-derous traitors" who had come to the city to circulate their Federalist lies and "provoke the people," the newspaper included in its list of offenders "the Swindling Harry Lee."[1] By 1812 Lee was a bankrupt, living on an annuity from funds bequeathed to his wife by her father. The decline of Lee's hopes for peacetime seemed to astonish him almost as much as the erosion of his revolutionary glory. Some of those who suffered by trusting him in business had a less charitable explanation for his dealings than he gave in his expressions of surprise. They called him a cheat. Lee's careless optimism as an investor, like his Federalism in politics, took him farther and farther from the harmonious, prosperous society he envisioned. Yet to abandon the pursuit seemed harder for Lee than to fail at it. Having long aspired to foster and exemplify the national happiness that would vindicate the Revolution's promise and efface the cruelty of war, he could only persevere in this effort to its end.

Neither the enthusiasm of Lee's enterprises nor the completeness of their collapse was unusual for the time. Many Americans, including entrepreneurs more astute than Lee, foresaw sure profits in the combination of peace, growing population, and open land. Profits were there, but they were not certain enough or big enough to justify the volume and the risk of all the get-rich-quick investments. Losses, bank-ruptcies, and imprisonments like Lee's became familiar stories. Lee's story, however, went beyond the wreck of speculation. In the process of failing to create the country and build the career that he expected, Lee betrayed many of the ideals by which he wanted to guide his own life and benefit others.

Lee combined a set of traits that remained compatible only during prosperity. His optimism encouraged him to fore-see success; his wartime audacity grew yet more daring in postwar enterprises, as his cautious calculation gave way to im-providence and carelessness; still, his integrity in financial transactions was a source of pride akin to his honor as an offi-cer. Optimism, audacity, improvidence, and integrity might flourish together as long as peace brought Lee's undertakings the sure rewards he counted on. Adversity would bring con-flicts among these traits which he was poorly prepared to reconcile.

The prospect of a boom in public securities when Hamil-ton's financial program took effect had briefly aroused Lee's interest even in the paper speculation that he deplored in prin-ciple. But he devoted his energy and money primarily to trans-actions in land. Land values in the 1780s and 1790s were at least as visionary as the traffic in government finance. Lee nevertheless shared a widespread conviction that real estate held a superior intrinsic worth and moral dignity arising from the tangible productivity of labor in the soil. However, only a fraction of the land he bought and lost ever saw a farmer while Lee owned it. He was speculating in its prospective value.

The high point of Lee's purchases and land holdings came in 1795. That year he joined in buying 200,000 acres at three shillings per acre from the Fairfax estate on the upper Potomac; he contracted to buy George Washington's rights in the Dismal Swamp Company's land for $20,000; and he helped Robert Morris, John Nicholson, James Greenleaf, and their North American Land Company buy a million acres of "cheap back lands" on credit at sixpence to a shilling per acre, designed for quick resale.[2] Lee felt confident in these transactions because "there are individuals of character & gold daily arriving in Philada. & N York from G. Britain & other European nations whose sole object is the purchase of lands."[3] Sure of his solvency and imminent profits, he accepted dubious bills of credit. He made large loans to friends at the same time that he was borrowing money from other friends. Both the dowry he had promised his daughter Lucy and an inheritance left to his goddaughter by her father went unpaid for years, swallowed by Lee's enterprises. He wanted his family as well as his friends "to share with me in a good bargain" like the purchase and resale of "our Georgia lands."[4] In a dozen ways—coal mines, canals, ore fields, reclaimed swamplands, a disputed inheritance in England, speculative property, productive property, currency transactions, interest-bearing loans—Lee always felt within striking distance of the lasting prosperity he sought from peace.

But Lee's diverse energetic activity heightened his vulnerability. His interlocking holdings depended on each other and on his financial improvisations for their uncertain security. He was not so much land poor as paper rich. If his paper lost its value, all of his wealth stood in danger. And the value of his vast holdings depended not so much on their productivity as on the market for quick speculative resale. Unfortunately for Lee and for many others, land investment in America began to turn downward in 1795. The fall of the continental credit empire of Robert Morris and his associates in 1797 hastened the contraction of Lee's assets. Contrary to the land speculators' hopes, too few European investors had rushed to buy American property. Capital had found more attractive returns from loans to European governments to help finance the Napoleonic Wars. The American speculators had banked on large, fast profits from big investors, not on small transactions with actual western settlers. Now they had property but too few buyers.

The default of men who owed money to Lee quickly showed how over-extended his transactions had grown. Lee had bought a 300,000-acre tract of Virginia land, then sold it to a group of New England investors. When the survey showed that the tract had only 133,874 acres, the purchasers stopped payments. Lee had to take losses elsewhere in order to get cash to cover some of his debts; his friends who had put up their property as collateral for his debts now faced forfeiture; his unpaid creditors could not meet their own obligations. By December of 1797, Lee was desperate for money with which to satisfy "those distressed individuals who are all about me now." He wrote to his agent, "they will be on me— shield me I pray." The following week: "If your expectations fail, I am gone."[5]

Lee was not gone yet. His agent settled the most pressing obligation. Lee had to give a lien on some of his Pennsylvania land in order to guarantee the New England investors a good title to the 300,000 acres of Virginia land he had sold them. Months later, he was still trying to get payments on Potomac land from John Nicholson, who had taken charge of the development of Matildaville. Nicholson and Morris owed Lee $21,500 on their Great Falls property; they finally forfeited title to the land because they could not pay the balance. Lee was slow to detect the signs of collapse in his risky plans for the prosperity of Matildaville, the Potomac, and the West. His optimism had enabled him to imagine no other outcome but success. He said that his losses were "as great as they were unexpected."[6] He attributed them not to his audacity and improvidence but to "the untoward & unexpected course of fiscal concerns in this country."[7] Having counted on expanding wealth, he blamed the surprise bursting of the land bubble for his "unprepared condition."[8] In October 1798, he admitted: "I have no money."[9]

While trying to use his District of Columbia lots to pay his debts, Lee had assured George Washington in September that "the time is fast approaching when property like mine must be in great demand."[10] In fact, Lee's losses had only begun. Early in 1801, his relatives were telling each other that "the most gloomy aspect hangs over all his affairs here."[11] His term in Congress was ending, and during the following twenty-four months Lee found himself a private citizen rapidly liquidating his assets. Again, as at the start of his reverses three years earlier, he found his losses "heavy & unexpected."[12] This time they would also be permanent. Two "distressing letters" to Robert Morris in search of repayment for a $40,000 loan yielded only Morris's final statement of bankruptcy, which he concluded by writing: "my good wishes is all that is left in my power."[13] Twenty years earlier, Morris's good wishes could have commanded cash. Now Lee was forced into "selling a great deal of property at half price to make up the heavy losses to which the failures of R. Morris Thos Thompson & others exposed me."[14] His taxable land holdings dropped sharply. In Westmoreland County, the site of the Stratford estate, they fell from 2,049 acres to 236. He was staving off creditors' suits by juggling new indebtedness: "good paper at 12 months" to one man; $6,000 to another in two-, four-, and nine-month installments; meanwhile looking for "a good note endorsed at 60 days" with which to pay $2,250 due in a week.[15] In his papers he found loose memoranda for large sums, the transfer of which he could not reconstruct, and he acknowledged in one instance that "the thing is so obscured & so mixed with my other transactions that I cannot speak with any precision thereon."[16]

Yet even this financial crisis could not completely suppress Lee's optimism and investments. At the same time that his new round of "unexpected" reverses began, he was obtaining from Gouverneur Morris a long testimonial to the promising opportunities for developing commerce with the West along the Potomac and Ohio rivers.[17] Early in 1802, while Lee was sacrificing Virginia property, he was also acquiring land in Georgia. Sure that it contained "the most convenient & productive iron estate in our country," he was determined to "bring into great use a great property."[18] Lee ought long ago to have asked himself why George Washington—one of America's most experienced and active land speculators—was selling rather than buying land in the boom of the early 1790s. Why did Washington decline an invitation to join in Robert Morris's land deals? Why was Washington willing to lower his original asking price in order to sell his Dismal Swamp Company shares to Lee? However, instead of reflecting on these questions, Lee had bought land from Washington, joined Morris's enterprises, and now continued to dream of growth when the contraction of investment had become severe. The fervor of Lee's transactions ran deeper than his intent to get rich or his surprise at setbacks. His eagerness to promote "great property" had become a large part—perhaps the mainstay—of his confidence in the country's future. His confidence was desperate because he had no avenue of retreat. To abandon it would leave the economic prospects as ominous as the political ones now looked under the ascendancy of Thomas Jefferson.

Lee's attempt to sustain enterprise amid adversity had a high cost, which was borne not only by him but also by those who trusted him. Like many other speculators caught in the frantic and hazy fixing of complex deals, he made false commitments. The Virginia land boom had few legal safeguards. Surveyors who were supposed to ascertain the dimensions and boundaries of claims were speculators themselves. Surveys were imprecise; titles overlapped each other; claims got certified without having been surveyed; men exchanged lands of whose outlines and attributes they knew little or nothing. Speculators bought and sold land warrants, which were not deeds to identifiable plots of land but rights to acquire property in the future. Thus purchasers acquired claims to vast acreage which no buyer, seller, or surveyor had seen. Lee tried to move boldly through this maze and got lost. Several men who bought property from him found that he had sold the same land to two different buyers. When his bills of credit bounced, he covered them with new ones that also went unhonored. His title to the land he was selling often stood in doubt. To protests from one buyer, he could only reply: "I was not responsible . . . you took my right good or bad."[19] In 1801, the federal government bought land and mining rights originally owned by Lee, only to find the title encumbered by a mortgage he had not paid before selling the land. A story "in general circulation" said that Lee had sold another man's farm without the owner's authorization.[20] Finally, in what Lee called "a trying & disagreeable scene," his unreliability passed the bounds that even his fellow speculators could forgive.[21] "It is a mode of dealing to which I am not accustomed," Washington complained when Lee gave him a bad note and depreciated bank shares in partial payment for the Dismal Swamp property. Washington grew suspicious of Lee's offers of land or of payment in kind and wrote to him, "I pray you not to deceive me."[22] By 1805, the agent for one of Lee's creditors warned that "all titles of land held under Genl. Lee may be supposed as precarious."[23]

Lee's protestations of good intentions were sincere. Wishing to give full value everywhere, he wanted to preserve his reputation for integrity. Nevertheless, as his financial crisis grew more pressing—as lawsuits loomed and threats of arrest increased—Lee became vaguer and shiftier. Having failed to win prosperity, he fell back on his gift for evasion and flight.

To a friend who was helping him meet his debts in 1802, he gave a bad check. For four years, from 1803 to 1807, Lee strung along the executor of William Ludwell Lee's estate, procrastinating the payment of a £5,000 bond while the interest due on it rose above $5,500. With new expedients, he persuaded the executor not to foreclose on the land that Lee had put up as collateral for the bond and for other obligations. He promised to pay with the proceeds of another land sale but then sold that land for promissory notes instead of cash; he promised that his brother Richard Bland Lee would settle the claims, but the executor could get no new offers there; Lee suddenly remembered that he had either an earlier understanding with William Ludwell Lee or a counter claim against the estate. Finally he started all over again and wrote to the executor in 1805: "if my plan pleases not give me another."[24] Almost two years later, he was still devising an "arrangement" to forestall the sale of the collateral property adjoining his Stratford estate.[25]

The play of wits that had always remained essential to Lee now was for the most part confined to a steadily shrinking circle of maneuver among more insistent creditors. No longer serving the freedom of his country in public office, Lee's mental energy was largely consumed in short-lived expedients to protect himself from the consequences of his improvidence. By the time that William Augustine Washington sent one of his estate managers to press Lee for payment of another procrastinated debt in 1805 and 1806, Lee's temporizing had almost reached its limit. He spoke of his own losses; in spite of them, he wanted to pay Washington—he had back lands, mills, and city lots in the District of Columbia; he said that he owned the back lands even though the patents were in someone else's name—he was sure that he had newer deeds to the land, but he could not find them at the moment; unfortunately, the Adelphi Mills were not in his name either, but Lee said he owned them, too. However, there were some small encumbrances to the title that he could not pay off until the mills were sold, and he could not clearly explain by what claim the mills belonged to him, or on what tenure; his city lots had to be sold to pay debts, but if Washington wanted them he could have them; still, Lee did not want to put anything in writing just now.[26]

The reputation for integrity on which Lee prided himself was gone. There had long been doubt about him. George Mason said in 1791 that Lee had sold his Occoquan Mills to some Quakers and then dreamed up the idea of a new road about to be built nearby from Dumfries to the port of Alexandria. This "Contrivance" was supposed to induce the Quakers "to offer him a high Price for some of his adjacent lands."[27] Men who started into transactions with Lee on friendly terms came out accusing him of resorting to "legal chimeras," "deceptions, misrepresentation and ——"[28] Now, after his schemes had run out, Lee became an object of contempt to some of his creditors. In July 1805, Nathaniel Pendleton, to whom Lee owed $25,000, offered $250 for the arrest of Lee in Fairfax County. Pendleton had decided that he had to use force or follow Lee "from place to place to get whatever occurs."[29] William Augustine Washington's agent called Lee "my *Exerciser*" and reported that "I have not been able to *twist* any offer of any thing like property from him."[30]

Lee was not a hardened confidence man. Just as his setbacks surprised him, his defaults shamed him. "I am vastly unhappy in being the instrument to such deep injury," he wrote about one unpaid creditor.[31] He felt especially mortified by the protested bill and unreliable bank shares that he had persuaded George Washington to accept in lieu of cash. "No event of my life has given me more anguish," he told Washington.[32] When Lee spoke of the "extreme misery" that he suffered in the ruin of his finances, he meant more than the sacrifice of property and the threat of jail.[33] His confidence in "the advancing prosperity of the country" had not only failed to make him rich but had also harmed many people whom he wanted to help, including the man he admired most and the son and daughter that Matilda Lee had left in his care.[34]

Beyond discrediting his financial competence, Lee's bankruptcy mirrored the dismantling of that vision of peacetime America to which he had devoted himself. He could take little consolation from knowing that other Americans remained solvent or that the country could still be prosperous. The national wealth he had anticipated was not an anarchic aggregation of private fortunes; rather, the inevitability of America's growth would link and guarantee the growing fortunes of everyone from the settler in the West to the enterprising genius at the hub of commerce. Lee's efforts to implement this opportunity arising from the Revolution had proven too weak. Despite his repeated protests that the blows were "unexpected," he knew that he shared responsibility for the damage done when his enterprises fell apart. The failure of his undertakings meant to him that he had misjudged the future of his country or, worse, had been unequal to the patriot's duty to create that future. This error or lapse left him without a new vision and with the blame for the hardships of others. These were the greatest of Lee's distresses. "The loss of money I am used to," he wrote Washington, "the loss of mental quietude I cannot bear."[35]

During the latter years of his financial crisis, Lee's health deteriorated. In July 1806, when he was fifty years old, his wife urged him: "guard your health with more care, than you have for several years past."[36] His neglect began after he left Congress, as his creditors grew more pressing while his resources shrank. Instead of remedying it, he seems to have remained negligent. Several of his letters written to fend off bankruptcy include phrases such as, "I am very sick," "sick as

I have been & am."[37] By February of 1809, shortly before he went to jail, he was saying, "My state of health continues precarious," and he was writing letters during "an interval of ease from pain."[38] Although Lee did not name his disorder, it confirmed the recurrent connection between his mental distress and his illnesses. The declining health that troubled Lee's last years began long before the Baltimore mob's beating. When Gilbert Stuart painted a portrait of the fifty-year-old Lee, he saw a man much changed in spirit from the twenty-six-year-old lieutenant colonel whom Charles Willson Peale had painted in 1782. The young man had firm features, wide-open eyes, and a frank, direct expression. The older man had heavier, looser jowls, a flushed reddish coloring, and eyes that looked out in a sidelong, guarded gaze.

During 1808, in the waning days of Lee's solvency, he tried to get out of the country. In February, he asked his old friend Secretary of State Madison to appoint him as an informal agent to Brazil. Failing that, he would be glad to accompany the American consul. Finally, in December, he asked just for permission to go through the embargo to the West Indies on his own. He gave different reasons for his requests: his own illness, his wife's illness, his need to procure a deposition in a lawsuit. But one can hardly doubt that in writing Madison about "my distressed condition" and "my very painful situation," Lee was thinking of his impending bankruptcy.[39] Now the only flight that could succeed would be an escape from the United States. In October he wrote more succinctly to his attorney, "do aid me to my friend in one of the British islands."[40]

As his creditors closed in, Lee felt primarily concerned about his family and what he called his "just debts." By taking an oath of insolvency, he might have avoided jail. But he would thereby have been forced to surrender all control over his assets and could no longer have paid some debts in full while defaulting completely on those he considered "an unjust demand."[41] As long as he retained his property and this right of choice, his unpaid creditors could have him committed to jail. Lee probably hoped that by going abroad he could both preserve some property for his family and avoid imprisonment. In writing Madison for help, he resorted, "with reluctance," to begging: "I have served in war & peace the U.S. I never asked for any office, or even favor before, from govt. or any member of govt. Nor shd I do it now, but for the peculiarity of my condition."[42]

But Lee's requests went unanswered. The more desperate he grew, the less willing were his old acquaintances to help him. They probably saw what he refused to see—that his fertile imagination had too few assets behind it, that his wits could not get him away from his creditors, that his old tactics no longer worked. He owed George Gilpin, a director of the Potomac Company, more than £3,000. "I wish you to see Gilpin & to negotiate with him for my debts," Lee wrote to a friend in January 1808. "I will give lands good lands."[43] Before long, George Gilpin would have him locked up.

Yet Lee did not go without a struggle. In his efforts to raise cash quickly, he turned to Robert Goodloe Harper for legal counsel. A leading Federalist politician, Harper had been an associate of Robert Morris in the six-million-acre North American Land Company promotion, the failure of which had assured Morris's bankruptcy and his default on Lee's large loan to him. Now, with Harper's help in a complex inheritance dispute, Lee hoped by the threat of litigation and the simultaneous offer of a settlement to get money sooner than was possible by administration of the estate and subsequent adversary proceedings against other claimants. The sooner he could get money with which to meet his immediate obligations, the longer he could delay the ultimate reckoning that would expose his insolvency. In September 1808 he told Harper, "My necessitys are such that every days gain in time, is momentous to me." However, the opposing attorney saw no advantage to his clients in a compromise, and Harper—whom Lee was not paying—reported in February 1809 that he could not speed up the legal process. On March 2, a few weeks before Lee was to surrender to the sheriff, he wrote Harper that, despite the prospect of "ultimate success" in the claim, he needed "money now out of it. This & this only is worthy of the pains & suffering I undergo." Lee still believed that a few thousand dollars would keep him out of jail and in control of his property. In the margin of the letter, Lee urged Harper to try again for a compromise, concluding: "My sit[uat]ion is dreadful." After reading the letter, Harper turned it over and wrote on the back: "No answer."[44]

There was no escape. Light-Horse Harry Lee was trapped. But he kept looking for a way out. His last days of freedom were a hectic sequence of pleas and schemes to evade a host of demands with a little cash. On March 4, he wrote a "serious entreaty" to James Breckinridge for help in another legal matter from which he expected to get some quick money. "I am miserable [in]deed," he said, "as I must prepare for jail." "In this hour of distress" he also turned again to James McHenry, his friend and fellow veteran, who had already tried to help him avoid imprisonment. On March 7, Lee asked McHenry for a loan of $4,000 which "would do" to avert "the deplorable condition to which I must soon be reduced." Finally, "brought to the last hour of the time allotted to me for my decision," Lee offered to sell McHenry "my ore bank" on the Potomac.[45] None of the last-minute shifts sufficed. Rather than give up all of his property, Lee went into the Westmoreland County Jail on April 24, 1809.

All of the aspirations by which Lee had shaped his plan for peace were now turning toward failure. His investments and his credit had deteriorated beyond salvage. Soon he would have to sign away everything, thereby acknowledging publicly that he and Matildaville and the Potomac and the burgeoning American continent would not prosper together. His own zealous enterprises had helped to cause his fall. Excesses of risk had corrupted peace, as excesses of violence had tainted war. Nor did the harmony and union that Lee sought for America seem more secure than the country's prosperity. Demagogues had risen to high office by pillorying revolutionary patriots with the charge of monarchism. Foreigners and the influence of foreign governments were gaining in power. Lee feared both disunion in America and unnecessary involvement in European war. Compounding these defeats, Lee left his family. By doing so he lost—for almost a year in jail and for the last five years of his life in the West Indies—the ties that most fully expressed the value of peace. This loss, even more than the others, was of his own making. From his "children & friends" he heard "entreatys" to make "an immediate sacrifice" of his property so that he could return to his family. He went to jail and stayed there because he believed that preserving "land and furniture" for his wife and children was better than living with them as a bankrupt.[46] In July 1809, he heard from his oldest son that Ann Lee and the children were well at Stratford and that Light-Horse Harry had not been forgotten during his absence. "I have your picture here executed by Stuart. It affords Mrs. L. the pensive satisfaction of paying to it, that adoration, which she has so constantly & so sweetly done to its original."[47]

At the suit of different creditors, Lee was imprisoned first in Westmoreland and then in Spotsylvania County. He called the Spotsylvania County Jail "this depot of misery."[48] Creditors followed him even there. William Augustine Washington sent another agent, who "requested to know when it would be Convenient for him to settle" his debt. Lee replied that "he was too much indisposed to attend to any business."[49] Almost a year after going to jail, he still had "not yet decided as to my conduct, so difficult is it for a man whose property is large to bring himself to deprive his family of it."[50] Inactive, unable to travel around Virginia and Maryland visiting people and making deals, arrested in his continental enterprises, Lee had much time to reflect. He could remember "those days when my recommendation would have weight" with the President of the United States.[51] Thomas Jefferson had ended that. Lately Lee had been thinking about Jefferson's embargo, which, by "the annihilation of value attached to property and to labour," had the effect of "consigning to jails and to the wheelbarrow" those citizens who were "thrown upon the mercy of the creditor." Having "changed his humble house into a lofty palace," Jefferson was now retiring "to ease and splendour, leaving to us the hard lot of penury and despair."[52]

Although Lee saw himself partly as a victim of Republican rule and the maladministration that was despoiling America, he could not evade all sense of responsibility for his own bankruptcy. He came closest to despair when he thought about his family. He reflected on the impending loss of land that "my dear wife wants," on his married daughter's unpaid dowry, on the sure profits from Potomac land that some creditor would now reap, on the "large property" intended for his children that now was "frittering away." He was immobilized amid conflicting pressures: wanting to secure property for his wife and children, watching it fall away for lack of payments, feeling "anxiety to return to my family," and knowing that he could do so only by further harming their estate. "These things hurt me deeply," he told his son-in-law; "indeed I fear the reflections they excite will destroy me."[53]

MR. JEFFERSON

Defending Federalist policies against Republican attack, Lee had written in 1799: "however perilous the crisis; however great the obstacles to be encountered; the pursuit of general happiness ought not to be abandoned in despair."[1] He obeyed that admonition in jail. The melancholy that overtook him between 1801 and 1810 owed much to his isolation and failure. While he was imprisoned, Lee found a new way to restore himself to a central role in defining and promoting the happiness that the American Revolution had promised. He began to write history. By narrating the part of the Revolutionary War that he had experienced, he could diffuse a correct understanding of the pursuit of the nation's independence and welfare. From this goal, as well as the love of his family, he derived a purpose that offset the reflections which oppressed him. Even when contemplating his own destruction in jail, he acknowledged, "I ought to hold up."[2]

Researching and writing his memoirs became Lee's main interest. Instead of devoting his energy to the disposition of his property and his early release from imprisonment, he stayed in jail, "not yet decided" about his finances but immersed in the story of the Revolutionary War.[3] Through this story he returned to the years in which his services had been most effective and his patriotism most conspicuous. By writing an account that would "record the truth fully," he would show

how the Revolutionary War had weighed merit more accurately than had the years that followed.[4]

Beyond reading other histories and relying on his memory, Lee did research for his memoirs primarily by asking for documents and narratives from other veterans. Some he approached anonymously, through a go-between, perhaps embarrassed to ask them to address their replies to the Spotsylvania Court House. But with others he established a direct correspondence. From Rhode Island, New York, New Jersey, Virginia, North Carolina, and South Carolina, Lee received long letters and some documents. Phebe Champe sent him the papers of her late husband, former sergeant John Champe, from Kentucky.

This correspondence contained not only information about the Revolutionary War but also expressions of praise and admiration such as Lee had not heard for a long time. The men whom he called "my brother soldiers" remembered Light-Horse Harry Lee as an "accomplished Scholar and renowned Hero and Statesman." They and their descendants felt grateful that "by a just Display of their Prowess and Patriotism in the Revolutionary War," Lee's memoirs would rescue them "from the Gulph of oblivion."[5] John Mercer accompanied his account of the 3rd Virginia Regiment at the Battle of Brandywine with assurances of his confidence that "whatever General Lee writes on this subject, will most probably from his genius & reputation bear a value with distant posterity."[6] Even before he finished writing his memoirs, Lee derived from such letters much of the gratification that the work offered him. Abandoning, for a while, the world of contemptuous creditors and hostile Jeffersonians, he found that among his old comrades he still enjoyed the stature that had seemed lost. Lee said of the veterans who had written him: "To these individuals I owe a heavy debt of personal gratitude."[7]

Lee's ability to make the heroes of the war immortal in history was the core of his new importance in the eyes of his fellow veterans. They felt that the achievements of the revolutionary soldiers, as well as the virtues that they represented, were being forgotten. Lee combined the personal experience and the literary gift to do justice to what one correspondent called "that ardour of patriotism which animated the friends you loved."[8] When William R. Davie received Lee's request, he replied: "this work seems to have been reserved by Providence for *your* pen."[9] By transmitting to posterity a correct knowledge of the wartime threats to independence and the means by which the war had been won—"the causes of failure and success, the consequences of enterprise & exertion"—Lee the historian could perpetuate the virtues demonstrated by Lee the soldier. As a spokesman for the victors of the Revolution, he would accomplish more than just reliving the past. He would restore himself to the front rank of contemporary patriots. "You will add a claim to the gratitude of your Country," Davie predicted, "perhaps, even more important, than the brilliant services you have rendered her in the field."[10] Lee accepted this compliment and proclaimed on his first page: "In usefulness to society, the degree is inconsiderable between the conduct of him who performs great achievements, and of him who records them; for short must be the remembrance, circumscribed the influence of patriotic exertions and heroic exploits, unless the patient historian retrieves them from oblivion, and holds them up conspicuously to future ages."[11]

In the years before his work on the memoirs began, Lee had several times recalled the exploits that he now planned to make conspicuous. They remained vivid in his mind even though they had arisen from a temperament that no longer governed his life—the temperament of a young officer in wartime. In his memoirs he called it "the ardor of youth," "the impetuosity of youth."[12] He used these terms to describe

Baron Steuben and Horatio Gates, older men who could still act like young ones. In recounting his own youth, Lee revived the ardor and impetuosity that had brought him glory. Recalling the high spirits with which he had fought the Revolution refreshed him when he confronted the harm done by time and politics. The war, Lee said in 1799, was "that manly struggle . . . which the American soldier styled a tory by the infants he then protected, cannot even now recollect without sensations which for a moment banish his age and infirmities."[13] His memoirs would contain a whole series of such moments, during which the fruits of independence and the prospects of his career still lay in the future.

Age and infirmities had no place in the excitement of danger, registered on the memory by indelible sensory experience. Patriotism, through the vividness of memory, again became the work of youth and daring and passion. Writing in jail, Lee recreated the flight of the young Harry Lee and Alexander Hamilton—neither of them yet twenty-one—from a British cavalry patrol. Hamilton swam the Schuylkill River, "while Lee put his safety on the speed and soundness of his horse." Back at camp, each was relieved to find the other safe; both were "united in friendship, which ceased only with life."[14] Now Hamilton had been dead for six years.

During the same period, Lee also wrote of the long, fast, dangerous flight of the Southern Army from Cornwallis in the race for the Dan River. He described the skill and poise with which Otho Holland Williams commanded the rear guard of light infantry, "enjoying the delight inspired by their manly ardor, and commending their devotion to their country." When the army's safety was certain, Williams's men, including Lee, knew a similar "delight" and suddenly no longer felt tired: "the whole corps became renovated in strength and agility; so powerful is the influence of the mind over the body."[15] The influence of this memory had afterward remained as vivid to Williams as to Lee. Ten years after the war, Williams, reminding Lee of "the ardour, activity, and enterprise with which you conducted the legion," told him that the Williamses would name their newborn son "Henry Lee, to perpetuate in my family the remembrance of that friendship which originated at a time when the test of merit could not be mistaken, when the exertions for liberty were most necessary, and when the arms of freemen were most effectual."[16] Lee, in giving the retreat to the Dan new life in his memoirs, might teach these lessons to the namesake he called "our Henry."[17] Otho Holland Williams could no longer do so; he had been dead for sixteen years.

Writing in jail, Lee recreated the Battle of Guilford Court House, which had made the 15th of March, 1781, "a day never to be forgotten by the southern section of the United States." The intensity of this experience for the man of twenty-one returned to the man of fifty-four as he described the morning of the 15th: "the atmosphere calm and illumined with a cloudless sun; the season rather cold than cool; the body was braced, and the mind high toned by the state of the weather. Great was the stake, willing were the generals to put it to hazard, and their armies seemed to support with ardor the decision of their respective leaders." Such ardor made the battle one of the most hard-fought of the war. Even in losing, Nathanael Greene and his army killed or wounded almost one-third of Cornwallis's force, leaving an aftermath as memorable to the survivors as the prelude had been exciting to many men who were no longer alive: "The night succeeding this day of blood was rainy, dark and cold: the dead unburied, the wounded unsheltered, the groans of the dying, and the shrieks of the living shed a deeper shade over the gloom of nature."[18] The horror had purpose because Nathanael Greene and his army eventually brought victory out of violence and secured American independence in the South. The story of the southern war was in large part Greene's story. Lee had first decided to tell it when he had heard of the death of his friend and commander, twenty-four years ago.

As Lee once again fully engaged his mind in intense activity, he could not altogether ignore his age—"I am well but troubled with constant pain in my eyes, in consequence of too much writing, so much more for the last year than was my habit"—yet he could produce the sensations of youth: not only ardor and impetuosity but also public service and glory.[19] When Lee wanted to put the best face on war, he spoke of a patriotic cause, served by the confident strength of a twenty-year-old. Not long before he went to jail, Lee, as a militia commander, had published an appeal for the 4th Virginia Division to prepare itself in case friction with Britain led to war. At the age of fifty-one, Lee addressed the young men of the division with special "earnestness," he said, "because he was once young, like them, and then experienced the honorable toils and perils of war. The season of youth, is the season for battle. War is upon us, and you are young."[20] When it came, the second war with Britain was not Lee's war. Even so, he did revive the season for battle as he recreated the first war with Britain and as he used its lessons to renew political war with the Republicans.

Lee announced in his first volume that "the object of these Memoirs" was, "by a faithful and plain elucidation of the occurrences of our war, connecting events with their causes, to enlighten the future defenders and rulers of our country."[21] The crucial enlightenment consisted of dramatizing the importance of the army in establishing American independence. Some of his most eloquent passages by turns denounced and lamented the lethal reliance on militia for battlefield combat. His strictures also discredited a sometimes temporizing populace and delinquent civil officials. He did not impose on his story schematic stereotypes of consistently careless civilians and unfailingly heroic soldiers. However, as he connected events with their causes, it became clear that unsteadfast citizens, constitutionally weak governments, and unwise officeholders had caused hardships and defeats, while persevering and far-sighted soldiers had sustained the struggle to victory. Thus Lee's history instructed future soldiers and rulers by presenting the advocates of military expertise and strong government as the central patriots and victors of the Revolution.

In 1812, Federalist reviewers praised Lee's memoirs for their usefulness "in diffusing more correct notions of our military policy, than have hitherto prevailed among us."[22] The initial reverses in the War of 1812—the Republican war, "the unhallowed war"—were the fruits of ignoring the lessons Lee's history taught. Modern historians have recently studied the Republican military policy that the Federalists denounced. As President, Jefferson set out to "republicanize" the army by replacing Federalist officers with Republicans. Among the commissions that lapsed in 1801 and went unrenewed was Lee's rank as major general. But Jefferson, even with a politically sound officer corps, did not want to use a large permanent force of professional soldiers to defend the country. Leading Republicans recognized that the changes in warfare visible in Europe rendered America's state militias an inadequate defense. Patriotism no longer seemed a sufficient substitute for professional competence. But the deep-seated suspicions of a nationally consolidated militia and of a larger regular army—suspicions the Republicans had long encouraged—left the United States militarily unprepared for the war that it declared on England. Federalist editors therefore welcomed Lee's memoirs as a vindication of their objections to Republican policy. Even if Lee could not persuade the Republicans of the importance of military professionalism in time to prevent the evils he had warned against, he could expose their folly. Even if he would not be restored to military command because he had been "proscribed as a tory," he could vindicate himself and other Federalist officers who had first decided "the cause of independence."[23]

Lee distilled his version of unsound military policy and unstable wartime conduct into his account of one man: Thomas Jefferson. The memoirs contain only two short sections on Jefferson's governorship during the British invasion of Virginia in 1780–1781. However, those passages had a significance disproportionately greater than their length both because they focused many of the assumptions that lay behind the whole work and because they opened some of the most important issues in the controversy over the legacy of the Revolutionary War. By the time that Lee wrote his account, he had formulated a version of his own place in the Revolution that made Governor Jefferson as fit to become a foil for Lee the historian as President Jefferson had become a preoccupation for Lee the politician. In Lee's retrospective self-portrait and in his prolonged concern with Jefferson lay the antecedents of his attack on Jefferson's effectiveness as a revolutionary patriot.

In sections of the memoirs that did not discuss Jefferson, Lee drew a self-portrait that subtly revised the character of the young officer who had left the army before the end of the war. He presented himself as a lieutenant colonel more accustomed to continental thinking and to planning for remote consequences than was the man whom one finds in Lee's wartime correspondence. The difference was one of emphasis and degree: during the war, Lee had shown an understanding of the connection between military operations and political support; he had also seen his Legion's activities as a subordinate part of Greene's plan to liberate the South. Nevertheless, the Lee of the letters thought more often of his own pride, glory, and advancement than did the Lee of the memoirs, who by comparison sounded like a mature strategist. The prolonged correspondence about Lee's resignation gets one sentence in the memoirs: "Lieutenant colonel Lee had become incapable from his ill health of continuing in command of the light troops, and had obtained leave of absence."[24] This disparity reflected Lee's later increased interest in the winning of the southern campaign and his decreased interest in the private resentments of a young officer. The change of interest helped cause his memory to err: he attributed one of the Legion's exploits to the period of his own command although it had occurred after his departure.

The most conspicuous of Lee's reinterpretations of his wartime services as a military thinker concerned Nathanael Greene's decision to return to South Carolina and resume the contest for control of the deep South after the Battle of Guilford Court House. This plan had occurred to a number of Greene's subordinates, including Lee; it was Greene's own decision and won praise as an important military and political stroke, making the Continental Army the core of resistance to British control. Lee, in his memoirs, gave credit for the strategy to an unnamed officer whom he called "the proposer," and he narrated that officer's hard-won victory in arguing for the policy during a council of war. Readers of the passage were evidently expected to admire Lee's modesty as much as his strategic insight. The manuscript draft of the memoirs shows that he had first intended to call himself "the projector," then had crossed that out and substituted "proposer" but had not liked that word either. He crossed it out, too, then finally settled for it and wrote it back in. As he reconstructed the debate among Greene's advisers over whether to pursue Cornwallis into Virginia or return to South Carolina, Lee revised the arguments of the proposer to make them more cogent and wrote an interlined comment on his opponents'

praise for Greene's ability to defeat Cornwallis in Virginia—
"flattery," Lee called it.[25] His implied claims for his own
originality and influence had strong evidence behind them,
including Greene's written expressions of gratitude. The significance of their prominence in the memoirs depends less on
the degree of their accuracy than on Lee's determination to
heighten his stature as a leading victor of the Revolution.

Beyond emphasizing his own accomplishments, Lee vi-
cariously placed himself within the inner circle of revolutionary patriots by becoming the spokesman for the fame of
Nathanael Greene and George Washington. Both generals
had shown him special favor. They had given him his own unit
with special assignments, under their immediate command.
Judging by the frequency and fervor of his comments, Lee's
pride in the two friendships he had formed was one of his most
valued legacies from the war—one that continued or grew
stronger after the deaths of Greene and Washington. This
pride, like Lee's outlook on most other aspects of his life, gave
personal qualities consequences of national significance. Lee
would, on the generals' behalf, represent to America the virtues that had guided the war to victory.

The career of Nathanael Greene, who never won a battle, showed the importance of stable character in the army's
survival and eventual triumph. When Lee heard of Greene's
death in 1786, he wrote: "How hard the fate of the U States,
to loose such a son in the middle of life—irreparable loss."[26]
In the Continental Congress, Lee served on the committee
planning a monument to Greene for the national capital. Lee
wanted to make sure that the United States, having lost
Greene, did not also lose the example of "his patriotism, valour and ability."[27] Soon afterward Lee and other officers decided to write a biography of Greene in order to transmit his
exploits "faithfully & fairly to posterity."[28] The projected biography was the beginning of Lee's memoirs. Twenty-three

years went by before Lee grew ready to devote his sustained effort to recreating the past. Then he found that he had too few sources to write a full biography of Greene. He wrote, instead, about the southern campaigns from his own point of view, adding an introductory account of the war from 1777 to 1780. Although Lee made himself the center of his history, he also carried out his plan to memorialize Greene. Greene's sound judgment formed a central theme in Lee's account: "Pure and tranquil from the consciousness of just intentions, the undisturbed energy of his mind was wholly devoted to the effectual accomplishment of the high trust reposed in him."[29] The tranquillity of Greene's mind in making momentous decisions aroused admiration in Lee, who envied it without attaining it. Lee's long discussion of the conflicting strategic counsel of "the proposer" and his opponents sought not so much to steal Greene's glory for Lee as to link Lee more closely with the equanimity, insight, and decisiveness of Greene. Far from being the unthinking instrument of Lee's genius, Greene, by his approval of Lee's proposal, confirmed Lee's possession of some of the gifts of high-level command, which Greene had in full measure.

Greene's self-mastery led the liberation of the South; Washington's had led a whole people both in the defense of liberty and in the implementation of self-government. In Lee's celebration of George Washington, he gave his fullest definition of the ideal American revolutionary and made his most frequent claim to share that stature. Lee was a representative in the United States Congress when Washington died in 1799. There he had urged the appropriation of money for a mausoleum. Americans' purpose in so honoring Washington would be to teach "our children's children . . . that the truest way to gain honor amidst a free people is to be useful, to be virtuous." Thus, "we may imitate his virtues and his great example" and thereby create "an opportunity of rearing some future WASHINGTON." Lee took this proposal as much to heart as he had the defense of Washington himself during the controversy over the Jay Treaty. Republicans in the House tried to substitute a less expensive monument. Lee considered $70,000 a "small" sum for honoring virtue; but Nathaniel Macon, in denouncing "this monument mania," called the expenditure excessive. Macon said that he, unlike Lee, was not carried away by "the visionary notions of speculation." Taunts like this committed Lee more intensely to his advocacy of Washington's virtues. The mausoleum would memorialize the dedication of both Washington and Lee to the public good rather than to private advantage. After the debate Lee wrote, "the opposition has been bitter & my feelings enlisted me so deeply in the business that I could not spare a moment."[30]

When Lee told the House of Representatives that "History will transmit to posterity the lustre of his fame, glittering with untarnished purity," he spoke as one who had already begun posterity's homage to Washington. Lee's funeral oration would soon be widely reprinted as a pamphlet and in newspapers. It was the fullest expression of his efforts to link himself to Washington. Often before, "at tavern and courthouse," he had rhetorically praised Washington. After the oration, for the rest of Lee's life, he would proudly be introduced to strangers and described in newspapers as "the confidential friend of Washington."[31]

From an early date, Lee had taken a proprietary interest in Washington's virtue and fame. Their correspondence contains many of Lee's expressions of respect, attachment, friendship, devotion, and love. After the ratification of the United States Constitution, Lee wrote a long letter urging Washington to accept the presidency. As Washington was leaving Virginia to enter that office, Lee wrote the congratulatory addresses for both the state legislature and the city of

Alexandria, commending him as "the instrument of general happiness."[32]

Among Washington's many admirable qualities, Lee, like other writers and orators, gave special attention to mental discipline and control over emotion, both of which had enabled Washington to be especially purposeful and effective. The funeral oration emphasized those attributes that made Washington "self-collected" as he planned to cross the Delaware River and surprise the enemy garrison in Trenton. Like Greene, Washington had "a clear and a penetrating mind, a strong and a sound judgment, calmness and temper for deliberation, with invincible firmness and perseverance." How had Washington's virtues become so uniquely and repeatedly beneficial to his country's happiness? Lee's words constantly rephrased the hero's self-discipline: "stability of system," "incorruptible integrity," "innate modesty," "purity of his private character," "unmoved by foreign intrusion, unshaken by domestic turbulence," "undismayed by disaster, unchanged by change of fortune." Washington was capable of "invigorating despondency" by his example; and even on his deathbed, "although in extreme pain, not a sigh, not a groan escaped him; and with undisturbed serenity he closed his well spent life."[33]

Unlike other writers and orators who praised Washington for the same qualities, Lee did not treat Washington's self-discipline as if it were an innate trait or a miraculous gift. He knew that Washington, like himself, was "ardent, and impetuous by nature." But Washington "subjected his passions to his reason; and could with facility, by his habitual self-control, repress his inclinations whenever his judgment forbade their indulgence: the whole tenor of his military life evinces uniform and complete self-command."[34]

This strength attracted Lee to Washington even though he could not emulate it. Through years of florid rhetoric, Lee propagated Washington's virtues by praising them more than by exemplifying them. Washington attained the three peaks of glory that Lee wanted for all revolutionary soldiers, including himself, but could claim for only one man: "First in war—first in peace—and first in the hearts of his countrymen."[35] These glories, for Lee, made a natural progression that went awry in his own life but that he could often validate "with a force and grandeur of eloquence" as he praised his "hero, his friend, and a country's preserver."[36]

In the memoirs, the British surrender at Yorktown, which Lee had witnessed, became a dramatic set piece in which to savor Washington's triumph and to review the six years of patience and self-denial by which Washington had been "lifted to the pinnacle of glory."[37] Lee's homage was an implied claim to share that glory, and the claim grew more urgent after Washington's death, as Lee himself moved toward political isolation and bankruptcy. He hoped to aid his faltering finances by profiting from the sale of printed copies of the funeral oration; however, he complied with Congress's wish to publish it without copyright, "much as I had flattered myself with a different disposition of it."[38] Instead of trading on his intimacy with Washington, Lee could take increasing consolation from having made such strength of character and successful patriotism a central legacy of the Revolutionary War. Washington's adopted son, George Washington Parke Custis—whose daughter married Lee's youngest son, Robert—described Light-Horse Harry Lee's later years: "The fame and memory of his chief was the fondly-cherished passion to which he clung amid the wreck of his fortunes—the hope, which gave warmth to his heart when all else around him seemed cold and desolate."[39] A portrait of Robert's mother, Ann Lee, shows her wearing a miniature—a likeness not of her husband but of George Washington.

The father of his country filled some of the functions of a father for the most famous of the Lees, even though Washington died eight years before Robert E. Lee was born. Growing up in Alexandria, Robert was surrounded by reminders of Washington, as well as by people who had known the master of nearby Mount Vernon. The Arlington mansion where Robert's wife, Mary Custis, grew up had many mementos of Washington, the memory of whom Mary's father assiduously promoted in speeches and writings. Robert and his wife named their first son George Washington Custis Lee. After entering Washington's family by marriage, Robert E. Lee cultivated, in himself and in his children, a strong sense of duty, integrity, responsibility, and self-discipline—all of which his mother had worked to instill in him after Light-Horse Harry left them. Robert was so exemplary in his demeanor that his contemporaries mentioned his resemblance to Washington. Finally, Robert E. Lee, like George Washington, became the commander of a revolutionary army.

Light-Horse Harry Lee's career was not the model for his son's. As a legacy to his youngest children he left mainly admonition—not property and not example. He gave signs of regretting this default on a father's duty; he tried to substitute for his own career the inspiring character of other heroes, especially Washington. Yet his default as a father ran deeper than the decline of his public stature and private fortune. Even in the achievements from which Lee took most pride—helping Washington to establish the American nation and to perpetuate its union—neither his own example nor his vicarious representation of Washington's example kept his sons from trying to destroy the union through civil war. This posthumous failure was not Lee's alone. The contrast was most extreme among the Lees because Harry, though singularly devoted to union, left a son uniquely prominent in the cause of disunion. But Henry Lee also shared this failure with Washington and with other patriots of the revolutionary generation. Despite their anxiety to preserve their republic, they neither exemplified its ideals nor defined its institutions clearly enough to win the united emulation of their children. Thus, many of their children eventually claimed that disunion and human slavery were honorable legacies of the American Revolution.

The greatest failure of Henry Lee and many of his contemporaries was not their descendants' departure from the fathers' revolutionary example, but rather their descendants' appeal to the fathers' example to justify destroying the fathers' work through disunion. The revolutionaries' conduct had created an equivocal legacy. They left the definition of their legacy for their children to settle. And the children, appealing to the precedent of the fathers, resorted to violence. The more honestly and legitimately Robert E. Lee could purport to embody the character of George Washington, the less effective was Washington's character—that is, the American Revolution's pre-eminent symbol of virtue—in perpetuating human freedom and national unity. The truer a son of Washington that Robert E. Lee could claim to be, the more deeply flawed was Washington as a model. Perhaps this was what Herman Melville saw when he wrote after the Civil War,

> Who looks at Lee must think of Washington;
> In pain must think, and hide the thought,
> So deep with grievous meaning it is fraught.[40]

For Henry Lee, the virtues of Washington always stood unquestioned; and they grew brighter when contrasted with the defects of Thomas Jefferson. While Jefferson grew in political importance and claimed to continue the revolutionary fight against monarchism, Lee became more bitter about Jefferson's success or, as he called it, "ambition." No other person in public or private life excited in Lee a comparably sustained and deep hostility, an enmity that intensified as Lee's own career declined. Jefferson became, to Lee, the primary cause and leading example of America's departure from the true legacy of the Revolutionary War. Lee had found himself unable to arrest Jefferson's career of deception and destruction—had, in fact, fallen victim to it. But he would, as a historian, ensure that posterity knew how Jefferson had failed the critical test of revolutionary patriotism—one in which Washington and Lee had conspicuously excelled—the test of war.

The short account of Jefferson's governorship in Lee's memoirs capped twenty years of Lee's opposition to Jefferson's rising influence. In this opposition Lee's embitterment grew until it found its final and most adept expression in his writing of history. During these earlier years, Jefferson was far less preoccupied with Lee than Lee was with Jefferson. After the publication of John Marshall's biography of George Washington in 1807 and Lee's memoirs in 1812, Jefferson intensified his own lasting concern over the interpretation of the Revolution that histories would perpetuate.

One of the most important and recurrent elements of Lee's animosity toward Jefferson was his insistence that Washington and Jefferson should be enemies. As Lee linked himself more closely to the Washington administration in 1793 and 1794, he warned the President against Jefferson: first, by implication, as one of those "perverse ambitious americans" who encouraged Citizen Genêt and the Democratic Societies; second, by name, as one who had made "derogatory" remarks in private about Washington's susceptibility to British influence.[41] Lee himself had written severe censures of the administration's domestic policies during its early years. Now he wanted to become its guardian against the machinations of Jefferson. Jefferson's presidential candidacies in 1796 and 1800 raised the level of hostility. In 1796, Lee warned Washington that Jefferson, despite his resignation from public office, was helping to prepare Republican manifestos for the newspapers and was "still engaged in the bustle of politics, & in turbulence & intrigue against the government."[42] In the summer of 1800, Lee told John Adams "that he knew Mr. Jefferson was using all his influence and intrigue, to supersede him in the Presidential chair."[43] In later years Lee described Jefferson's advance to the presidency as the fruition of a "plan" of "political treachery" executed by "a veteran gambler." Only by these means could Jefferson have succeeded men whose "revolutionary services" had won them wider public esteem.

Thus Lee first tried to prevent Jefferson's elevation to the presidency and then sought to distinguish between those Federalist patriots who had won the office through revolutionary merit and Jefferson, who had risen by "unprincipled" ambitious scheming. This distinction preserved the title of Lee and the Federalists and especially Washington as winners of the Revolutionary War and custodians of independence. Jefferson's political success, despite the Republicans' claim to be "protectors of the rights and liberty of our common country," did not make him the primary spokesman for the Revolution.[44] Lee would make sure that Washington always held that place. On Christmas Day in 1812, Lee called after dinner at Charles J. Catlett's house in Alexandria and, as usual, monopolized the conversation, even though he was still suffering from the wounds inflicted by the Baltimore mob. A traveler recorded: "He told several anecdotes of Washington." Lee linked himself to his hero by bragging, somewhat inaccurately, that he had been Washington's "primary agent for the spy department." And he assured the traveler that "Washington some time before his death spoke to him plainly of the deceitfulness and hypocrisy of Jefferson."[45]

Lee was one of the last Americans to accept Jefferson's election to the presidency. As a one-term congressman from the Northern Neck of Virginia, Lee was a member of the House that settled the electoral vote tie between Jefferson and

Aaron Burr in 1801. The Virginia delegation's majority cast
the state's vote for Jefferson, while Lee persisted, against the
advice of his old friend Hamilton, in voting for Burr. Lee said
of the two candidates: "In morality both are alike, in the
power of doing ill, the Virginian surpasses." Preventing the
election of Jefferson would continue the political war, even
after the recent defeat, "by a diversion in the enemys country."[46] Lee's partisan resistance went beyond that of most
Federalists in the House, who only hoped to substitute Burr
for Jefferson. Lee joined those whom Albert Gallatin called
"the most desperate of the federalists." They planned to continue the deadlock in the House voting and thereby prevent a
choice between the two Republicans. The lame-duck Federalist majority in Congress could then "pass a law by which they
would vest the Presidential power in the hands of some man of
their party," by making either the Chief Justice of the Supreme Court or the president pro tempore of the Senate next
in line for the unfilled presidency. This plan had little support,
even among Federalists, and further isolated Lee. Not only
did a Republican like Gallatin later recall him as "a desperate
character and held in no public estimation," but even Hamilton privately scorned the motives for supporting Burr: "A
H——Lee &c. &c. may find their account in it but good men
in the Country never will."[47]

Lee may have hoped to receive some political reward
from his old Princeton friend and fellow Continental officer
Aaron Burr. However, he was "desperate" primarily because
much of his objection to the Republicans' replacement of the
Federalists centered on the antipathy he felt toward Thomas
Jefferson. He told the House of Representatives in January
1801 "that a great change had been made in the direction of
our affairs; he did hope (though he did not believe) this change
would be productive of much good to the people."[48] And privately he told Hamilton in February, "our best interests will

be jeopardized shd. Mr. J. succeed. . . . I feel disturbed for our poor country." Lee said he would "resign to the public will," but he tried to thwart that will.[49] Only the refusal of other Federalists to risk political upheaval resolved the deadlock in favor of Jefferson. Lee's dalliance with Burr was a futile kind of opposition that revealed the extent to which Lee was blaming Jefferson's rise for his own fall. In 1807, Lee wrote to the President to complain about a report, which Jefferson disavowed, that Jefferson had privately named Lee as one of the supporters of Burr's plan to form a new empire in the West. Lee's protest summarized the threat to his own stature as a revolutionary patriot that he attributed to his political opponent: "I had supposed that my loyalty was so well established as to defy the most rancorous calumny."[50]

During Jefferson's presidency he, rather than Lee, was the principal object of calumny. In this abuse Lee took an indirect part, ostensibly to help stop one source of it. In 1802 and again in 1805, the Federalist press circulated a story that Jefferson in earlier years had cuckolded one of his oldest friends, John Walker. Jefferson was willing to admit privately that he had "offered love" to Mrs. Walker before his own marriage; John Walker wanted a document in which Jefferson would acknowledge his fault and thus soothe the family's pride and rescue Mrs. Walker's reputation.[51] Lee, whose wife was Mrs. Walker's niece, acted as a go-between. A newspaper report said that he took to the President Walker's challenge to a duel. Lee claimed that his main purpose as an emissary was to conclude an amicable settlement. He drafted John Walker's first-person narrative of Mrs. Walker's charges that Jefferson had propositioned her repeatedly for eleven years.

Jefferson's biographers have called Lee a "troublemaker" in this matter and accused him of "malice toward Jefferson."[52] Lee's public attacks on Jefferson, the most bitter of which followed the Walker affair by three years, were directed

against Jefferson's character as a politician. But even though
he did not retail the more salacious charges publicly, his intense partisanship made him a less suitable agent to settle ami-
cably a controversy that had arisen through Federalist attacks.
Jefferson, who wanted "to consign this unfortunate matter to
all the oblivion of which it is susceptible," was obliged to meet
Lee in 1803 and again at Monticello in 1806.[53] He probably
read, in Lee's hand, the account of himself slipping Mrs.
Walker a paper "to convince her of the innocence of promis-
cuous love," sneaking to her bedroom to catch her undressing,
and, while a guest of the Walkers, leaving his own wife in bed
as he waited in the hall for Mrs. Walker, "ready to seize
her."[54] In negotiating with Jefferson over how to acknowledge the truth of at least part of Walker's story, Lee
acted either as a troublemaker or as one who gravely misjudged his own fitness to be a peacemaker. In later years,
when John Marshall tried to explain the sources of "the bitterness displayed" toward Lee in Jefferson's writings, Marshall included among its causes "the part he took in the affair
of Mrs. Walker."[55]

While he engaged in negotiation and writing about Jefferson's sexual activity as a young man, Lee was also very
busy trying to forestall his own bankruptcy. In the following
years, Lee's financial trouble seemed not to distract him from
thinking about Jefferson but to increase his preoccupation.
Imprisonment in 1809 and 1810 would give Lee time to fix
Jefferson's place in the history of the Revolution. Yet even
while Lee was urgently juggling assets in an attempt to avoid
jail, he took time, in November 1808, to write a thirty-eight-
page pamphlet that was a sustained diatribe against Jefferson.
Lee said that he wanted to prevent Jefferson from causing a
war with Britain during the last months of his presidency.
However, the pamphlet, published anonymously in 1809, laid
to Jefferson's charge all the "heart-rending adversity" that the

nation and, by implication, Lee were both suffering. It was a short, acid history of the Early National Period that blamed Jefferson for the country's having "been suddenly tumbled from the summit of prosperity." Lee attributed the growth of political parties, the outcome of elections, and the fall from popularity of leading Federalists to the schemes of Jefferson.

Lee's bitterness toward Jefferson—accusing him of conceit, self-aggrandizement, obliquity, agitation, corruption, demagoguery, and political treachery—arose from his inability to find any other adequate explanation for Jefferson's success at supplanting the Federalists, both in political office and as the defenders of the American Revolution. Jefferson had perverted the legacy of the Revolution: first, by discrediting its real heroes with the false charge of monarchism; second, by pursuing "the wildest projects of the most visionary theory"; and third, by exploiting Americans' wartime hostility toward Britain to foster a new, unjust war against Britain in obedience to the dictates of absolutist France. In pursuit of Jefferson's plan, "the name of liberty was prostituted to consecrate personal exaltation." Lee used the Revolution's strongest symbol for betrayal by numbering Jefferson among the "Arnolds" whom Washington had overcome. Lee also blamed "the negligence of the majority" and the folly of "the deluded many" for Jefferson's success, but these interpretations did not satisfy him. To be the victim of public ignorance was hardly more reassuring than to be its beneficiary. Lee dignified his political defeat and his economic failure by uniting his own ruin to the impending ruin of his country. Jefferson had sabotaged "our lost happiness." Now, retiring to his "grotesque mansion," he "mocks at our distress."

Lee could no longer struggle, even from political retirement, against the destruction of his vision of peace, because that destruction was now complete. The final blast at Jefferson before Lee went to jail, although ostensibly provoked by the danger of war during the presidential transition, in fact spoke for a dead cause, not a current emergency. Lee was giving up the contest for control of national affairs, as well as his hope that he could unite his own and the nation's prosperity. "Let us then not despond," he wrote; but he could expect, at best, that America would avoid war with Britain, and the vision of bloodshed that concluded his pamphlet cast doubt even on that solace. Jefferson would complete his destruction of peace by fixing on his successor a policy that brought both poverty and war to Americans.[56]

Lee turned away from contemporary politics to write history. In doing so, he found a setting in which he could dispute Jefferson's primacy as a patriot far more successfully than he had ever done in politics. No longer trying to rescue Washington and Adams from Jefferson's hypocrisy or struggling to prevent Jefferson's election as President or dealing in slander, Lee would give up the attempt to protect Americans from false leaders. Instead of trying to prevent or explain political defeat, he would take up a more congenial task—explaining how the American Revolution had been won. By comparing his services with Jefferson's conduct, Lee could establish for posterity their respective merits. The chaotic and deceit-ridden contests of politics would give way to the "conviction of truth" in history.[57]

Lee put his account of Benedict Arnold's invasion of Virginia at the beginning of the second volume of his memoirs. It was less than thirty pages long and mentioned Jefferson by name or title only a few times, but it denigrated Jefferson far more effectively than a longer, more personal attack could have done. The story was simple. An enemy force had come up the James River in transport ships and had sent out raiding parties, which destroyed crops, buildings, public stores, and official papers, causing the legislature and the executive to abandon Richmond. The invaders returned to their ships and departed with few casualties. Later, a raiding party from Cornwallis's army caused the officials to move from Charlottesville across the Blue Ridge to Staunton.

Lee held Virginia officials, especially Jefferson, responsible for the success of the enemy incursions. First, despite a warning from Washington that the state might be invaded, Jefferson had left Virginia "unprepared." "Had the governor fortunately prepared," Richmond would have been saved, the traitor Arnold might have been captured, and his detachment destroyed. Lee repeated that "a little reflection," "the most common reflection," would have shown the danger and the need for readiness, but "hope . . . prevailed over vigilance." "The government, which does not prepare in time," Lee charged, "sports with the lives of its citizens." Second, when the invading force arrived, the government's confused reaction had enabled the enemy to increase the raid's destructiveness. Archives, munitions, and stores were concentrated rather than dispersed and thus were "yielded to the will of the invader." Those that survived owed their safety to "accident, more than precaution." The government had not warned planters to keep their tobacco out of accessible warehouses; "our towns were filled with our staple commodity, ready to be burnt, or to be exported, as might best comport with the enemy's views." The invading force "spread desolation all around." Third, Jefferson had bungled the defense of the state or, rather, had failed to put up a defense. Lee emphasized the weakness of the British—"a small corps conducted by a traitor." Despite the enemy's vulnerability, they got away "without meeting even the semblance of resistance." The militia was "never . . . judiciously conducted"; an enemy detachment destroyed the state's only cannon foundry "undisturbed by even a single shot." When Lee summarized "the supineness of the government," he called his narrative "incredible," but "nevertheless true."

Lee did not allow Jefferson the plea of lack of resources. The memoirs stressed how much more ably the defense of Virginia could have been managed. The state's weakness came "not from the want of means, but from the want of wisely husbanding and wisely applying our resources." Who could have saved the state? Obviously, not Jefferson. The governor ought to have relied on those Continental "officers, bred under Washington," who had returned to their homes in Virginia when the army had been reduced in size: "they were devoted to the great cause for which they had fought, and with alacrity would have rallied around the standard of their country." And who could have led such men? An unnamed but easily recognizable "soldier of genius," commanding a "legionary corps of three hundred horse and three hundred musketry, with a battalion of mounted riflemen, accompanied by a battalion of infantry." That commander would have prevented "these injurious and debasing incursions." As Lee thought about the missed chance to protect Virginia, he wrote: "Never in the course of the war was a more alluring opportunity presented for honorable enterprise, with so fair a prospect of success."[58]

When the nation's survival depended on armed combat, a leader like Jefferson would always shrink in stature. In writing the pamphlet attack on Jefferson the year before starting his memoirs, Lee had taken some consolation from Jefferson's unfitness for war. Lee opposed a second war with Britain and hoped that Jefferson would avoid one. Yet, in imagining such a war, Lee still found fault with the reason for Jefferson's reluctance. "War, however necessary, never can be acceptable to him whose envious mind sickens in observing merit rising to eminence. . . . A military leader of brilliant abilities would be very apt to obscure presidential eminence."[59] The prospect of another war with Britain, like Lee's recounting of the Revolutionary War, brought back into prominence the nation's dependence on the soldier—a dependence that had too often been denied or forgotten in the Jeffersonians' claim to represent the American Revolution in partisan politics.

The soldier's importance to his country was fresh in Lee's mind as he contrasted his own gifts with Jefferson's failures during the war. One of William R. Davie's letters to Lee in jail had not only encouraged him to write history but also warned him to stand ready for further military service when America entered the Napoleonic Wars: "your talents must again be brought into action."[60] When war came, Lee did not regain a command. However, as he imagined in his memoirs the "timidity and impotence" of Jefferson being replaced by "a discriminating officer" who maneuvered his "inferior force" with "dexterity" and brought "a retreating foe . . . to submission," Lee did fight a new war.[61] Through it he vindicated the value of military virtue in contrast with political ambition. By this achievement, if not by a return to active duty, Lee could prove Davie correct in writing, "I cannot permit myself to believe that your career is finished."[62]

Jefferson's reaction to the enemy invasion looked very different from the one Lee imagined for the "soldier of genius." Jefferson ran. Lee did not explicitly accuse Jefferson of cowardice; nor did he directly fault the Virginia authorities for retiring before the enemy. Nevertheless, he constructed an artful portrait of irresolution and retreat that conveyed an accusation more effectively than polemical attack would have done. The accusation was embedded by innuendo within the narrative. Lee described the state authorities "driven from the seat of government; chased from Charlottesville; and at length interposing the Blue Ridge between themselves and the enemy." More specifically, he depicted "the governor of the oldest state in the Union, and the most populous . . . driven out of its metropolis, and forced to secure personal safety by flight." Lee attributed the invaders' success to "the supineness of the government" and emphasized "these truths" by repeating that the invasion was never "seriously opposed." If posterity had only this behavior by which to judge its ancestors, it would pronounce them "destitute" of "courage and love of country." The reader of Lee's narrative could hardly blame the citizens of Virginia when, "finding the metropolis gone, and the enemy unresisted," they "followed the example of the government" and took to "flight." In Lee's mind, this failure of courage undermined the reputation that Jefferson had won as a thinker, writer, and politician. Lee began his account of Jefferson's governorship by referring to Jefferson's "early and distinguished part in the revolution." Then he concluded it by remarking that, in rulers, "attachment to the common cause is vain and illusory, unless guided in times of difficulty by courage, wisdom, and concert."[63] He wanted to make sure that his readers did not miss the import of the narrative, which demonstrated how ineffective Jefferson's attachment to the cause had become. In the manuscript draft of the memoirs, when Lee came to his summary of "the disgraces and distresses" that the government's failure had brought on the state, he headed the section with a note to his copyist: "Take care how you copy here."[64]

Of the many attacks to which Thomas Jefferson was subjected during his career, few troubled him as much as the ones that Lee tried to incorporate into the history of the Revolution. The publication of Lee's memoirs began a new debate over Jefferson's war record and Lee's reliability as a historian. Jefferson took a leading part in his own defense and in denouncing Lee. Lee, on the other hand, spent his last years out of the country; his cause rested on his previous writings until his sons took up the campaign after his death. As often happens in disputes over military events, the controversy descended into details that tax the patience of anyone who is not a participant in the debate. However, the most significant disagreements between Lee and Jefferson concerned not so much the facts of the invasion as the interpretation of effective service to the revolutionary cause. In the differing interpretations, the contest of historians succeeded the contest of politicians in defining the meaning of the Revolutionary War.

The link between political campaigns and the writing of history was especially clear in the argument over Jefferson's governorship. Lee's memoirs perpetuated, with somewhat greater subtlety and accuracy, the charges of Jefferson's "want of firmness" that had begun with his first presidential candidacy in 1796.[65] Federalists contended that Jefferson's failure as governor demonstrated his unfitness for the presidency: "he does not possess fortitude for the station."[66] In the face of danger, "he fled for safety from a few light-horsemen, and shamefully abandoned his trust!" Rumor said that he had been so anxious to escape Tarleton's dragoons as they neared Monticello that he fell off his horse in trying to reach Carter's Mountain nearby. The Federalists magnanimously conceded that "his flight" arose "not from any criminality, but from a constitutional weakness of nerves."[67] Lee's memoirs described the British "chasing our governor from hill to hill."[68] By the year that the memoirs were published, the *New-York Evening Post* was referring to Jefferson as "THE COWARD OF CARTER'S MOUNTAIN."[69] The editors could omit his name, confident that readers would recognize the character. These accusations of weakness had originated in print with the Alexandria Federalist and former Continental Army officer Charles Simms in 1796. Fourteen years later, Simms was one of Lee's most active helpers in gathering source material for the memoirs and in planning their publication. While Lee was still in jail, writing, he told Simms that the account of "the Virga. campaign" would be "the most tasteless part of my work & yet as I always presumed full of rich matter."[70]

Thomas Jefferson felt as much concern about the political implications of historical interpretation as did Lee or Simms. As Jefferson got older, he, like other leaders of the revolutionary generation, grew increasingly preoccupied with the version of the Revolutionary War that history would pass on to those who could not know the truth from their own experience. Among other revolutionaries, the manifestations of this solicitude ranged from John Adams's argument with Mercy Otis Warren over her history's account of his own career to the growing number of veterans writing autobiographies. With the publication of John Marshall's *Life of Washington,* followed in a few years by Lee's memoirs, Jefferson worried that the Federalists were framing a distorted, yet uncontested, interpretation of the war. He warned: "we have been too careless of our future reputation; while our tories will omit nothing to place us in the wrong."[71]

For Jefferson, as for Lee, American history's central question was, Which Americans had won the Revolutionary War? Implicit in the question lay the assumption that the answer would determine who had the best claim to preserve and govern the republic. Jefferson believed that the histories and biographies, rather than the surviving revolutionary documents from which they were drawn, would shape future generations' assessment of the participants in the war. Ten years after the publication of Lee's memoirs, Jefferson wrote with alarm: "this book had begun to be quoted as history."[72] Only rival books could correct such error because from a "congeries" of documents, written by men with varied motives, "history may be made to wear any hue, with which the passions of the compiler, royalist or republican, may choose to tinge it." As an example, Jefferson cited "the party feelings" of Washington's biographer Marshall, "a leading mountebank" in political contests. The biography, Jefferson charged, praised officers who had "done nothing military," but who had later "become heroes in party, altho' not in war"; similarly, Marshall slighted the wartime services of those "who rendered signal services indeed, but did not earn his praise by apostatizing in peace from the republican principles for which they had fought in war."[73]

Despite his warning that documents could be distorted to yield partisan accounts, Jefferson was not a relativist. He knew that there was a truth of the Revolutionary War, and he saved his greatest scorn for "the lying Lee."[74] In 1796, after the charges against Jefferson were first published, and again in 1816, after reading Lee's memoirs, Jefferson reworked his diary and notes on his conduct during the invasion of Virginia. His own accounts of the truth sometimes contradicted each other, but he remained sure that Lee's version was "parody," "romance," and "a tissue of errors from beginning to end."[75] To refute Lee's lies, Jefferson encouraged the work of two other historians: William Johnson, a Republican Supreme Court justice who wrote a biography of Nathanael Greene, and Louis Girardin, who continued John Burk's *History of Virginia* through the Revolutionary War years. The two works accomplished Jefferson's wishes: Johnson frequently challenged Lee's accuracy as a historian and his pretensions as a commander or strategist; Girardin wrote a long, detailed vindication of Jefferson's actions as governor. Girardin worked with Jefferson's papers at Monticello, and in May 1815, Jefferson read and corrected Girardin's chapters on the Revolution. After Johnson's biography was published, Jefferson congratulated him on "a fair history of the Southern war. . . . Lee's military fable you have put down."[76]

More was at stake in this war of histories than individual reputations. The survival of republicanism depended on Americans' ability to defend it. Drawing lessons from conduct in war and in political contests, historians could discredit a whole course of policy by purporting to describe the ineffectiveness of its adherents. Marshall and Lee believed that weak governments and popular laxness in wartime had endangered the republic. Their histories would show that American independence and liberty required able leaders who wielded coercive authority. Jefferson, on the other hand, believed that wartime difficulties arose "not from luke-warmness in our citizens or their functionaries, as our military leaders supposed; but from the pennyless condition of a people, totally shut out from all commerce." He feared that partisan history, by wrongly impugning the ability of public virtue and decentralized governments to defend themselves, would use the crises of the war years to discredit self-government.

In upholding his own reputation as governor, Jefferson was protecting for future generations the republicanism of the Revolution. To dramatize this connection, Jefferson, in his accounts of his governorship, exaggerated the support among his wartime critics in the Virginia General Assembly for creating an executive with dictatorial powers to replace him. Thus he implied that his administration had functioned as effectively as republican institutions would permit. Anyone who demanded more would subvert the Revolution. As soon as Jefferson had seen, in Johnson's work, "the Romance of Lee removed from the shelf of History to that of Fable," he expressed his "anxiety" that Johnson write a history of political parties. The story of how the Republicans had worked "to arrest our course towards monarchy" would, like the correct account of the war, show who had done most "to secure the result of our revolutionary sufferings and sacrifices in a government, bottomed on the only safe basis, the elective will of the people."[77]

The publication of Girardin's history in 1816 and Johnson's biography in 1822 did not still Jefferson's concern about Lee's account of his governorship. In the last year of his life he was still drafting a long, detailed, hour-by-hour justification of his conduct during the invasion of 1780–1781. In 1826,

Lee's oldest son edited a second edition of the memoirs. Later, when some of Jefferson's comments about Light-Horse Harry Lee were published posthumously, the younger Lee would write a harsh attack on Jefferson's character and career. Now, however, he hoped to reconcile contradictions, and he invited Jefferson to write a rebuttal to the accusations in the original version of the memoirs. For such a reply, Jefferson referred the younger Lee to Girardin's account. At the same time, in his impassioned letter, he complained about the injustice of his being "under the reproach of history" for not having repelled the invaders. The enemy had held Richmond for only a day; the British had occupied many other state capitals; Napoleon had taken the capitals of Europe. Why should the Virginia authorities "alone" be criticized? By the end of Jefferson's narrative of the invasion, the legislature had abandoned him, the executive council had abandoned him; finally, even his horse collapsed, and he had to carry his saddle until he could borrow an unbroken colt in order to return to Richmond within a few hours of the enemy's departure. Jefferson described to Lee the "memorandums" made at the time on "scraps of paper" that were now "tattered and tender." He invited Lee to come to Monticello and consult these, as well as his other papers, all of which would confirm his "fidelity."[78] Furthermore, he knew that the State Department archives and George Washington's papers would contain corroboration in the form of Jefferson's weekly reports. The younger Lee was one of the last guests at Monticello before Jefferson's death. On Thursday, June 29, Jefferson, though already weakened by his final illness, felt "able to converse" with Lee about his record as war governor. Lee did not get to look at the documents; Jefferson wanted "to examine the papers with him."[79] But Jefferson's health grew steadily worse. Lee did not see him again; five days later he was dead.

The most thorough students of Jefferson's career—

Dumas Malone, Julian P. Boyd, and Merrill D. Peterson—
have not stressed, to the same degree that Jefferson did, his
exact movements and activities during the invasion as a vindication of his merit in the governorship. Having shown that
Jefferson was not a coward, they give most of their attention
not to his bravery but to his administrative work. They rightly
emphasize his record as a diligent governor, which rebuts
most charges of negligence put forth in political campaigns
and in Light-Horse Harry Lee's memoirs. Jefferson and his
contemporaries, however, attached more importance than do
modern historians to the issue of his personal conduct in the
face of enemy attack. Revolutionaries saw in this issue a crucial measure of the legitimacy of their competing versions of
the Revolution and its lessons. Jefferson's effectiveness as an
administrator, writer, or politician could not offset a failure of
courage, in his contemporaries' assessment of his merit as a
defender of liberty. Although an institution—an army, a republican government, a political party—might help to secure
liberty, the value of the institution could not adequately be
weighed by asking only how effectively it functioned in fighting, governing, or winning elections. The revolutionary generation did not put their greatest faith in the operation of organizations. Rather, the true guarantor of liberty was the moral
character of the soldiers, officials, or political partisans who
could, by their actions, save or lose American independence.
Institutions might be created or altered with the intent to assure that virtuous men filled positions of responsibility. But
the moral character of individuals, not the workings of the impersonal organization, enabled an institution to protect liberty
and claim public support.
    Opposing partisans within the revolutionary generation
might differ in their estimates of each other's virtue and in
their choice of ways to preserve the nation's strength. Still,
they perpetuated the premise on which they had undertaken

the Revolution—America's survival depended on their courage. When Henry Lee contrasted the timid governor with the soldier of genius, he was not implying that an army necessarily created more effective patriots and ought therefore to supplant civil government, which created cowards. Rather, his attack on Jefferson implied that the patriot who had most fully met the challenge of personally defending liberty had thereby proven himself best qualified to design and man the institutions that would preserve it. Thus Lee concluded not that Virginia should have had a military government but that his advocacy of a more powerful, centralized civilian government carried more weight than Jefferson's defense of decentralization, in light of their contrasting credentials as courageous patriots. Lee and Charles Simms conceded that Jefferson—as his modern biographers demonstrate—had for the most part served effectively as governor, especially in supplying the Southern Army from Virginia's resources. But if Lee and Simms could still show that Jefferson, under the duress of administrative crisis or personal danger, had proven weak, they could challenge his claim to be a fit defender of the Revolution—as governor, party leader, or President and Commander in Chief. When Jefferson, in the last weeks of his life, labored over the record of what he called "these minute details," he knew that, by the standards of his contemporaries, the record contained one of the critical measurements of his character.[80] And on the strength of his character rested much of the conviction that his career would carry for posterity. To perpetuate the true legacy of the Revolution—the faith in liberty and republicanism that he had striven to express in documents and institutions—Jefferson would have to show that his conduct had not betrayed the ideals he claimed to have defended.

Jefferson's main problem, when writing his self-justifications, was to clarify the distinction between personal courage and military competence. He could refute some of Lee's account by demonstrating his own diligence during the invasion. Even more important, he could adduce the state government's lack of resources in order to show that "the total destitution of means" rather than "mismanagement of them" explained the state's vulnerability.[81] He still had to respond to the accusation implied by the recurrent word "flight." Jefferson freely acknowledged that the invasion called for military skills—"no services but military of any avail"—and that he did not have them—"unprepared by his line of life and education for the command of armies."[82] He deferred to experienced men by naming the senior Continental Army officer, Baron Steuben, to command the militia and by declining re-election to a third one-year term as governor so that General Thomas Nelson could succeed him.

There remained the charge summarized by Jefferson in these words: "but I was not with the army !"[83] In staying out of the reach of Arnold at Richmond and of Tarleton at Charlottesville, he had failed to face the enemy in the field. Lee's memoirs said that Jefferson "very readily saved himself" from Tarleton "by taking shelter in an adjacent spur of the mountains."[84] A Federalist writer had put Lee's implied accusation more explicitly in 1796: "the proof of a steady attachment to the civil rights of one's fellow-citizens ought not to rest merely on *writings;* this attachment ought to be evinced by *public conduct,* by *action* and in *times of danger;* then the hazarding of *personal safety* for the preservation of our civil rights is the highest testimony of patriotism. . . . Mr. Jefferson has generally sacrificed the civil rights of his countrymen to his own personal safety."[85] Jefferson could respond to such an attack partly by describing his administrative work—"I was engaged in the more important function of taking measures to collect an army." Even so, he also needed to document his personal courage. He said that during Arnold's invasion he had been away from Richmond "3 days only," that he had stayed "always within observing distance of the enemy," and that he had gone "every where, where my presence could be of any service."[86] His self-justification paid special attention to the stories of his escape from Tarleton outside of Charlottesville. Girardin, while hoping that "these details will be excused" in order to correct misrepresentations, explained in his history that Jefferson had walked from Monticello to Carter's Mountain less than ten minutes before the British arrived at his home.[87] Jefferson wrote sarcastically of his critics: "These closet heroes forsooth would have disdained the shelter of a wood, even singly and unarmed, against a legion of armed enemies."[88]

Jefferson, when he accused his critics of demanding that he act like Don Quixote, was not belittling the idea of heroism. Rather, he was directing against his critics the same kind of charge they had made against him; they were only "closet" heroes, not real ones. Similarly, he censured Marshall's biography of Washington not because it praised military men but because it praised some officers who were "heroes in party, altho' not in war," while it slighted the military merits of men who had remained faithful to "the republican principles for which they had fought in war."[89] Jefferson shared his contemporaries' assumption that dedication to revolutionary principles included the heroism of physical courage. He claimed wartime courage for some Republican civilians and denied it to some Federalist officers.

For the revolutionary generation, courage lay at the heart of the survival of republicanism. Neither Jefferson nor any other signer of the Declaration of Independence served in the Continental Army during the Revolutionary War. Yet all knew that their signatures on the declaration exposed them to the penalty for treason if the Revolution failed. Thus, by signing they pledged their lives, as the declaration said. The success of the cause—they and their contemporaries believed—

would always depend on bravery of this kind, among civilians as well as soldiers.

In characterizing the politics of the Early National Period as a continuation and re-enactment of the revolutionary contest, the wartime generation perpetuated this emphasis on individual moral strength as the ultimate defender of liberty. Seeing a political world beset by foreign influence and domestic conspiracy, they cast their patriotism in the language of struggle and honor. At the same time, defining politics as a legacy of war helped predispose adversaries to see each contest as a critical test of their survival. Political war demanded a courage akin to combat because each domestic controversy, like the original fight with Britain, could end with the death of liberty and of independence. Partisans defended or rewon the Revolution against enemies who, by definition, intended to destroy it.

To the revolutionary generation, the strengths that had won the War of Independence would remain crucial to Americans' implementation of their vision of the future. Consequently, describing wartime courage and identifying its most successful exemplars became an important source of confidence that the revolutionaries' posterity could perpetuate a correct goal, undeterred by partisan lies about the past. For this purpose, those who had won the war must leave behind accurate histories of it. Posterity would imitate the virtues and would respect the heroes there portrayed. On these histories would depend, in part, the outcome of the revolutionary struggle over the character of America.

Jefferson's varied grounds for resentment of Lee finally focused on Lee's role as a historian. When Jefferson at last turned a rancor toward Lee comparable to Lee's hostility, his censure made up in bitterness some of what it lacked in quantity. John Marshall, later trying to explain the "asperity" with which Jefferson spoke of Lee, commented—on his own behalf as well as Lee's—"Those Virginians who opposed the opinions and political views of Mr. Jefferson seem to have been considered rather as rebellious subjects than legitimate enemies entitled to the rights of political war."[90] Marshall was saying, in a partisan way, that Jefferson saw in Federalists, especially Virginia Federalists like Lee, betrayers of the Revolution. Jefferson had detected Lee's "malice" as early as 1796 when Lee, using "the slander of an intriguer," had tried to alienate Washington from Jefferson. Lee ought "either to have been of more truth, or less trusted by his country."

When "this miserable tergiversator" embodied his untruths in history, his power to do evil, in Jefferson's eyes, far exceeded the holding of political office.[91] His falsehoods, unless exposed, could undermine Americans' faith in self-government. Jefferson praised Johnson's biography of Greene especially because it repeatedly, in Johnson's words, "brought in question Colonel Lee's . . . accuracy as an historian." Johnson professed to "impeach Colonel Lee's *recollection,* not his *veracity.*"[92] But Jefferson was ready to impeach Lee's truthfulness. The "imputations" in Lee's memoirs arose not from error but from a design to deny Jefferson's firmness in the revolutionary cause.[93] But the lies had failed, and five years after Lee's death, Jefferson reassured Johnson that the liar had been crushed. Johnson was worrying that Lee's relatives, some of whom had provided material for the biography of Greene, would, with other Virginians, attack the book in order to "espouse the fame of Colo. Lee."[94] Jefferson told him: "the family of enemies, whose buzz you apprehend, are now nothing . . . and their military relation has long ago had the full-voiced condemnation of his own state. Do not fear these insects."[95]

While Lee was writing his memoirs he planned to publish them anonymously. He thought that they were "written with too much freedom for the times." They "will occasionally displease & I have no desire to engage in duels in my last period of life."[96] However, after he left jail and when publication drew near, he decided to put his name on the title page. Perhaps Lee's reputation as an officer and his work as a historian would enhance each other and together would remind his countrymen of his stature as a revolutionary. The publisher's advertisement announced that the work "bears in every part the ingenuous stamp of a patriot soldier; and cannot fail to interest all who desire to understand the causes, and to know the difficulties of our memorable struggle."[97]

The book received favorable reviews in the periodicals, especially from Federalist editors, one of whom said that Lee's memoirs "will, we trust, soon be, on every account, in the hands of all his countrymen."[98] Lee had more motive to hope that the publishers and reviewers were right than just his pride as an author and a patriot. The copyright to the memoirs was held by his brother Richard Bland Lee. The profits would go first to repaying Harry's debt to Richard, contracted during his bankruptcy, and thereafter "to the use of his children."[99] Light-Horse Harry might again, on the strength of his revolutionary services, contribute to the welfare of his family. Before the book came out, he wrote: "I indulge a hope that it will take a great run when published."[100] Within months of its release, even before all the reviews had appeared, he was saying: "A second edition is contemplated in the spring."[101]

The book, despite its many minor errors of fact and despite the "freedom" with which it criticized contemporaries, became a standard authority. However, it did not make money. When Lee left America for the West Indies, he took his papers with him, planning to write biographies of George Washington and Nathanael Greene.

PEACE

SPOTSYLVANIA COUNTY COURT HOUSE, VIRGINIA, March 20, 1810: "Henry Lee was this day discharged from the custody of the Sheriff or Keeper of the jail of the said County, being charged in executions agreeably to the within list, he the said Lee having complied with the act of the General Assembly for relief of Insolvent Debtors." Lee returned to Stratford, where his wife and children, as promised, had waited for his release. But the family did not stay there long. To secure the payment of one of his debts, Lee had signed over to his oldest son his life interest in the estate, and "also all his personal property in the farm & in the house of Stratford."[1] The father did not become his son's permanent guest. Ann Lee intended to leave Westmoreland County no matter what her husband did, and for the rest of her life—despite financial difficulty and offers of hospitality—she stuck to "her determination not to move again into the country."[2]

In 1811 Ann, Harry, and their children moved to a rented house in Alexandria. A "little vessil" carried their belongings up the Potomac.[3] On the way, Lee's papers got wet; and, as the family moved into its new home, one of the unfurnished rooms was filled with manuscripts spread out to dry. In Alexandria, Lee, living on his wife's income, completed his memoirs and arranged for their publication.

Lee still wanted to leave the country. To some correspondents he said that his financial affairs called him to the West Indies; to others he spoke of his health. In the islands, he said, he had "a fast friend who had offered me his house even purse."[4] In April of 1812, three months before his trip to Baltimore, Lee again asked President Madison to make him a special envoy.

During the last months of 1812, Lee slowly regained strength from what he called "the extraordinary atrocity of the unpunished Baltimore mob."[5] Some Federalists wanted him to write an account of the Baltimore riot. But in October his health remained "so deranged & inconvenient" that he said, "I write with much irksomeness," and he could hardly complete letters.[6] A "Correct Account" of the riot published under his name in 1814 seems to have been written by another member of Hanson's party without special help from Lee. Lee left no sign that he paid attention to the praise with which the Federalist press described his character and career in order to discredit the mob, the Baltimore authorities, and the Madison administration. Despite the reverses that the Republicans suffered in the elections of 1812, Lee saw in 1813 a "dark political horizon which envelopes our miserable country."[7] Any writing that he might undertake would be additions and corrections to his memoirs. And he planned to do that as soon as possible, because above all he wanted to get out of the United States.

At first, in January 1813, Lee said that he only intended to spend the winter at sea in a warm climate in hopes of repairing his health. Yet, as he acknowledged during the same month, he did not expect "speedy restoration" and would have to plan a longer stay in the West Indies. The United States and Britain were at war, so Lee had to wait until the British admiral of the fleet blockading the Chesapeake gave him a pass, which came in April. Then he had to wait until he could, "without money," get passage on a vessel.[8] By the end of April he was ready to leave. One of his brothers, Edmund

Jennings Lee, tried to persuade him not to go until he had been officially discharged as an insolvent debtor in all the jurisdictions where he owed money. Unlike modern bankruptcy, the liquidation or transfer of Henry Lee's property had not freed him from his unpaid debts, for which he was still liable. Edmund had posted bail for Harry's personal appearance, and he said: "If I should be obliged to pay this money, it will be almost my ruin."[9] Nevertheless, around the 1st of May, Harry left for the West Indies, saying that he expected to be back in August.

When Lee wrote, in November 1813, that the beating by the Baltimore mob "has for a time exiled me from home," he was referring to his search for a healthy climate.[10] Even so, his five years in the West Indies became more than an ease to his physical pain. They took him away from political enemies he could not defeat, a war he deplored, a family he could no longer support, and a country in which he would never again prosper. The Caribbean did more for his spirit than for his body. In fact, its heat did not seem very beneficial. By November he had decided that "some temperate climate in the south of Europe instead of this tropical region" would have done his health more good.[11] He had left Virginia during its most temperate and beautiful season, the spring.

Lee repeatedly expressed dissatisfaction with his absence from America: he hoped to return to his family; he offered to accept a command in the army; he wanted to know "the lowest price Lee & Wilson will take for the Rappahannock estate."[12] Still he stayed in the islands, exiled not only by intense, intermittent pain but also by "bitter . . . reflexions on the past."[13] The story of Lee's last five years is one of internal struggle between a revolutionary, who still wanted to shape the destiny of his children and his country, and a sick, broken man, who wanted to escape the scenes of his shame. The story ends with his return to America.

Often during the five years Lee announced his intent to

go home. Usually he wrote such letters when his health was improving; but in August 1816, while his disease remained "obdurate & painful," he said, "I mean to return home in a few months, determined there to abide my fate."[14] Yet he remained. He continued to suffer a recurrent cycle of pain so keen that he felt near death and then of relief that "restored me nearly to my former state of health."[15] All the while, putting faith in the curative powers of the sea, Lee traveled: from Port-au-Prince to Barbados, then to Guadeloupe, then to Havana, then to Puerto Rico, then to San Pedro, back to Port-au-Prince, then to the Bahamas—first Turks Island, then Caicos, then New Providence—then a trip to the Windward Islands, and then back to New Providence. Physicians gave him medicines to take and regimens to follow. With each of them he hoped that his cure was imminent or at least that his pain was ending. But after meeting Lee in 1813, the governor of Barbados wrote: "he will never recover."[16]

Despite his pain—perhaps, in part, because of it—activity remained as important to Lee as it had ever been. Although he could travel by boat, he could not move about with ease: "I must have a friend with me to take care of me."[17] His most important form of activity was still in his mind; he devoted most of his energy to thinking about America's war with Britain and about his children's futures. His attempts to assure prosperity for his family and to prevent war with Britain had played a large part in reducing him to exile. At the same time that he sought distance from these failures, they engrossed his mind.

Lee, like other Americans, had long seen the danger that the United States would become involved in the Napoleonic Wars. It was in the interest of both Britain and France for each to prevent America from trading with the other. The United States insisted on its right to trade with both but lacked the armed power to enforce that right against either

belligerent. The Jefferson and Madison administrations tried
to coerce the European powers economically, by withholding
the American trade which they assumed to be vital to the
more industrialized nations' well-being. Lee described this policy as "determining to fix upon their own country the palsy,
provided they can but knock Britain down with an apoplectic
fit."[18] Federalists who opposed the policy believed that Jefferson and Madison were obsessed with excessive hostility toward Britain. Moreover, the Republicans wrongly assumed
that the British were equally obsessed with undermining the
independence of the United States. The Federalists were not
persuaded by one of the main pieces of evidence that Republicans cited to prove this counter-revolutionary design: Britain's
refusal to accept the concept of naturalization, by which Britons could, in the eyes of the United States, become American
citizens. Britain claimed and exercised the right to stop
American merchant ships, in the same way that the Royal
Navy stopped British merchant ships, and impress into their
navy men whom the British deemed to be their subjects. The
United States regarded this procedure as the seizure of
American citizens. Lee treated impressment as the fundamental source of contention between America and Britain. This
outlook gave the war, when it came in 1812, an especially bitter futility because Lee believed that no American victory
short of conquering the British Isles could induce Great Britain to abandon a principle it considered essential to the maintenance of its navy. As it turned out, the problem of defining
the extent of American victory in the War of 1812 never
arose.

Both before the war and during it, Lee's concern was divided into two parallel lines of thought. On the one hand, he
took a keen and detailed interest in preparation and strategy.
If war came, he wanted the United States to win as much as
possible, especially by invading Canada. Still more important,

he wanted to minimize the casualties from disease and inexperience that he knew to be particularly severe among undisciplined soldiers. After the war began, he wanted American success to "uphold our countrys honor."[19] Even in an "unfortunate war," he still felt "the sacred duty we all owe to our country"; and as his health improved temporarily in 1814, he thought of returning to America to serve in the army.[20]

On the other hand, Lee was anxious to prevent the war and, once it started, to end it. Not only did he foresee American defeat but he also believed that the impressment issue was "not worth fighting" for and could be compromised "without treading upon the nation's honor."[21] "My heart so honestly deplores the war," he wrote in November 1813, as he grew ever more certain that America's mistaken position on impressment was alone prolonging it.[22] Lee's hostility toward immigrants intensified. Neither they nor the principle of naturalization were worth fighting for. He called the beneficiaries of naturalization "acti-citizens" and said that "the error ought to be renounced." If it caused war, it became "a cruel wrong inflicted by our rulers on our native people the only stock of the nation to be primarily regarded." Lee advised James Monroe to help the naturalized seamen if the British would concede any rights to them, "but do not expose us to war for them."[23] Not content with intruding in American politics and rioting in American cities, the foreign-born were now causing the deaths of native-born Americans in an unnecessary war.

But when Lee, echoing Edmund Burke, lamented "war, with its iliad of woe," he called up feelings that went far deeper than his resentment of immigrants.[24] The conduct of Napoleon confirmed Lee's long-time conviction that France had become the principal threat to liberty. In 1808, Lee had praised the Spaniards' resistance to "the proud conqueror"—a resistance that would be supported by the "virtuous" even if not by Thomas Jefferson.[25] Now America and Britain, "the only two nations of the many in the world who understand the meaning of liberty," were "cutting each other's throats." Even though Lee hoped that the United States would succeed in its fighting in North America, he believed that, across the Atlantic, Britain was fighting "for the safety of Europe, of the independance of most of its nations, in short for the maintenance of all those rights dear to civilized man."[26] Following the vain theories and mistaken policies of Thomas Jefferson, in defense of unneeded immigrants at the cost of probable defeat and humiliation, America was fighting a war on the side of the power that most threatened the survival of the principles of the American Revolution.

Three days after Congress had declared war, Lee had urged Madison to "hold back yr. ships of war & privateers." Lee had believed that the British government might soon repeal the Orders in Council, which imposed restrictions on neutral trade that America refused to concede. Such a repeal, Lee had said, "may stop war, unless it is hastened on our part." The Orders in Council had in fact been suspended; but news of this decision had not stopped the war after it had begun, and Madison had not replied to Lee's appeal that: "You immortalize yr. name too by shewing yr. deep reluctance to wade in human blood." Now Lee waited in the West Indies, reading the American and London newspapers, talking to travelers, watching the "encrease of venom" in the hostilities and "the abuse & roughness bordering on atrocity" in the command of the American army.[27] The revulsion toward war that had come upon Lee during the Revolution—that had moved his attachment to a permanent union of the states, that had given extra urgency to public order and to Federalist predominance, that had turned his recurring eagerness for combat toward a yet greater enthusiasm for the promises of peace—now filled the periods of his remission from physical pain. "Whenever I experience the flood tide of health however little . . I forget my own sorrows in those of our afflicted country. . . . God of Heaven, infuse love of peace into our rulers, & save our land from the tragic scenes which must follow, with increased fury and extent, continuance of the war."[28]

When Lee heard that Britain was sending an army of veterans to attack America in 1814, he anticipated a strike against "the Chesapeake & perhaps the potomac." If it came, he wanted his wife to move out of Alexandria to her brother's home, both for her safety and for her peace of mind. "If you wait," he warned her, "you will encounter disagreeable scenes should we be provided to defend the country, not an easy thing with raw troops agst. veterans."[29] Invasion threatened his family as well as the region to which he had devoted most of his peacetime energies; and it promised further lethal confirmation of his unheeded arguments for military training. A war which Lee could neither prevent, for the welfare of his country and of liberty, nor fight, in obediencc to the duty he felt, had finally destroyed the peace whose steady deterioration he believed he had suffered to a unique degree. Republicans might see in it a second War of Independence, a proof that the nation's honor, interests, and liberty rested on their courage and patriotism, not on faint and treasonable Federalists. Lee saw in it a "fatal labyrinth into which we have been winded."[30] One of the greatest regrets he felt as he left America for the Caribbean was that "anxious as I am for the happiness of my country, it is not in my power to aid it."[31]

And yet, as he spent the autumn of 1813 at Barbados, he decided to try peacemaking. Lee, on his own initiative, opened a brief correspondence with the British governor, Sir George Beckwith, in which he deplored "the sad and wanton war, waged by my Country against yours," and offered the draft of a peace treaty. Lee hoped that each country would agree not to use seamen who were citizens of the other. Once this was assured, he believed that impressment—which he treated as

the sole question delaying peace—could be suspended in practice and thereby removed as a source of contention, even
though still claimed as a right. Lee told Beckwith that, if Britain would accept this plan, "infirm as I am, I would hasten to
my Country and hasten back to you, with the wished for Answer, which I am persuaded would be in the Affirmative." In
reply, Beckwith pointed out that the Madison administration
had rejected more direct avenues of negotiation, that Great
Britain would never abandon impressment, and that Lee's
proposal did not address the issue of naturalization. As long
as the United States insisted on naturalization and Britain rejected it, the nationality of seamen would remain a subject of
dispute.

On each of the three days after submitting his treaty to
Beckwith, Lee wrote a long letter—one to President Madison, one to Secretary of State Monroe, and one to Senator
Rufus King. The letters lamented the effects of the war, al-
luded to the correspondence with Beckwith, and urged the
start of negotiations. Lee sent a copy of his treaty to Monroe.
None of his letters accomplished its purpose. Beckwith seems
to have been the only person who would reply and then just
"as a private Man, but without any Authority whatever."[32]
Two months later, in January 1814, Lee wrote to Monroe
again, enclosing a copy of his previous letter and saying, "I
shall be happy to hear should you think my efforts toward
peace worthy of your attention. . . . But not a moment ought
to be lost." No answer came. Six weeks later, Lee wrote again
to tell Monroe that he had written before and to assure him:
"Peace can even now be had."[33]

Lee probably broke American law by trying to open negotiations with the British as a private citizen. Yet he preferred to pursue a vain effort for peace rather than watch the
war's havoc inactive. Lee was ready to return to America,
when healthy, to do his duty in the war. But he was ready to
return to America while sick if he could end the war. How-

ever, Light-Horse Harry Lee was not born to be a peace-maker. He wanted to end the War of 1812, as he had wanted to prevent it and had tried to promote and prolong the years of peace that preceded it. But his temperament was combative even when his judgment turned him away from war. He always remained a revolutionary—though neither a violent opponent of all authority nor an ally of all who were poor—a revolutionary who could not give up struggle because American independence remained precarious and its visionary promises of happiness had not yet been won. In this struggle, Lee continually confronted two threats: immobility and chaos. He worked to save both his country and himself from these dangers. He could not stop striving; one of them might overtake him—tyranny by the king, capture by the enemy, panic by the militia, stagnation in enterprise, disorder in politics, oblivion in history, madness in war, death in exile. Lee praised peace like a man who knew how hard it was to live at peace; Lee dreaded combat like a man who felt its attraction.

Few of his fellow revolutionaries felt equal alarm or faced defeat so complete. Perhaps they avoided his fate partly by temporizing more judiciously. The virtuous character of George Washington and the eloquent writings of Thomas Jefferson might embody the Revolution. But could imitating Washington or endorsing Jefferson suffice to preserve a country dedicated to revolutionary ideals? Might not the example of the revolutionary generation—even of the greatest of them—be ambiguous and flawed? The conduct of these and other contemporaries of Lee's, like his own career, had failed to match their ambitions. The conduct of their posterity might fail even more gravely. This discrepancy troubled Washington and Jefferson. It destroyed Lee. And it left unanswered the question of whether a country founded on revolution could long endure.

That Lee would die uncertain about the survival of vir-

tue and the union gave him more concern than his financial
reverses. To prevent such uncertainty, he had devoted his life
to the American Revolution. His family, his property, his political career, even his stature as a patriot suffered from this
single-minded ambition that he was unable to fulfill. In later
generations, other Americans—with other interpretations of
the legacy of the Revolution and better judgment in politics
and business—would try to prove that a country founded on
revolution could endure. But with the deaths of Lee and his
contemporaries, the cause no longer rested on the strength of
the men who had declared and won independence. In the future, the perpetuation of the Revolution would seem to depend less on the character of individuals and more on parties,
constitutions, organizations, armies, and impersonal objective
guarantees of progress—all of which seemed less vulnerable to
the weaknesses of character that might undermine a cause
based on heroes. Lee's striving to prove that a hero could permanently secure the Revolution failed more spectacularly than
did most revolutionaries' efforts. Yet others also tried this impossibility, and they too failed to leave the legacy they had envisioned.

In the last part of his life, Lee's plans for the distant future
centered on his family. Throughout his five years away from
home, his concern for them never abated. He had left his wife
and children, but he wanted them not to forget him, just as he
thought constantly of them. "My heart never turns from you
a moment," he wrote, "& all dear to it pass hourly in review
of my minds eye."[34] He repeatedly asked for more letters,
longer letters, more detailed letters. Those he received from
his sons he showed to his hosts, who complimented him on his
children. On the anniversary of his marriage to Ann Hill
Carter, he recalled "that happy day" at Shirley which had

been so hot.[35] From Barbados he sent Ann a brooch containing a lock of his hair. He strongly regretted his inability to shape the developing characters of his youngest sons, Sydney Smith Lee and Robert Edward Lee, who had been eleven and six years old, respectively, when their father last saw them. He was sure that Robert was "as good as ever . . . it is his nature," but Lee felt that he did not know Smith "thoroughly" and said that the boy was "ever in my thoughts."[36] He kept asking for reports on "my dear Smith and Robert; their genius, temper, their disposition to learn, their diligence and perseverance in doing what is assigned to them."[37]

The children grew up with their father's concern but without his presence. Still, he remained vivid for them long after his death. Robert E. Lee's greatest manifestation of interest in his father came late in life, after he, too, had suffered reverses—long absences from his family, slow advancement in the United States Army, defeat and surrender of the Confederate Army of Northern Virginia. He visited his father's grave at Dungeness in 1862 and again in 1870, six months before his own death. He thanked William B. Reed for sending him a letter that Light-Horse Harry had written during the Revolutionary War. Robert said that he had not seen the distinctive handwriting of his father since the federal government had seized his papers among the family's possessions at Arlington. Much had happened since then to bring him closer to Light-Horse Harry. Robert wanted, like his father, to write a history of the army he had commanded; it would vindicate his conduct of the campaigns. His publisher planned to issue Robert's book and Robert's new edition of Light-Horse Harry's memoirs as a matched set. Having too few source materials and too little leisure, Robert E. Lee did not write the history he had planned. He did write a short biography of his father for the new edition of the memoirs, using primarily the letters that Harry had written from the West Indies. Light-Horse Harry

finally won the emulation of his son through their shared defeat. Robert, like his father, spent his greatest eloquence not
on extenuating failure but on linking Lee to "the vast and
matchless character of Washington," thereby receiving with
Washington "the veneration of remotest posterity."[38]

Although Light-Horse Harry could write letters of in-
quiry and advice from exile, he saw that the younger boys
would never know him well if he died in the West Indies. He
wrote to his oldest son: "Take care of my wife & children."[39]
Unable to see them, Lee liked to hear about the family's domestic incidents and personal feelings. He "daily re-perused"
the letters that described them.[40] But some of the news was all
too predictable. Ann Lee's income was dwindling; the Bank of
Virginia twice decreased the dividends that made up her main
support; in 1816 she was spending money set aside for the
education of her oldest son, whom Harry had insisted on
sending to Harvard—she urged Charles Carter Lee to cut his
expenses at school and warned him, "We cannot borrow
money, because we cannot repay it."[41] She was getting rid of
first the slaves, then the horses, and was having daily confer-
ences with her younger children about what food they could
afford to buy for supper. When Harry heard about her econo-
mies he wrote to Ann, in May 1817, "Your self privations
cannot be permitted. If I ever approach you, I must alter the
condition." But he could not forget that he had created the
condition yet had felt unable to remain in Alexandria and endure it. "God of heaven, how cutting to my heart the knowledge of yr. situation."[42]

Unable to contribute to the welfare of his children by
money or by his presence, Lee devoted his regular letters to
expressions of love and moral counsel. His son Carter received
most of the advice; Lee wanted him to copy the letters into a
stitched book. Lee kept up a steady flow of recommendations
for Carter's reading—"the best poets, the best orators, and

the best historians."[43] Lee knew the authors of whom he
wrote and liked nothing better than a debate with Carter over
the relative merits of Sophocles and Shakespeare or Pope and
Milton. Lee intended for this reading to improve his son primarily by inculcating correct moral principles. If Carter would
"dwell on the virtues & labor of the good & great men which
history presents to view," he would be able to imitate them.

To the precepts of authors whom he recommended, Lee
added his own, on which he placed special emphasis. They
were truths he had learned with pain. He wanted his son to
"abhor lying & deception," which were the "bitterest foes" of
virtue.[44] He held up his "favorite Grecian," the Theban general Epaminondas, as the best example of truthfulness, and returned to this admonition in several letters. He also warned
Carter: "Avoid debt, the sink of mental power and the subversion of independence, which draws into debasement even
virtue, in appearance certainly, if not in reality." Carter should
imitate the frugality of Frederick the Great—"he never
wanted money, and never missed the opportunity of advancing his nation's prosperity, because the means were not
ready." Above all, Lee urged on his son "the acquirement of
complete self-command. It is the pivot upon which the character, fame, and independence of us mortals hang." Self-command gave the greatest men a "splendor of virtue," which was
their pre-eminent attribute.[45]

Lee saw in his solicitude for his children the opportunity
to perpetuate the moral character that had strengthened men
and nations throughout history. On such strength, particularly
virtue—that is, self-control and self-sacrifice for the public
good—would rest the survival of the qualities that had won
the American Revolution. When Carter was fifteen years old,
Lee wanted him to study "Washingtons official letters
wherein the just good honorable man is plainly to be seen even
by a young reader."[46] Lee's letters of advice served, in part, as

a continuation of the efforts of his memoirs; he would ensure for his family the lesson he had tried to teach his country: Virtue alone made men great. "Fame in arms or art," he told Carter, "is naught, unless bottomed on virtue. Think, therefore, of fame, only as the appendage to virtue, and be virtuous, though poor, humble, and scorned."[47]

Clearly, in his letters Lee was looking back over his own past while writing about his son's future. If he could inspire his children to imitate the revolutionary generation while avoiding his own mistakes and misfortunes, he would have ensured their happiness even though he had not secured their prosperity. Perhaps, as he wrote, these principles temporarily replaced the "bitter . . . reflexions" that dominated his view of his life. In his last years, after the War of 1812 had ended, Lee's mind was more often turning back beyond the Revolution and beyond his own past to a world of literature containing permanent truths, vivid characters, and beautiful expression. He had brought all his papers with him to the islands, intending to write biographies of Washington and Greene. But he did not undertake those projects. Instead, as he wrote Carter, "I indulge every hour I am able in reading, more with a view of yours, Smith's, and Robert's good than any satisfaction to myself." Yet he derived much satisfaction from the books: he wanted his son to read Homer over and over. Lee himself read the *Iliad* and the *Odyssey* "with Homeric rapture."[48] He told himself that he was working for his children's improvement. At the same time he took increasing delight in a world of intellect and imagination, which he endowed with a moral clarity and a reward for virtue that had proven to be deeply alloyed in the world of men he had known. The more he read, the more he wanted to read and reread. He wrote to a friend, "I scarcely ever leave my room."[49]

Lee had favorites among authors who wrote in English. He commended Locke for philosophy, Hume for history,

Pope for poetry, and Dean Swift for being "truly instructive, as well as infinitely agreeable."[50] But his deeper interests lay elsewhere. Pope's translation of Homer appealed to him more than *Paradise Lost* did; however, Lee could still read Homer and Demosthenes "in their own language with entire knowledge of their stile & meaning," and to them he returned. He would have read Homer a hundredth time before he would have read a novel of Sterne's once. Recalling his preparation for Princeton and his stay there, he said that "the time I devoted when a youth to the greek language & to those authors was the best period of my academic life."[51] He retained his interest in military men and contrasted the commanders among the ancients with the men who had fought the Napoleonic Wars. After Lee's death, newspaper obituaries reported that he had left in manuscript a history of the War of 1812. Actually, the manuscript he had composed during his illness was a diary and commonplace book, in which he copied favorite quotations and wrote commentaries. Although his fascination with combat still survived, he preferred to go back before Wellington, before Hannibal, to the siege of Troy and its aftermath. In "the immortal Homer and his coadjutor Virgil," and in the greatest of dramatists, Sophocles, he found heroism celebrated and tragedy dignified.[52] He had learned the truth of the lines of Sophocles that he copied in translation—the goddess Athena's comment on the madness of Ajax:

> And, if perchance, in riches or in power
> Thou shinest superior, be not insolent;
> For, know, a day sufficeth to exalt
> Or to depress the state of mortal man.[53]

Lee was about to join the ancients. His letters were hardly for his son's benefit any more; in his last one, a few weeks before his death, he said to Carter, "I fear you will be puzzled." He had been studying "oriental authors"—the Persian poet Hafiz, Confucius, and Hindu teachings—to confirm the universality of the Golden Rule and to show "that the immortality of the soul has been generally believed by all nations from our first records of man."[54] Lee, who by the age of twenty-five had seen the deaths of more men than most of his countrymen would witness in a lifetime, wanted to be ready for his own. He had been reading Alexander Pope's "Epitaphs," and he copied in his journal two lines from one of them that compared the present life to the one to come:

> Calmly he looked on either life & here
> Saw nothing to regret, & there to fear.

Lee said that he had "always thought" that this "applied . . . to me."[55]

In the summer of 1817, Lee was growing more anxious to return to America. He booked passage from Nassau on a series of vessels, but each time some problem arose: he could not get a cabin to himself, which his illness required, or the ship was going to the wrong port on the Atlantic coast, or the vessel, "in which I had a small interest," had been seized.[56] By January 1818, he was ready to take the ship *Betsey* "to some Southern port, which not yet decided."[57] Again, however, though Lee was now ready to go in any vessel to any port, something prevented his departure. Finally, on March 1, 1818, he met James H. Causten in Nassau, and Causten agreed to land him at Cumberland Island, Georgia.

EPILOGUE

THE DAY AFTER GENERAL LEE DIED, PHINEAS SAW many rough-looking sailors, soldiers, and marines come to Dungeness. With them were officers who wore bands of black crepe. Men and women from Cumberland Island, Amelia Island, and St. Mary's arrived to attend the burial of General Lee.

Commodore Henley of the naval squadron in the Sound and General Gaines of the army detachment at Fernandina ordered an interment with full military honors. A long procession formed at the mansion—six of the officers who had stayed with Lee during his illness now served as his pall bearers; behind them were other officers, a marine guard, the army band, the civilian mourners, and a contingent of soldiers and sailors who wore clean uniforms and stood, looking respectful and solemn, carrying reversed arms.

Two of the pall bearers placed their sheathed swords, crossed, on the coffin, and the procession headed toward the family burial ground on the edge of the Dungeness estate. The customary noises of Cumberland Island—waves on the beach, sea breezes in the live oaks, and sounds from the inhabitants of the salt marsh: egrets, herons, chattering waterhens—were broken by the discharge of a naval gun from the U.S.S. *John Adams*. Regularly, once every minute as the funeral procession moved in the direction of the beach, the gun was fired again.

The column followed the route that Phineas and General Lee had taken on their daily walks as it passed through the garden of Dungeness. The army band set the pace, playing the Dead March from Handel's oratorio *Saul.* When the column left the walkway among the flowers and fruit trees, it cut across an open field. Until recently—that is, until Phineas turned twelve, three years ago—the field had been an orange orchard. But in January of 1815, a contingent of British soldiers had cut the orchard down during their skirmishes with American forces on Cumberland Island in one of the last engagements of the war.

From the field the funeral procession took a winding path along the bank of the salt marsh, passing under the moss-hung branches of large water oaks. Halfway from the mansion to the beach, in the southern corner of an olive orchard, lay the family cemetery—a small plot, about forty by fifty feet, separated from overhanging trees by a low wall. In one corner of the lot was an open grave. There the concluding portion of the burial service was read. "Mr. Taylor performed the religious duties, in which all were reminded that we must die." The marine guard fired a salute in volley. Not until Lee's body was in the earth did the flag ship's minute gun cease echoing over the island.

NOTES

BIBLIOGRAPHICAL ESSAY

ACKNOWLEDGMENTS

INDEX

NOTES

WITH A FEW EXCEPTIONS, THESE NOTES SERVE ONLY TO IDENTIFY THE sources of quotations. I have placed the reference numbers at the end of sentences or paragraphs in the text for convenience, without intending to imply that the quoted document always constitutes the main evidence for everything in the sentence. I have not used the three dots of elision at the ends of quotations which close my sentences. Light-Horse Harry Lee's father, Henry Lee (1729–1787), is referred to as Henry Lee II, and Light-Horse Harry Lee's son Henry Lee (1787–1837) as Henry Lee IV.

PROLOGUE

The narrative of Lee's death is based on the following sources: Charles C. Jones, Jr., *Reminiscences of the Last Days, Death and Burial of General Henry Lee* (Albany, N.Y., 1870); Frederick A. Ober, "Dungeness, General Greene's Sea-Island Plantation," *Lippincott's Magazine,* XXVI (1880), 241–249; John F. Stegeman and Janet A. Stegeman, *Caty: A Biography of Catharine Littlefield Greene* (Providence, R.I., 1977), 174–180; Lucian Lamar Knight, *Georgia's Landmarks, Memorials and Legends,* I (Atlanta, Ga., 1913), chap. 1; " 'Light Horse Harry' Lee's Grave," *Confederate Veteran,* III (1895), 214–215; George White, *Historical Collections of Georgia . . . ,* 3d ed. (New York, 1855), 286–288; William Barnwell to Henry Lee [IV], Mar. 27, 1818, James Shaw to Henry Lee [IV], Mar. 26, 1818, James H. Causten to Ann Lee, Apr. 11, 1818, Robert E. Lee to Mary Custis Lee, Jan. 18, 1862, and Apr. 18, 1870, Lee Family Papers, Virginia Historical Society, Richmond; [?] to [?], Mar. 1818 [erroneously attributed to Catharine Greene], Henry Lee Personal Miscellany, Library of Congress, Washington, D.C.; Henry Lee to James Monroe, Mar. 15, 1818,

James Monroe Papers, Library of Congress; *New-York Evening Post,* Apr. 9, 1818; *Connecticut Gazette* (New London), Apr. 15, 1818; *Richmond Enquirer,* Apr. 24, 1818; *Niles' Weekly Register,* Apr. 24, 1818, XIV (1818), 151.

1: PARTISAN WAR

1 Henry Lee, *Memoirs of the War in the Southern Department of the United States* (Philadelphia, 1812), I, 287–289.

2 Charles Lee, "Proposals for the Formation of a Body of Light Troops Ready to be Detach'd on Emergent Occasions," [1778], *The Lee Papers,* (New-York Historical Society, *Collections,* IV–VII [New York, 1872–75]), III, 287.

3 On Princeton, see Sheldon S. Cohen and Larry R. Gerlach, "Princeton in the Coming of the American Revolution," *New Jersey History,* XCII (1974), 69–92.

4 Henry Lee to Charles Lee, July 5, 1775, Thomas Gage Papers, William L. Clements Library, Ann Arbor, Michigan.

5 George Washington Parke Custis, *Recollections and Private Memoirs of Washington, by His Adopted Son* . . . , ed. Benson J. Lossing (New York, 1860), 356; Henry Banks, *The Vindication of John Banks of Virginia . . . Also, The Vindication of General Henry Lee, of Virginia* . . . (Frankfort, Ky., 1826), 61; George Weedon to Richard Henry Lee, Feb. 1, 1778, Lee Family Papers (Accession No. 38–112), University of Virginia Library, Charlottesville.

6 Board of War to George Washington, Apr. 3, 1780, George Washington Papers, Library of Congress, Washington, D.C.

7 James Tilton, *Economical Observations on Military Hospitals; and the Prevention and Cure of Diseases Incident to an Army* (Wilmington, Del., 1813), 45.

8 Dixon & Nicolson's *Virginia Gazette* (Williamsburg), Oct. 30, 1779.

9 Banks, *Vindication of Banks,* 61.

10 Joseph Reed to Henry Lee, Aug. 1, 1780, Brock Collection, Box 4, Henry E. Huntington Library, San Marino, California.

11 Lee, *Memoirs of the War,* II, chap. 30, quoted at 165–166. See also Henry Lee to George Washington, [September], Oct. 21 and 25, 1780, Washington Papers, Library of Congress. The account in Lee's memoirs may also have been based on Champe's papers, loaned to Lee by Champe's widow. See William Buckner McGroarty, "Sergeant

John Champe and Certain of His Contemporaries," *William & Mary Quarterly*, 2d ser., XVII (1937), 165.

12 *New Jersey Gazette*, Jan. 14, 1778, in Frank Moore, ed., *Diary of the American Revolution from Newspapers and Original Documents*, II (New York, 1860), 7.

13 George Washington to President of Congress, Apr. 3, 1778, John C. Fitzpatrick, ed., *The Writings of George Washington from the Original Manuscript Sources, 1745–1799* (Washington, D.C., 1931–40), XI, 205–206.

14 Henry Lee to Allen McLane, July 3, 1779, Allen McLane Papers, New-York Historical Society Library, New York.

15 *Daily National Intelligencer* (Washington, D.C.), Apr. 8, 1818.

16 Lee, *Memoirs of the War*, I, 394.

17 Henry Lee to Nathanael Greene, Jan. 25, 1781, Nathanael Greene Papers, Clements Library.

18 Lee, *Memoirs of the War*, I, 251.

19 Dixon & Nicolson's *Virginia Gazette*, Oct. 30, 1779.

20 Henry Lee to George Washington, Mar. 31, 1778, Washington Papers, Library of Congress.

21 George Washington to President of Congress, Apr. 3, 1778, Fitzpatrick, ed., *Writings of Washington*, XI, 206.

22 John André, "The Cow Chace," *Royal Gazette* (New York), Aug. 16, 1780, in William Nelson, ed., *Documents Relating to the Revolutionary History of the State of New Jersey*, IV (Trenton, N.J., 1914), 586.

23 Henry Lee to George Washington, Jan. 20, 177[8], Washington Papers, Library of Congress.

24 George Weedon to Richard Henry Lee, Feb. 1, 1778, Lee Family Papers, University of Virginia.

25 Lee, *Memoirs of the War*, I, 42.

26 Henry Lee to Charles Carter Lee, Apr. 19, 1817, in Robert E. Lee, "Life of General Henry Lee," *Memoirs of the War in the Southern Department of the United States*, ed. Robert E. Lee (New York, 1869), 68.

27 Henry Lee to James Madison, Mar. 4, 1790, James Madison Papers, Library of Congress.

28 Henry Lee to Anthony Wayne, August 1778, Anthony Wayne Papers, Historical Society of Pennsylvania, Philadelphia; Henry Lee to George Washington, Jan. 20, 1778, Washington Papers, Library of Congress; Henry Lee to Thomas Sim Lee, Sept. 18, 1780, Emmet

Collection (Emmet No. 1102), Manuscripts and Archives Division, New York Public Library, Astor, Lenox and Tilden Foundations, New York.

29 Henry Lee to Thomas Sim Lee, Sept. 18, 1780, Emmet Collection, New York Public Library.

30 Marquis de Lafayette to Henry Lee, Oct. 29, 1780, in Henry Lee [IV], *The Campaign of 1781 in the Carolinas With Remarks Historical and Critical on Johnson's Life of Greene* (Chicago, 1962 [orig. publ. Philadelphia, 1824]), Appendix, ii.

31 *Dunlap's Pennsylvania Packet, and General Advertiser* (Philadelphia), Apr. 8, 1780.

32 Henry Lee, Rough General Orders, June 30, 1794, William P. Palmer, *et al.,* eds., *Calendar of Virginia State Papers and Other Manuscripts* (Richmond, Va., 1875–92), VII, 203.

33 Lee, *Memoirs of the War,* I, 267, 126, II, 94n.

34 Henry Lee to Nathanael Greene, June 4, 1781, Nathanael Greene Papers, William R. Perkins Library, Duke University, Durham, North Carolina.

35 Lee, *Memoirs of the War,* II, 35; Henry Lee, Manuscript Memoirs, Virginia Historical Society.

36 Henry Lee to James Madison, Nov. 17, 1813, Madison Papers, Library of Congress.

37 Lee, *Memoirs of the War,* II, 252.

38 Anne King Gregorie, *Thomas Sumter* (Columbia, S.C., 1931), 148; Peter Horry and Mason Locke Weems, *The Life of Gen. Francis Marion* . . . (Philadelphia, 1837 [orig. publ. 1809]), 223. See also entry of May 17 and 19, 1781, William Seymour, "A Journal of the Southern Expedition, 1780–1783," Historical Society of Delaware, *Papers,* II, No. 15 (Wilmington, Del., 1896), 27.

39 Alexander Garden, *Anecdotes of the American Revolution, Illustrative of the Talents and Virtues of the Heroes and Patriots, Who Acted the Most Conspicuous Parts Therein,* 2d ser. (Charleston, S.C., 1828), 125, 130–131.

40 Charles Royster, *A Revolutionary People at War: The Continental Army and American Character, 1775–1783* (Chapel Hill, N.C., 1979), 80–82.

41 Archibald Henderson, "The Transylvania Company: A Study in Personnel," *Filson Club History Quarterly,* XXI (1947), 345.

42 Lee, *Memoirs of the War,* I, 312–313n.

43 John C. Dann, ed., *The Revolution Remembered: Eyewitness Accounts of the War for Independence* (Chicago, 1980), 201–202; Christopher Ward, *The War of the Revolution*, ed. John Richard Alden (New York, 1952), II, 918, n.6.

44 Lee, *Memoirs of the War*, I, 311.

45 [Henry Lee], *A Cursory Sketch of The Motives and Proceedings of The Party Which Sways the Affairs of the Union* . . . (Philadelphia, 1809), 8.

46 Nathanael Greene to Henry Lee, Jan. 28, 1782. Compare texts of draft (HM 22701), Huntington Library, and final copy, Greene Papers, Clements Library.

47 Henry Lee to Nathanael Greene, Feb. 19, 1782 (HM 22708), Huntington Library.

48 Anthony Wayne to Henry Lee, Aug. 24, 1779, Wayne Papers, Historical Society of Pennsylvania.

49 [John Eager Howard to William Johnson], n.d., Notes on errors in Volume I of Johnson's Life of Greene, Lee Family Papers, Robert E. Lee Memorial Association, Stratford Hall, Virginia.

50 George Washington to James Duane, June 5, 1780, Fitzpatrick, ed., *Writings of Washington*, XVIII, 479.

51 Nathanael Greene to Henry Lee, Feb. 18, 1782 (HM 22706), Huntington Library.

52 Joseph Johnson, *Traditions and Reminiscences Chiefly of the American Revolution in the South* . . . (Charleston, S.C., 1851), 405–406.

53 Henry Lee to Jonathan Clark, Aug. 22, 1779, Jonathan Clark Papers, Draper Manuscripts, State Historical Society of Wisconsin, Madison.

54 Nathanael Greene to Henry Lee, Oct. 7, 1782, Greene Papers, Clements Library.

55 Edmund Pendleton to William Woodford, Oct. 11, 1779, quoted in Mrs. Catesby Willis Stewart, *The Life of Brigadier General William Woodford of the American Revolution*, II (Richmond, Va., 1973), 1105.

56 Henry Lee [II] to Charles Lee, Sept. 8, 1779, Lee Family Papers, Virginia Historical Society.

57 Quoted in Anthony Wayne to Henry Lee, Aug. 7, 1781, Wayne Papers, Historical Society of Pennsylvania; Nathanael Greene to Henry Lee, Oct. 7, 1782, Greene Papers, Clements Library.

58 Nathanael Greene to Henry Lee, Mar. 12, 1782, Greene Papers, Clements Library.

59 Henry Lee to [?], Oct. 2, 1781, Lee Family Papers, Virginia Historical Society.

60 Thomas E. Templin, "Henry 'Light Horse Harry' Lee: A Biography" (Ph.D. diss., University of Kentucky, 1975), 136–139, 185–189.

61 Henry Lee to [?], Oct. 2, 1781, Lee Family Papers, Virginia Historical Society; Lee, *Memoirs of the War,* II, 290.

62 Banks, *Vindication of Banks,* 62.

63 Alexander Garden, *Anecdotes of the Revolutionary War in America, with Sketches of Character of Persons the Most Distinguished, in the Southern States, for Civil and Military Services* (Charleston, S.C., 1822), 63.

64 Garden, *Anecdotes of the Revolution,* 2d ser., 121.

65 Henry Lee to Anthony Wayne, Aug. 24, 1778, Wayne Papers, Historical Society of Pennsylvania.

66 Nathanael Greene to Henry Lee, Dec. 21, 1781, Greene Papers, Clements Library; Lee, *Memoirs of the War,* II, 387–401; Henry Lee to Nathanael Greene, Dec. 29, 1781 (HM 22697), Huntington Library.

67 Henry Lee to Nathanael Greene, Dec. 28, 1781, Greene Papers, Clements Library.

68 Henry Lee to Nathanael Greene, Feb. 13, 1782 (HM 22704), Huntington Library.

69 Ichabod Burnett to Henry Lee, June 20, 1782, New-York Historical Society, New York.

70 Lee, *Memoirs of the War,* I, 276, 392.

71 Henry Lee to Nathanael Greene, Aug. 17, 1782 (HM 22730), Huntington Library.

72 Ichabod Burnett to Henry Lee, June 20, 1782, New-York Historical Society; Nathanael Greene to Henry Lee, Jan. 28 and Apr. 22, 1782, Brock Collection, Box 4, and HM 22701, Huntington Library.

73 Henry Lee to Nathanael Greene, Feb. 19, 1782, Huntington Library.

74 Henry Lee to Nathanael Greene, Feb. 13, 1782, *ibid.*

75 Ichabod Burnett to Henry Lee, June 20, 1782, New-York Historical Society.

76 Henry Lee to [Richard Henry Lee], Apr. 1, 1792, Lee Family Papers, University of Virginia.

77 Henry Lee to Charles Carter Lee, Apr. 19, 1817, in R. E. Lee, "Life of Henry Lee," *Memoirs of the War* (1869 ed.), 68; [Henry Lee], *The*

Address of the Minority in the Virginia Legislature to the People of that State . . . [Richmond, Va., 1799], 3.

78 Henry Lee to Nathanael Greene, Feb. 19, 1782, Huntington Library.

79 Henry Lee to Nathanael Greene, Feb. 13, 1782, *ibid.*

80 Nathanael Greene to Henry Lee, Apr. 22, 1782, *ibid.*

81 Henry Lee to Nathanael Greene, Feb. 10, 1782 (HM 23426), *ibid.*

82 Ichabod Burnett to Henry Lee, June 20, 1782, New-York Historical Society.

83 Henry Lee to Nathanael Greene, Oct. 5, 1782, Greene Papers, Clements Library; Henry Lee to Nathanael Greene, Feb. 17, 1782 (HM 23424), Huntington Library.

84 Nathanael Greene to Henry Lee, Apr. 22, 1782, Huntington Library.

85 Nathanael Greene to Henry Lee, Feb. 12, 1782, Greene Papers, Clements Library.

86 Nathanael Greene to Henry Lee, Feb. 18, 1782, Huntington Library.

87 Henry Lee to Joseph Reed, Aug. 6, 1780, Lee Family Papers, Virginia Historical Society.

88 John Stewart to Henry Lee, July 13, 1782, Lee Family Papers, *ibid.*

2: THE QUEEN OF STRATFORD

1 Henry Lee to Charles Lee, Apr. 4, 1781, Lee Papers, Virginia Historical Society.

2 John P. Kennedy, *Memoirs of the Life of William Wirt, Attorney-General of the United States,* I (Philadelphia, 1851), 35; Nathanael Greene to Henry Lee, June 6, 1782, Greene Papers, Clements Library; [Recollections of Stratford by Charles Carter Lee], Lee Family Papers, Stratford Hall.

3 Ichabod Burnett to Henry Lee, June 20, 1782, New-York Historical Society.

4 Henry Lee to James Madison, Jan. 8, 1792, Madison Papers, Library of Congress.

5 Lee, *Memoirs of the War,* I, 199–201.

6 *Ibid.,* II, 382, 396.

7 Henry Lee to [Allen McLane], June 10, 1780, Allen McLane Papers, New-York Historical Society.

8 Henry Lee to James Madison, Feb. 11, 1809, Madison Papers, Library of Congress.

9 Henry Lee to Joseph Reed, Aug. 27, 1779, Lee Papers, Virginia Historical Society.

10 Henry Lee to George Washington, Mar. 31, 1778, Washington Papers, Library of Congress; Henry Lee to Nathanael Greene, Oct. 25, 1780, Greene Papers, Clements Library.

11 Henry Lee, *A Funeral Oration on the Death of General Washington, Delivered in Philadelphia, at the Request of Congress* (Philadelphia, 1800), 12–13.

12 Lee, *Memoirs of the War*, II, 367.

13 Nathanael Greene to Henry Lee, Oct. 7, 1782, Greene Papers, Clements Library.

14 *Virginia Gazette and General Advertiser* (Richmond), June 26, 1793.

15 Lucy Grymes Lee Carter to Alice Lee Shippen, Dec. 1812, Lee Family Papers, Stratford Hall; Douglas Southall Freeman, *R. E. Lee: A Biography*, 4 vols. (New York, 1934–35), III, 496, n. 34.

16 Henry Lee [IV] to Ann Lee, Apr. 7, 1818, Lee Family Papers, Virginia Historical Society.

17 Nathanael Greene to Henry Lee, May 22, 1781, Lee Family Papers, Stratford Hall.

18 Henry Lee to George Washington, June 15, 1792, Washington Papers, Library of Congress.

19 Henry Lee to George Washington, Dec. 16, 1791, Washington Papers, Library of Congress; Dixon & Nicolson's *Virginia Gazette*, Oct. 30, 1779.

20 Henry Lee to Alexander Hamilton, Sept. 10, 1792, Harold C. Syrett, *et al.*, eds., *The Papers of Alexander Hamilton* (New York, 1961–79), XII, 352.

21 Henry Lee to George Washington, Apr. 23 and May 15, 1793, Washington Papers, Library of Congress; Henry Lee to Alexander Hamilton, May 6, [1793], Syrett, *et al.*, eds., *Papers of Hamilton*, XIV, 416.

22 Henry Lee to James Madison, Jan. 23, 1792, Madison Papers, Library of Congress.

23 Henry Lee to George Washington, Apr. 23, 1793, Washington Papers, Library of Congress.

24 George Washington to Henry Lee, May 6, 1793, Fitzpatrick, ed., *Writings of Washington*, XXXII, 450.

25 William Lee to Henry Lee, Apr. 20, 1793, Brock Collection, Box 4, Huntington Library.

26 Henry Lee to Alexander Hamilton, May 6, 1793, Syrett, *et al.*, eds., *Papers of Hamilton*, XIV, 416.

27 Lee, *Memoirs of the War*, II, 461.

28 Henry Lee to Alexander Hamilton, June 15, 1793, Syrett, *et al.*, eds., *Papers of Hamilton*, XIV, 549.

29 Henry Lee to George Washington, Feb. 28, 1799, Washington Papers, Library of Congress.

30 Henry Lee to James Madison, Oct. 29, 1788, Madison Papers, Library of Congress.

31 Lee, *Funeral Oration*, 14.

32 Henry Lee to John Milledge, Jan. 12, 1806, John Milledge, Jr., Papers, Duke University.

33 Garden, *Anecdotes of the Revolutionary War*, 1st ser., 127–128.

34 Henry Lee to the Senators in Congress, Apr. 19, 1794, Executive Letter Books, Virginia State Library, Richmond.

35 *Virginia Herald and Fredericksburg Advertiser*, Aug. 8, 1793.

36 Tobias Lear, *Observations on the River Potomack, the Country Adjacent, and the City of Washington*, ed. Samuel T. Chambers (Baltimore, Md., 1940 [orig. publ. New York, 1793]), 14.

37 Henry Lee to George Washington, Sept. 8, 1786, Washington Papers, Library of Congress.

38 Henry Lee to Messrs. Nicklin & Griffith, Feb. 19 and Mar. 15, 1802 (Accession nos. 4170 and 9210-c), University of Virginia; Henry Lee to James Greenleaf, July 23, 1794, Historical Society of Pennsylvania; Henry Lee to James Madison, Oct. 29 and Nov. 19, 1788, Madison Papers, Library of Congress; Henry Lee to Patrick Henry, Feb. 4, 1795 (HM 19957), Huntington Library.

39 Henry Lee to James Madison, Oct. 29 and Dec. 8, 1788, Madison Papers, Library of Congress.

40 Henry Lee to Zachariah Johnston, Mar. 27, 1792, Zachariah and Thomas Johnston Papers, Duke University.

41 James Madison to George Washington, Nov. 5, 1788, Gaillard Hunt, ed., *The Writings of James Madison*, V (New York, 1904), 301–302.

42 George Washington to James Madison, Nov. 17, 1788, Fitzpatrick, ed., *Writings of Washington*, XXX, 129–130.

43 Henry Lee to James Madison, Sept. 8, 1789, Madison Papers, Library of Congress.

44 Jonathan Elliot, ed., *The Debates in the Several State Conventions, on*

the Adoption of the Federal Constitution . . . 2d ed., III (Philadelphia, 1863), 182.

45 Henry Lee to James Madison, Sept. 8, 1789, Madison Papers, Library of Congress.

46 Henry Lee to [?], Mar. 6, [?], Robert E. Lee Papers, Duke University.

47 Henry Lee to James Madison, Sept. 8, 1789, Madison Papers, Library of Congress.

48 Robert Morris to John Nicholson, Nov. 1797, quoted in Ellis Paxson Oberholtzer, *Robert Morris: Patriot and Financier* (New York, 1968 [orig. publ. 1903]), 343.

49 Franklin B. Sawvel, ed., *The Complete Anas of Thomas Jefferson* (New York, 1903), 61.

50 *Daily National Intelligencer,* Apr. 8, 1818.

51 Henry Lee to George Washington, Feb. 28, 1799, Washington Papers, Library of Congress.

52 Richard Bland Lee to James Madison, Mar. 6, 1816, Richard Bland Lee Papers, Library of Congress.

53 Henry Lee [IV], *Observations on the Writings of Thomas Jefferson, With Particular Reference to the Attack they Contain on the Memory of the Late Gen. Henry Lee,* 2d ed. (Philadelphia, 1839), 179.

54 Henry Lee to William Sullivan, July 14, 1797, Miscellaneous Papers, New York Public Library.

55 Ann Lee to Carter Berkeley, Nov. [26?], 1809, Henry Lee Personal Miscellany, Library of Congress.

3: UNION

1 Henry Lee to Theodorick Bland, Apr. 25, 1777, Charles Campbell, ed., *The Bland Papers: Being a Selection from the Manuscripts of Colonel Theodorick Bland, Jr., of Prince George County, Virginia* (Petersburg, Va., 1840–43), I, 53.

2 [Henry Lee], *Plain Truth: Addressed to the People of Virginia, Written in February 1799 By a Citizen of Westmoreland County, (Virg.)* [Richmond, ?1799], 5–6.

3 Henry Lee to Anthony Wayne, Jan. 7, 1781, R. E. Lee, "Life of Henry Lee," *Memoirs of the War* (1869 ed.), 33–34.

4 Lee, *Memoirs of the War,* II, 94n.

5 Lee, *Plain Truth,* 6–7; Lee, *Memoirs of the War,* I, 212.

6 Lee, *Memoirs of the War,* II, 304.

7 Henry Lee to Thomas Sim Lee, Sept. 18, 1780, Emmet Collection, New York Public Library.

8 Henry Lee to Nathanael Greene, July 20, 1780, Greene Papers, Clements Library.

9 Lee, Manuscript Memoirs, Virginia Historical Society. Compare Lee, *Memoirs of the War,* II, 190

10 Lee, *Memoirs of the War,* I, 23; II, 304

11 Henry Lee to Nathanael Greene, July 20, 1780, Greene Papers, Clements Library.

12 Lee, *Plain Truth,* 21.

13 Henry Lee to Henry Lee [II], Apr. 19, 1786, Lee Family Papers, Virginia Historical Society.

14 Lee, *Plain Truth,* 19.

15 Elliot, ed., *Debates on the Constitution,* III, 183.

16 Henry Lee to George Washington, Oct. 17, 1786, Washington Papers, Library of Congress; Henry Lee to [St. George Tucker], Oct. 20, 1786, Tucker-Coleman Papers, Swem Library, College of William and Mary, Williamsburg, Virginia.

17 Henry Lee to George Washington, Sept. 8, 1786, Washington Papers, Library of Congress; Henry Lee to Richard Bland Lee, Apr. 4, 1786, Lee Family Papers, Stratford Hall.

18 Henry Lee to George Washington, Feb. 16, 1786, Washington Papers, Library of Congress.

19 Henry Lee to [St. George Tucker], Oct. 20, 1786, Tucker-Coleman Papers, College of William and Mary.

20 *A Circular Letter, Addressed to the State Societies of the Cincinnati, by the General Meeting, Convened at Philadelphia, May 3, 1784* (Philadelphia, 1784), 3.

21 Henry Lee to George Washington, [Oct. 1, 1786], Washington Papers, Library of Congress.

22 Norman K. Risjord, *Chesapeake Politics, 1781–1800* (New York, 1978), 315–316.

23 Elliot, ed., *Debates on the Constitution,* III, 178, 187.

24 Lee, *Funeral Oration,* 12.

25 Henry Lee to George Washington, Sept. 8, 1786, Washington Papers, Library of Congress.

26 Elliot, ed., *Debates on the Constitution,* III, 185.

27 Henry Lee to George Washington, Sept. 13, 1788, Washington

Papers, Library of Congress; George Washington, Circular Letter to the States, June 8, 1783, Fitzpatrick, ed., *Writings of Washington,* XXVI, 487–488.

28 Elliot, ed., *Debates on the Constitution,* III, 42, 586; Lee, *Plain Truth,* 13, 15, 16.

29 Kenneth M. Stampp, "The Concept of a Perpetual Union," *Journal of American History,* LXV (1978), 5–33. See also Paul C. Nagel, *One Nation Indivisible: The Union in American Thought* (New York, 1964).

30 Elliot, ed., *Debates on the Constitution,* III, 585–586.

31 Henry Lee to George Washington, Apr. 21, 1786, Washington Papers, Library of Congress.

32 Elliot, ed., *Debates on the Constitution,* III, 43–45.

33 Henry Lee to George Washington, Sept. 13, 1788, Washington Papers, Library of Congress.

34 Quoted in Thomas Boyd, *Light-horse Harry Lee* (New York and London, 1931), 187; Henry Lee to [Richard Henry Lee], May 17, 1789, Lee Family Papers, University of Virginia.

35 Henry Lee to George Washington, July 24, 1788, Washington Papers, Library of Congress.

36 Henry Lee to James Madison, Nov. 19, 1788, Madison Papers, Library of Congress.

37 Henry Lee to Richard Henry Lee, Aug. 10, 1788, Lee Family Papers, University of Virginia.

38 Henry Lee to James Madison, Oct. 29 and Dec. 8, 1788, June 10 and Sept. 8, 1789, Mar 4, 1790, Madison Papers, Library of Congress.

39 Henry Lee to [Richard Henry Lee], May 17, 1789, Lee Family Papers, University of Virginia; Henry Lee to James Madison, Mar. 4, 1790, Madison Papers, Library of Congress; Henry Lee to George Washington, June 12, 1790, Washington Papers, Library of Congress.

40 George Washington to Henry Lee, Aug. 27, 1790, Lee Family Papers, Stratford Hall.

41 Henry Lee to George Washington, Mar. 14, 1789, Washington Papers, Library of Congress.

42 [Henry Lee], *The Address of the Minority in the Virginia Legislature to the People of that State* . . . [Richmond, Va., 1799], 2; Lee, *Funeral Oration,* 20.

43 James Madison to Henry Lee, Apr. 13, 1790, Madison Papers, Library of Congress.

44 Henry Lee to James Madison, Jan. 8, 1792, *ibid.*

45 *The Aurora; or General Advertiser* (Philadelphia), Nov. 24, 1794, Mar. 1, 1800.

46 Henry Lee to James Madison, Mar. 4, 1790, Jan. 8, 1792, Madison Papers, Library of Congress.

47 Henry Lee to Richard Bland Lee, Apr. 4, 1786, Lee Family Papers, Stratford Hall.

48 Henry Lee to James Madison, Mar. 4, 1790, Aug. 14, 1791, Madison Papers, Library of Congress.

49 John Marshall to [Henry Lee IV], Jan. 18, 1834, Papers of John Marshall, Institute of Early American History and Culture, Williamsburg, Virginia.

50 *Aurora*, Mar. 1, 1800.

51 Henry Lee to Alexander Hamilton, Sept. 10, 1792, Syrett, *et al.*, eds., *Papers of Hamilton*, XII, 352.

52 Henry Lee to Alexander Hamilton, May 6, [1793], *ibid.*, XIV, 416.

53 Henry Lee to James Madison, Mar. 4, 1790, Jan. 8 and 23, 1792, Madison Papers, Library of Congress.

54 David Stuart to George Washington, Mar. 15, 1790, Fitzpatrick, ed., *Writings of Washington*, XXXI, 28n.

55 Henry Lee to James Madison, Mar. 4 and Apr. 3, 1790, Jan. 8 and 17, 1792, Madison Papers, Library of Congress.

56 Henry Lee, Manuscript note headed "Federal Writ," [c. 1792], Executive Papers, Virginia State Library.

57 R. E. Lee, "Life of Henry Lee," *Memoirs of the War* (1869 ed.), 46.

58 R. E. Lee to George W. Jones, Mar. 22, 1869, quoted in Freeman, *R. E. Lee*, IV, 303.

59 Lee, *Plain Truth*, 35.

60 Henry Lee to Alexander Hamilton, Feb. 20, 1800, Syrett, *et al.*, eds., *Papers of Hamilton*, XXIV, 288.

4: THE MOB

1 Merrill D. Peterson, *The Jefferson Image in the American Mind* (New York, 1960), 116.

2 Lee, *Memoirs of the War*, I, 11, 11–13n; Henry Lee to Nathanael Greene, Apr. 2, 1781, Nathanael Greene Letters, Library of Congress; Lee, *Plain Truth*, 45.

3 Henry Lee to Charles Carter Lee, Apr. 19, 1817, R. E. Lee, "Life of Henry Lee," *Memoirs of the War* (1869 ed.), 67.

4 Lee, *Memoirs of the War*, I, 84n.

5 Henry Lee to Charles Carter Lee, June 18, 1817, R. E. Lee, "Life of Henry Lee," *Memoirs of the War* (1869 ed.), 71.

6 *The Odes of Horace,* Book III, Ode iii, lines 1–4; Lee, *Funeral Oration,* 16–17; *Aurora,* Feb. 14, 1800.

7 Alexander Hamilton to John Laurens, [Sept. 11, 1779], Syrett, *et al.,* eds., *Papers of Hamilton,* II, 168.

8 Ethel Armes, *Stratford Hall: The Great House of the Lees* (Richmond, Va., 1936), 314.

9 Henry Lee to James Madison, July 19, 1807, Madison Papers, Library of Congress.

10 Henry Lee to Anthony Wayne, Jan. 7, 1781, R. E. Lee, "Life of Henry Lee," *Memoirs of the War* (1869 ed.), 33; Henry Lee to Joseph Reed, Jan. 9, 1781, Henry Lee to Nathanael Greene, Aug. 20, 1781, Lee Family Papers, Virginia Historical Society; Henry Lee to Nathanael Greene, June 4, 1781, Nathanael Greene Papers, Duke University.

11 See Bibliographical Essay.

12 Henry Lee to James Madison, Oct. 19, 1786, Madison Papers, Library of Congress.

13 Lee, *Memoirs of the War,* I, 343–344; Elliot, ed., *Debates on the Constitution,* III, 178.

14 Henry Lee to James Madison, July 19, 1807, Madison Papers, Library of Congress.

15 Lee, *Memoirs of the War,* I, 191.

16 Lee, *Plain Truth,* 39.

17 Lee, *Memoirs of the War,* I, 186.

18 United States, *Annals of the Congress of the United States. Sixth Congress. The Debates and Proceedings in the Congress of the United States* ... (Washington, D.C., 1851), col. 275.

19 Henry Lee to Robert Goode, May 17, 1792, Executive Letterbooks, Virginia State Library.

20 Lee, *Memoirs of the War,* I, 204n.

21 Henry Lee to James Madison, Jan. 23, 1792, Madison Papers, Library of Congress.

22 Lee, *Funeral Oration,* 16.

23 Lee, *Memoirs of the War,* I, 233, 233–234n.

24 United States, *Annals of the Sixth Congress,* cols. 229–231.

25 Lee, *Memoirs of the War,* I, 234n.

26 Henry Lee to Smith Snead, May 10, 1792, Henry Lee to County

Lieutenants of Princess Anne, Northampton, Accomack, Elizabeth City, and Norfolk, May 18, 1792, Executive Letterbooks, Virginia State Library.

27 United States, *Annals of the Sixth Congress,* cols. 276–277.

28 Lee, *Memoirs of the War,* I, 234n.

29 Henry Lee to James Madison, Oct. 19 and 25, 1786, Madison Papers, Library of Congress; Henry Lee to Richard Bland Lee, Nov. 11, 1786, Lee Family Papers, Stratford Hall.

30 Elliot, ed., *Debates on the Constitution,* III, 180; Henry Lee to George Washington, Oct. 17, 1786, Washington Papers, Library of Congress; Henry Lee to Richard Bland Lee, Nov. 11, 1786, Lee Family Papers, Stratford Hall; Henry Lee to [St. George Tucker], Oct. 20, 1786, Tucker-Coleman Papers, College of William and Mary.

31 Virginia, *The Virginia Report of 1799–1800 Touching the Alien and Sedition Laws* . . . (New York, 1970 [orig. publ. Richmond, 1850]), 109.

32 Henry Lee to the Delegates, Militia Commandants, Courts, and Commandants of Volunteer Militia in the District of Monongalia, Aug. 20, 1794, Executive Letterbooks, Virginia State Library.

33 Thomas McKean to Jared Ingersoll, Aug. 29, 1794, "Papers Relating to What Is Known As the Whiskey Insurrection in Western Pennsylvania, 1794," John B. Linn and William H. Egle, eds., *Pennsylvania Archives,* 2d ser., IV (Harrisburg, Pa., 1876), 217.

34 Henry Lee to Committee of Conference, Nov. 1, 1794, *ibid.,* 437.

35 [Henry Lee to ?], Sept. 1794, Executive Papers, Virginia State Library.

36 Henry Lee to General Fitzgerald, Nov. 9, 1794, Lee Family Papers, Stratford Hall; Henry Lee to Inhabitants of Four Western Counties, Nov. 8, 1794, "Papers Relating to Whiskey Insurrection," Linn and Egle, eds., *Pennsylvania Archives,* 2d ser., IV, 444–445.

37 Henry Lee to James Iredell, Jan. 21, 1795, James Iredell Papers, Duke University.

38 Alexander Hamilton to Rufus King, Sept. 17, 1794, Syrett, *et al.,* eds. *Papers of Hamilton,* XVII, 242.

39 Lemuel Cocke to James A. Bradley, Sept. 12, 1794, Sherwin McRae and Raleigh Colston, eds., *Calendar of Virginia State Papers and Other Manuscripts* . . . ,VII (Richmond, 1888), 308.

40 [Henry Lee] to Col. Avery, [Sept. 1794], [Henry Lee] to Lemuel Cocke, [Sept. 1794], [Henry Lee], Draft of Address, [Sept. 1794],

[Henry Lee to ?, Oct. 1794], Executive Papers, Virginia State Library.

41 William Findley, *History of the Insurrection in the Four Western Counties of Pennsylvania* . . . (Philadelphia, 1796), 218.

42 *Aurora*, Feb. 14, 1800. See also [James Thomson Callender], *The Prospect Before Us*, II (Richmond, Va, 1801), part ii, 75n.

43 *Aurora*, Nov. 24, 1794.

44 James Madison to Thomas Jefferson, Nov. 16, 1794, Madison Papers, Library of Congress.

45 See Bibliographical Essay.

46 *Aurora*, Nov. 24, 1794.

47 St. George Tucker to James Monroe, Mar. 8, 1795, Monroe Johnson, "Washington Period Politics," *William & Mary Quarterly*, 2d ser., XII (1932), 164.

48 William Branch Giles to James Madison, Apr. 12, 1795, Madison Papers, Library of Congress.

49 Henry Lee to Alexander Hamilton, Jan. 5, 1795, Syrett, *et al.*, eds., *Papers of Hamilton*, XVIII, 11.

50 *Ibid.*

51 Henry Lee to Patrick Henry, Feb. 4, 1795, Huntington Library.

52 Alexander Hamilton to George Washington, Dec. 24, 1795, Syrett, *et al.*, eds., *Papers of Hamilton*, XIX, 515.

53 Timothy Pickering to Alexander Hamilton, Nov. 17, 1795, *ibid.*, 453.

54 Merrill D. Peterson, *Thomas Jefferson and the New Nation: A Biography* (New York, 1970), 709.

55 Lee, *Plain Truth*, 14–15, 24, 54.

56 See Bibliographical Essay.

57 Henry Lee to Alexander Hamilton, May 6, [1793], June 15, 1793, Francisco de Miranda to Alexander Hamilton, Apr. 6–[June 7], 1798, William S. Smith to Francisco de Miranda, Nov. 24, 1792, Syrett, *et al.*, eds., *Papers of Hamilton*, XIV, 416, 550, XXI, 401, 401n. The phrase "wishing to enter the service of the Republic" reads in the original "Souhaitant d'entrer au Service de la Repl." On Miranda, see William Spence Robertson, "Francisco de Miranda and the Revolutionizing of Spanish America," *Annual Report of the American Historical Association for the Year 1907*, I (Washington, D.C., 1908), and William Spence Robertson, *The Life of Miranda*, I (Chapel Hill, N.C., 1929).

58 Henry Lee to [?], Jan. 16, 1793, Miscellaneous Papers, New York Public Library.

59 Lee, *Plain Truth*, 8–10.

60 Henry Lee to Alexander Hamilton, Mar. 6, 1791, Syrett, *et al.*, eds., *Papers of Hamilton*, XVI, 122; Henry Lee to George Washington, Apr. 23, 1793, Washington Papers, Library of Congress.

61 Henry Lee to George Washington, June 14 and Sept. 17, 1793, Washington Papers, Library of Congress.

62 United States, *Annals of the Sixth Congress*, col. 364.

63 Lee, *Address of the Minority*, 3.

64 Risjord, *Chesapeake Politics*, 434.

65 Virginia, *Journal of the House of Delegates of the Commonwealth of Virginia* (Richmond, 1793), 69.

66 Henry Lee to Secretary of War, Feb. 5, 1794, Executive Letterbooks, Virginia State Library.

67 Henry Lee to [?], Apr. 27, 1794, College of William and Mary.

68 *Virginia Herald and Fredericksburg Advertiser*, Aug. 7, 1794.

69 Henry Lee to George Washington, May 31, 1794, Executive Letterbooks, Virginia State Library.

70 Henry Lee to John Jay, June 30, 1795, mentioned in John Jay to Henry Lee, July 11, 1795, Henry P. Johnston, ed., *The Correspondence and Public Papers of John Jay*, IV (New York, 1893), 178.

71 Quoted in Boyd, *Lee*, 240–241; Henry Lee to George Washington, Dec. 4 and 9, 1795, Washington Papers, Library of Congress; Lee, *Cursory Sketch*, 14 and n.

72 Garden, *Anecdotes of the Revolutionary War*, 1st ser., 421.

73 Virginia, *Virginia Report of 1799–1800*, 98, 105.

74 Lee, *Plain Truth*, 27.

75 Virginia, *Virginia Report of 1799–1800*, 103–105, 109; Lee, *Address of the Minority*, 4, 11.

76 Henry Lee to James Madison, [1808], Madison Papers, Library of Congress.

77 Lee, *Plain Truth*, 28.

78 Richard H. Kohn, *Eagle and Sword: The Federalists and the Creation of the Military Establishment in America, 1783–1802* (New York, 1975), esp. 284.

79 Henry Lee to George Washington, Oct. 5, 1798, Washington Papers, Library of Congress.

80 Archibald Blair to Henry Lee, July 13, 1798, Archibald Blair Papers, Library of Congress.

81 Lee, *Plain Truth,* 50.

82 Virginia, *Virginia Report of 1799–1800,* 108; Lee, *Address of the Minority,* 5, 14; United States, *Annals of the Sixth Congress,* col. 275.

83 Lee, *Plain Truth,* 45–47; Lee, *Address of the Minority,* 5.

84 Lee, *Cursory Sketch,* 9–10.

85 *Ibid.,* 15–16.

86 *Ibid.,* 22.

87 Henry Lee to James Madison, Aug. 19, 1811, Madison Papers, Library of Congress.

88 Lee, *Memoirs of the War,* I, 46.

89 Lee, *Cursory Sketch,* 37–38.

90 Maryland, *Report of the Committee of Grievances and Courts of Justice of the House of Delegates, On the Subject of the Recent Mobs and Riots in the City of Baltimore* (Annapolis, Md., 1813), 15, 165.

91 Quoted in J. Thomas Scharf, *The Chronicles of Baltimore; Being A Complete History of 'Baltimore Town' and Baltimore City from the Earliest Period to the Present Time* (Baltimore, Md., 1874), 309–310.

92 Maryland, *Report of the Committee,* 14–15.

93 Entry of Dec. 25, 1812, John Pierce, "December 1812. Journey to Washington," Massachusetts Historical Society *Proceedings,* 2d ser., XIX (1905), 378.

94 *Federal Republican* (Baltimore), Aug. 7, 1812, quoted in *New-York Evening Post,* Aug. 10, 1812.

95 *Federal Republican,* July 27, 1812, quoted in J. Thomas Scharf, *History of Maryland from the Earliest Period to the Present Day,* III (Baltimore, Md., 1879), 5–6.

96 Maryland, *Report of the Committee,* 3, 163.

97 *Alexandria Daily Gazette, Commercial & Political,* July 7, 1812.

98 *The Supporter* (Chillicothe, Ohio), Aug. 15, 1812.

99 Maryland, *Report of the Committee,* 172, 63.

100 Quoted in *Virginia Argus* (Richmond), Aug. 3, 1812.

101 *Maryland Gazette* (Annapolis), Dec. 31, 1812.

102 *Aurora,* July 30, 1812.

103 Maryland, *Report of the Committee,* 46.

104 Frank A. Cassell, "The Great Baltimore Riot of 1812," *Maryland Historical Magazine,* LXX (1975), 251.

105 Maryland, *Report of the Committee,* 58.

106 Cassell, "Baltimore Riot," *Maryland Historical Magazine,* LXX (1975), 254.

107 Maryland, *Report of the Committee,* 193.

108 Entry of Dec. 25, 1812, Pierce, "Journey to Washington," Massachusetts Historical Society *Proceedings,* 2d ser., XIX (1905), 378.

109 "Henry Lee," *A Correct Account of the Conduct of the Baltimore Mob* . . . (Winchester, Va., 1814), 8.

110 Maryland, *Report of the Committee,* 192.

111 "Lee," *Correct Account,* 7.

112 Maryland, *Report of the Committee,* 243.

113 "Lee," *Correct Account,* 12.

114 Maryland, *Report of the Committee,* 195.

115 "An Exact and Authentic Narrative of the Events Which Took Place in Baltimore on the 27th and 28th of July . . . ," in Scharf, *Chronicles of Baltimore,* 322.

116 Maryland, *Report of the Committee,* 252.

117 *National Intelligencer,* Sept. 5, 1812.

118 "Exact and Authentic Narrative," in Scharf, *Chronicles of Baltimore,* 320.

119 "Lee," *Correct Account,* 13.

120 *Federal Republican,* quoted in *New-York Evening Post,* Sept. 17, 1812.

121 Pierce, "Journey to Washington," Massachusetts Historical Society *Proceedings,* 2d ser, XIX (1905), 384.

122 *Federal Republican,* quoted in *New-York Evening Post,* Aug. 8 and Sept. 17, 1812.

123 Narrative of John E. Hall, *Maryland Gazette,* Aug. 27, 1812.

124 *Connecticut Journal* (New Haven), Aug. 6, 1812.

125 *Norfolk Gazette and Publick Ledger,* Aug. 3, 1812.

126 *New-York Evening Post,* Aug. 11, 1812.

127 *Albany Register,* Aug. 4, 1812, quoted in *New-York Evening Post,* Aug. 8, 1812.

128 *Federal Republican,* quoted in *New-York Evening Post,* Aug. 8, 1812.

129 *Providence Gazette,* Aug. 15, 1812.

130 *American Watchman and Delaware Republican* (Wilmington), Aug. 5, 1812.

131 *Providence Gazette,* Aug. 15, 1812.

132 *Pennsylvania Republican* (Harrisburg), Aug. 4 and 11, 1812.

133 Quoted in *American Watchman and Delaware Republican,* Aug. 5, 1812.

134 James C. Boyd to James McHenry, Aug. 2, 1812, quoted in Cassell, "Baltimore Riot," *Maryland Historical Magazine,* LXX (1975), 257; Henry Lee to Bernard M. Carter, Oct. 27, 1812, Virginia State Library; Henry Lee to James Monroe, Jan. 7, 1813, James Monroe Papers, New York Public Library; Henry Lee to [Henry Lee IV], Sept. 3, 1813, Lee Family Papers, Stratford Hall; Elizabeth Jane Stark, ed., *Recollections of Old Alexandria and Other Memories of Mary Louisa Slacum Benham* (Starkville, Miss., 1978), 34.

135 *Connecticut Journal,* Aug. 27, 1812.

5: "THE SWINDLING HARRY LEE"

1 Quoted in *American Watchman and Delaware Republican,* Aug. 5, 1812.

2 Henry Lee to Patrick Henry, Apr. 22, 1795, Papers of Patrick Henry, Library of Congress.

3 Henry Lee to Patrick Henry, Feb. 4, 1795, Huntington Library.

4 Henry Lee to [?], Dec. 27, 1795, John Heise Autograph Collection (38–342), University of Virginia.

5 Henry Lee to William Sullivan, Dec. 3, 1797, New-York Historical Society; Henry Lee to William Sullivan, Dec. 10, 1797, New York Public Library.

6 Henry Lee to John Nicholson, Mar. 15, 1798, Clem D. Johnston Collection (Accession No. 6693–a), University of Virginia.

7 Henry Lee to George Washington, Feb. 2, 1798, Washington Papers, Library of Congress.

8 Henry Lee to George Washington, Feb. 28, 1799, *ibid.*

9 Henry Lee to Henry Banks, Oct. 19, 1798, Henry Banks Papers, Virginia Historical Society.

10 Henry Lee to George Washington, Sept. 28, 1798, Washington Papers, Library of Congress.

11 John James Maund to Robert Carter, Jan. 3, 1801, Kate Mason Rowland, "Letters of John James Maund, 1790–1802," *William & Mary Quarterly,* 1st ser., XX (1912), 279.

12 Henry Lee to Thomas Jefferson, Feb. 24, 1806, Jefferson Papers, Library of Congress.

13 Robert Morris to Henry Lee, Aug. 27, 1801, Virginia Historical Society.

14 Henry Lee to [?], Feb. 27, 1804 (HM 22930), Huntington Library.

15 Henry Lee to [Jonathan] Rhea, [Oct. 1802] (HM 24719), *ibid.*

16 Henry Lee to [?], Nov. 8, 1800 (HM 3617), *ibid.*

17 Gouverneur Morris to Henry Lee, Jan. 22, 1801, Jared Sparks, *The Life of Gouverneur Morris* . . . , III (Boston, 1832) 146–150.

18 Henry Lee to Messrs. Nicklin & Griffith, Feb. 10, 1802, Lee Family Papers, Virginia Historical Society; Henry Lee to Nicklin & Griffith, Mar. 15, 1802 (Accession No. 9210-c), University of Virginia. See also Henry Lee to Nicklin & Griffith, Mar. 3, [1802], and May 2, 1802, Historical Society of Pennsylvania.

19 Henry Lee to Henry Banks, Oct. 19, [1798], Henry Banks Papers, Virginia Historical Society.

20 Levi Lincoln to Henry Dearborn, Jan. 25, 1802, Walter Lowrie and Matthew St. Clair Clarke, eds., *American State Papers, Class V, Military Affairs,* I (Washington, D.C. 1832), 159; James P. Cocke to Thomas Jefferson, Sept. 19, 1806, Jefferson Papers, Library of Congress.

21 Henry Lee to George Washington, Feb. 28, 1799, Washington Papers, Library of Congress.

22 George Washington to Henry Lee, Jan. 25, 1798, Fitzpatrick, ed., *Writings of Washington,* XXXVI, 140.

23 Charles Blackburn to William Augustine Washington, Apr. 30, 1805, Tracy W. McGregor Library, Manuscripts Department, University of Virginia.

24 Quoted in William Hodgson to Henry Lee, Sept. 8, 1805, William Hodgson Letterbook, Virginia State Library.

25 Henry Lee to Charles Lee, Apr. 18, 1807, Leesburg Families Papers, University of Virginia.

26 Charles Blackburn to William Augustine Washington, Apr. 30, 1805, University of Virginia.

27 George Mason to Zachariah Johnston, Nov. 18, 1791, Robert A. Rutland, ed., *The Papers of George Mason, 1725–1792,* III (Chapel Hill, N.C., 1970), 1245.

28 Henry Banks to Henry Lee, Mar. 9, 1794, Henry Banks Papers, Virginia Historical Society; Benjamin Haskell to William Sullivan, Jan. 1, 179[8], Robert E. Lee Papers, Duke University.

29 Nathaniel Pendleton to George Deneale, July 18, 1805, George Deneale Papers, Virginia Historical Society.

30 Charles Blackburn to William Augustine Washington, June 6, 1806, University of Virginia.

31 Henry Lee to John Nicholson, Mar. 15, 1798, *ibid.*

32 Henry Lee to George Washington, May 22, 1799, Washington Papers, Library of Congress.

33 Henry Lee to James Wilson, n.d., New-York Historical Society.

34 Henry Lee to George Washington, Feb. 28, 1799, Washington Papers, Library of Congress.

35 Henry Lee to George Washington, May 22, 1799, *ibid.*

36 Ann Lee to Henry Lee, July 8, 1806, Lee Family Papers, Stratford Hall.

37 Henry Lee to George Deneale, Oct. 20, [1805?], George Deneale Papers, Virginia Historical Society; Henry Lee to [?], Mar. 22, [?], Henry Lee Personal Miscellany, Library of Congress.

38 Henry Lee to James Madison, Feb. 11, 1809, Madison Papers, Library of Congress.

39 Henry Lee to James Madison, Mar. 21, 1808, *ibid.*

40 Henry Lee to Robert Goodloe Harper, Oct. 22, 1808 (Accession No. 7131), University of Virginia.

41 Henry Lee to James Breckinridge, Mar. 4, 1809, James Breckinridge Papers, Virginia Historical Society.

42 Henry Lee to James Madison, [1808], Madison Papers, Library of Congress.

43 Henry Lee to Charles Simms, Jan. 15, 1808, Papers of Charles Simms, Library of Congress.

44 Henry Lee to Robert Goodloe Harper, Sept. 20, 1808, Lee Family Papers, Virginia Historical Society; Henry Lee to Robert Goodloe Harper, Mar. 2, 1809, Lee Family Papers, Stratford Hall.

45 Henry Lee to James Breckinridge, Mar. 4, 1809, James Breckinridge Papers, Virginia Historical Society; Henry Lee to James McHenry, Mar. 7, 1809 (MH 48), Huntington Library; Henry Lee to James McHenry, n.d., James McHenry Papers, Library of Congress.

46 Henry Lee to B[ernard] M. Carter, Mar. 7, 1810, Virginia State Library.

47 Henry Lee [IV] to Henry Lee, July 3, 1809, New-York Historical Society.

48 Henry Lee to Bernard M. Carter, Mar. 10, 1810, Virginia State Library.

49 William Brook to William Augustine Washington, Dec. 5, 1809, Beverley Family Papers, Virginia Historical Society.

50 Henry Lee to B[ernard] M. Carter, Mar. 7, 1810, Virginia State Library.

51 Henry Lee to James Madison, Mar. 6, 1809, Madison Papers, Library of Congress.

52 Lee, *Cursory Sketch*, 36–37.

53 Henry Lee to Bernard M. Carter, Mar. 13, 1810, Virginia State Library.

6: MR. JEFFERSON

1 Lee, *Plain Truth*, 1.

2 Henry Lee to Bernard M. Carter, Mar. 13, 1810, Virginia State Library.

3 Henry Lee to B[ernard] M. Carter, Mar. 7, 1810, *ibid.*

4 Henry Lee to Charles Simms, Jan. 6, 1809 [1810], Simms Papers, Library of Congress.

5 Henry Lee to Charles Simms, Jan. 6, 1809 [1810], *ibid.*, William Goddard to Richard Jackson, Mar. 12, 1810, William Goddard to Henry Lee, Apr. 2, 1810, Lee Family Papers, Stratford Hall.

6 John Mercer to Henry Lee, Nov. 16 [10?], 1809, *ibid.*

7 Lee, *Memoirs of the War*, I, 3.

8 Christopher R. Greene to [Henry Lee], [1809], Lee Family Papers, Stratford Hall.

9 William R. Davie to [Henry Lee], Feb. 21, 1810, *ibid.*

10 William R. Davie to Henry Lee, Jan. 9, 1810, *ibid.*

11 Lee, *Memoirs of the War*, I, 1.

12 *Ibid.*, I, 232n, 161.

13 Lee, *Plain Truth*, 39.

14 Lee, *Memoirs of the War*, I, 20–21.

15 *Ibid.*, 291–292.

16 Otho Holland Williams to Henry Lee, [c. December 1791–February 1792], Lee [IV], *Campaign of 1781*, 125–126.

17 Henry Lee to Otho Holland Williams, Feb. 1792, *Calendar of the General Otho Holland Williams Papers in the Maryland Historical Society* (Baltimore, 1940), 250.

18 Lee, *Memoirs of the War*, I, 352–354, 358.

19 Henry Lee to B[ernard] M. Carter, Mar. 7, 1810, Virginia State Library.

20 Henry Lee, *Fourth Division—You are called upon . . .* [Richmond? 1807], Broadside, Virginia Historical Society.

21 Lee, *Memoirs of the War*, I, 192.

22 *The Port Folio,* n.s., VIII (1812), 564.

23 *The American Review of History and Politics,* IV (1812), 230; Theodore Crackel, "Mr. Jefferson and His Army: Politics, Reform and the Military Establishment, 1801–1809," unpublished essay quoted in Don Higginbotham, "The Debate Over National Military Institutions," in W. M. Fowler and Wallace Coyle, eds., *The American Revolution: Changing Perspectives* (Boston, 1979), 162–163. I have also relied on Lawrence Delbert Cress's manuscript, "Arms and Ideas: Political Ideology and the Evolution of American Military Institutions to the War of 1812."

24 Lee, *Memoirs of the War,* II, 424.

25 Lee, Manuscript Memoirs, Virginia Historical Society.

26 Henry Lee to George Washington, July 11, 1786, Washington Papers, Library of Congress.

27 Worthington C. Ford, *et al.,* eds., *Journals of the Continental Congress, 1774–1789,* XXXI (Washington, D.C., 1934), 504.

28 Henry Lee to Col. Rhea, Mar. 10, 1811, Miscellaneous Papers, New York Public Library.

29 Lee, *Memoirs of the War,* I, 294.

30 United States, *Annals of the Sixth Congress,* cols. 802–804; Henry Lee to [?], Jan. 8, 1800, Henry Lee Personal Miscellany, Library of Congress.

31 United States, *Annals of the Sixth Congress,* col. 802; *Aurora,* Feb. 14, 1800; entry of Dec. 25, 1812, Pierce, "Journey to Washington," Massachusetts Historical Society *Proceedings,* 2d ser., XIX (1905), 378.

32 Virginia, *Journal of the House of Delegates of the Commonwealth of Virginia . . .* [*1789*] (Richmond, Va., 1790), 14.

33 Lee, *Funeral Oration.*

34 Lee, *Memoirs of the War,* I, 26.

35 Lee, *Funeral Oration,* 19. On the orations after Washington's death, see Robert P. Hay, "George Washington: American Moses," *American Quarterly,* XXI (1969), 780–791.

36 Custis, *Recollections of Washington,* 363.

37 Lee, *Memoirs of the War,* II, 372.

38 Henry Lee to Theodore Sedgwick, Dec. 28, 1799, United States, *Annals of the Sixth Congress,* col. 223.

39 Custis, *Recollections of Washington,* 363.

40 Herman Melville, "Lee in the Capitol," lines 71–73, *Collected Poems of Herman Melville,* ed. Howard P. Vincent (Chicago, 1947), 148.

41 Henry Lee to George Washington, Sept. 17, 1793, and Aug. 17, 1794, Washington Papers, Library of Congress.

42 Quoted in Thomas Jefferson to George Washington, June 19, 1796, Paul Leicester Ford, ed., *The Writings of Thomas Jefferson,* VII (New York, 1896), 82.

43 George Gibbs, *Memoirs of the Administrations of Washington and John Adams,* II (New York, 1846), 366.

44 Lee, *Cursory Sketch,* 4–5, 10.

45 Pierce, "Journey to Washington," Massachusetts Historical Society *Proceedings,* 2d ser., XIX (1905), 384.

46 Henry Lee to Alexander Hamilton, Feb. 6, 1801, Syrett, *et al.,* eds., *Papers of Hamilton,* XXV, 331.

47 Albert Gallatin to Mrs. Gallatin, Jan. 15, 1800 [1801], Papers of Albert Gallatin, Elmer Holmes Bobst Library, New York University, New York; Albert Gallatin to Henry A. Muhlenberg, May 8, 1848, Henry Adams, ed., *The Writings of Albert Gallatin,* II (New York, 1879), 664; Alexander Hamilton to James McHenry, Jan. 4, 1801, Syrett, *et al.,* eds., *Papers of Hamilton,* XXV, 292.

48 United States, *Annals of the Sixth Congress,* col. 963.

49 Henry Lee to Alexander Hamilton, Feb. 6, 1801, Syrett, *et al.,* eds., *Papers of Hamilton,* XXV, 331.

50 Henry Lee to Thomas Jefferson, Jan. 17, 1807, Jefferson Papers, Library of Congress.

51 Thomas Jefferson to Robert Smith, July 1, 1805, quoted in Dumas Malone, *Jefferson and His Time,* I: *Jefferson the Virginian* (Boston, 1948), 154.

52 Malone, *Jefferson and His Time,* I, 448; Peterson, *Jefferson and the New Nation,* 709.

53 Thomas Jefferson to John Walker, Apr. 13, 1803, Virginia State Library.

54 John Walker's Narrative, [1805?], Jefferson Papers, Library of Congress.

55 John Marshall to Henry Lee [IV], Oct. 25, 1830, Marshall Papers, Institute of Early American History and Culture, Williamsburg.

56 Lee, *Cursory Sketch,* 3–4, 9–10, 17, 17n, 13, 36, 23.

57 Henry Lee to Charles Simms, Mar. 12, 1810, Simms Papers, Library of Congress.

58 Lee, *Memoirs of the War*, II, 1–24.

59 Lee, *Cursory Sketch*, 22.

60 William R. Davie to Henry Lee, Apr. 20, 1810, Brock Collection, Box 4, Huntington Library.

61 Lee, *Memoirs of the War*, II, 14–15.

62 William R. Davie to Henry Lee, Apr. 20, 1810, Huntington Library.

63 Lee, *Memoirs of the War*, II, 232–233, 1–24.

64 Lee, Manuscript Memoirs, Virginia Historical Society.

65 [William Loughton Smith], *The Pretensions of Thomas Jefferson to the Presidency Examined* . . . ([Philadelphia], 1796), 34n; *Columbian Mirror and Alexandria Gazette*, Sept. 29, 1796; *Virginia Gazette*, Oct. 12, 1796.

66 *Virginia Gazette*, Oct. 12, 1796.

67 Smith, *Pretensions of Jefferson*, 34.

68 Lee, *Memoirs of the War*, II, 234.

69 *New-York Evening Post*, Aug. 15, 1812.

70 Henry Lee to Charles Simms, Mar. 12, 1810, Simms Papers, Library of Congress.

71 Thomas Jefferson to William Johnson, Mar. 4, 1823, Jefferson Papers, Library of Congress.

72 Thomas Jefferson to William Johnson, Oct. 27, 1822, *ibid.*

73 Sawvel, ed., *Anas of Jefferson*, 24–25, 38–39.

74 Thomas Jefferson to James Monroe, Jan. 1, 1815, Jefferson Papers, Library of Congress.

75 Thomas Jefferson, The 1816 Version of the Diary and Notes of 1781, Julian P. Boyd, *et al.*, eds., *The Papers of Thomas Jefferson* (Princeton, N.J., 1950–), IV, 264–265.

76 Thomas Jefferson to William Johnson, Oct. 27, 1822, Jefferson Papers, Library of Congress.

77 *Ibid.*

78 Thomas Jefferson to Henry Lee [IV], May 15, 1826, *ibid.*

79 Entry of July 7, 1826, *The Diary of John Quincy Adams, 1794–1845*, ed. Allan Nevins (New York, 1951), 358.

80 Thomas Jefferson to Henry Lee [IV], May 15, 1826, Jefferson Papers, Library of Congress.

81 Thomas Jefferson to James Monroe, Jan. 1, 1815, *ibid.*

82 Thomas Jefferson, Diary of Arnold's Invasion and Notes on Subsequent Events in 1781: The 1796? Version, Boyd, *et al.*, eds., *Papers of Jefferson*, IV, 260.

83 Thomas Jefferson to Henry Lee [IV], May 15, 1826, Jefferson Papers, Library of Congress.

84 Lee, *Memoirs of the War*, II, 211. The word "spar" has been corrected to read "spur."

85 Smith, *Pretensions of Jefferson*, 33.

86 Thomas Jefferson to Henry Lee [IV], May 15, 1826, Jefferson Papers, Library of Congress.

87 [L. H. Girardin], *History of Virginia . . .*, IV (Petersburg, Va., 1816), 502n.

88 Thomas Jefferson, 1816 Version of Diary of 1781, Boyd, *et al.*, eds., *Papers of Jefferson*, IV, 265.

89 Sawvel, ed., *Anas of Jefferson*, 25.

90 John Marshall to Henry Lee [IV], Oct. 25, 1830, Marshall Papers, Institute of Early American History and Culture, Williamsburg.

91 Thomas Jefferson to George Washington, June 19, 1796, Ford, ed., *Writings of Jefferson*, VII, 82–83.

92 William Johnson, *Sketches of the Life and Correspondence of Nathanael Greene, Major General of the Armies of the United States in the War of the Revolution* (Charleston, S.C., 1822), II, Postscript, 1; II, 174.

93 Thomas Jefferson to James Monroe, Jan. 1, 1815, Jefferson Papers, Library of Congress.

94 William Johnson to Thomas Jefferson, Dec. 10, 1822, *ibid.*

95 Thomas Jefferson to William Johnson, Mar. 4, 1823, *ibid.*

96 Henry Lee to Charles Simms, Jan. 6, 1809 [1810], Dec. 4, 1809, Simms Papers, Library of Congress.

97 Quoted in *Daily National Intelligencer*, Apr. 8, 1818, from A. & G. Way, *An Interesting Work, Entitled Memoirs of the War in the Southern Department of the United States* [Washington, D.C., 1810].

98 *American Review*, IV (1812), 230.

99 Richard Bland Lee to John Jay, Oct. 1812, Richard Bland Lee Papers, Library of Congress.

100 Henry Lee to Col. Rhea, Mar. 10, 1811, New York Public Library.

101 Henry Lee to John Rutledge, Jan. 9, 1813, John Rutledge Papers, No. 948, Southern Historical Collection, Library of the University of North Carolina at Chapel Hill.

7: PEACE

1 Quoted in John James Chew to William Selden, Aug. 8, 1835, Brock Collection, Box 5, Huntington Library.

2 Richard Bland Lee to [?], Feb. 13, 1819, Richard Bland Lee Papers, Library of Congress.

3 Charles Carter Lee to George Henry Moore, Feb. 29, 1860, George Henry Moore Papers, Duke University.

4 Henry Lee to James Madison, [1808?], Madison Papers, Library of Congress.

5 Henry Lee to Rufus King, Nov. 19, 1813, Rufus King Papers, New-York Historical Society.

6 Henry Lee to Bernard M. Carter, Oct. 27, 1812, Virginia State Library.

7 Henry Lee to Rufus King, Nov. 19, 1813, Rufus King Papers, New-York Historical Society.

8 Henry Lee to James Monroe, Jan. 13, 1813, James Monroe Papers, New York Public Library.

9 Edmund Jennings Lee to Luther Martin, May 14, 1813, Brock Collection, Box 4, Huntington Library.

10 Henry Lee to Rufus King, Nov. 19, 1813, Rufus King Papers, New-York Historical Society.

11 Henry Lee to James Madison, Nov. 17, 1813, Madison Papers, Library of Congress.

12 Henry Lee to [Henry Lee IV], July 7, 1813, Lee Family Papers, Virginia Historical Society.

13 Henry Lee to Rufus King, Nov. 19, 1813, Rufus King Papers, New-York Historical Society.

14 Henry Lee to [William] Goddard, Aug. 29, 1816, Lee Family Papers, Virginia Historical Society.

15 Henry Lee to James Monroe, Feb. 23, 1814, James Monroe Papers, New York Public Library.

16 George Beckwith to Earl Bathurst, Nov. 26, 1813, "Major-General Henry Lee and Lieutenant-General Sir George Beckwith on Peace in 1813," *American Historical Review*, XXXII (1927), 285.

17 Henry Lee to James Monroe, Jan. 13, 1813, James Monroe Papers, New York Public Library.

18 Lee, *Cursory Sketch*, 13n.

19 Henry Lee to James Monroe, Jan. 13, 1813, James Monroe Papers, New York Public Library.

20 Henry Lee to James Monroe, June 8, 1814, *ibid*.

21 Henry Lee to James Madison, Feb. 11, 1809, Madison Papers, Library of Congress.

22 Henry Lee to James Madison, Nov. 17, 1813, *ibid.*

23 Henry Lee to James Monroe, Nov. 18, 1813, James Monroe Papers, New York Public Library.

24 Henry Lee to Sir George Beckwith, Nov. 10, 1813, "Lee and Beckwith on Peace," *American Historical Review*, XXXII (1927), 287.

25 Lee, *Cursory Sketch*, 21.

26 Henry Lee to James Madison, Aug. 19, 1811, Madison Papers, Library of Congress; Henry Lee to Rufus King, Nov. 19, 1813, Rufus King Papers, New-York Historical Society.

27 Henry Lee to James Madison, June 21, 1812, and Nov. 17, 1813, Madison Papers, Library of Congress.

28 Henry Lee to Rufus King, Nov. 19, 1813, Rufus King Papers, New-York Historical Society.

29 Henry Lee to Ann Hill Carter Lee, Sept. 12, 1814, Lee Family Papers, Virginia Historical Society.

30 Henry Lee to Rufus King, Nov. 19, 1813, Rufus King Papers, New-York Historical Society.

31 Henry Lee to James Monroe, May 13, [1813?], James Monroe Papers, New York Public Library.

32 Henry Lee to Sir George Beckwith, Nov. 10, 1813, Sir George Beckwith to Henry Lee, Nov. 18, 1813, "Lee and Beckwith on Peace," *American Historical Review*, XXXII (1927), 287–288, 292.

33 Henry Lee to James Monroe, Jan. 10 and Feb. 23, 1814, James Monroe Papers, New York Public Library.

34 Henry Lee to [Henry Lee IV], Sept. 3, 1813, Lee Family Papers, Stratford Hall.

35 Henry Lee to Charles Carter Lee, June 18, 1817, R. E. Lee, "Life of Henry Lee," *Memoirs of the War* (1869 ed.), 71.

36 Henry Lee to Ann Hill Carter Lee, May 6, 1817, Lee Family Papers, Virginia Historical Society.

37 Henry Lee to Charles Carter Lee, Sept. 30, 1816, R. E. Lee, "Life of Henry Lee," *Memoirs of the War* (1869 ed.), 60.

38 R. E. Lee, "Life of Henry Lee," *ibid.,* 50–53.

39 Henry Lee to [Henry Lee IV], July 7, 1813, Lee Family Papers, Virginia Historical Society.

40 Henry Lee to Ann Hill Carter Lee, May 6, 1817, *ibid.*

41 Ann Hill Carter Lee to Charles Carter Lee, July 17, 1816, Henry Lee Personal Miscellany, Library of Congress.

42 Henry Lee to Ann Hill Carter Lee, May 6, 1817, Lee Family Papers, Virginia Historical Society.

43 Henry Lee to Charles Carter Lee, Sept. 30, 1816, R. E. Lee, "Life of Henry Lee," *Memoirs of the War* (1869 ed.), 60.

44 Henry Lee to Charles Carter Lee, Aug. 8, 1816, Lee Family Papers, Stratford Hall.

45 Henry Lee to Charles Carter Lee, Feb. 9, Aug. 25, Sept. 3, and May 5, 1817, R. E. Lee, "Life of Henry Lee," *Memoirs of the War* (1869 ed.), 63, 72–73, 69–70.

46 Henry Lee to [Henry Lee IV], Sept. 3, 1813, Lee Family Papers, Stratford Hall.

47 Henry Lee to Charles Carter Lee, Feb. 9, 1817, R. E. Lee, "Life of Henry Lee," *Memoirs of the War* (1869 ed.), 63.

48 Henry Lee to Charles Carter Lee, Nov. 20 and May 5, 1817, *ibid.*, 74, 69.

49 Henry Lee to Nicholas Fish, [Nov.] 4, 1816, Nicholas Fish Papers, Library of Congress.

50 Henry Lee to Charles Carter Lee, Dec. 1, 1816, R. E. Lee, "Life of Henry Lee," *Memoirs of the War* (1869 ed.), 61.

51 Henry Lee to [Henry Lee IV], Sept. 3, 1813, Lee Family Papers, Stratford Hall.

52 Henry Lee to Charles Carter Lee, May 5, 1817, R. E. Lee, "Life of Henry Lee," *Memoirs of the War* (1869 ed.), 69.

53 Henry Lee to Charles Carter Lee, Aug. 8, 1816, Lee Family Papers, Stratford Hall; Sophocles, *Ajax*, lines 127–132.

54 Henry Lee to Charles Carter Lee, Feb. 9, 1818, R. E. Lee, "Life of Henry Lee," *Memoirs of the War* (1869 ed.), 77–78.

55 Alexander Pope, "On Mr. Elijah Fenton," lines 7–8. Lee's version quoted in Armes, *Stratford Hall*, 352.

56 Henry Lee to Charles Carter Lee, Sept. 3, 1817, R. E. Lee, "Life of Henry Lee," *Memoirs of the War* (1869 ed.), 72.

57 Henry Lee to Charles Carter Lee, Jan. 24, 1818, *ibid.*, 78.

EPILOGUE

The epilogue is drawn from the same sources as the prologue. The quotation comes from the narrative dated March 1818 in the Henry Lee Personal Miscellany, Library of Congress, erroneously attributed to Catharine Greene.

BIBLIOGRAPHICAL ESSAY

BECAUSE HENRY LEE'S CAREER TOUCHED MUCH OF AMERICAN HISTORY from 1776 to 1815, a full bibliography for his life and times—or even a list of works that I have read—is not practical here. Instead, I will mention a few studies that have been especially useful, including the work of those historians mentioned in the text.

The most important sources for this book are the surviving Henry Lee manuscripts, which are widely scattered, as well as Lee's publications issued during his lifetime. All of the manuscript repositories that I used, though not all the documents that I consulted, are mentioned in the notes.

The latest and most thorough biography of Lee is Thomas E. Templin's doctoral dissertation at the University of Kentucky, "Henry 'Light-Horse Harry' Lee: A Biography" (1975). Although my concerns and my analysis of Lee differ from Templin's, I have found his study reliable and valuable. An earlier biography, Thomas Boyd, *Light-horse Harry Lee* (New York, 1931), remains useful. Cecil B. Hartley, *Life of Major General Henry Lee* (New York, 1859), and Noel B. Gerson, *Light-Horse Harry: A Biography of Washington's Great Cavalryman, General Henry Lee* (Garden City, N.Y., 1966), have little to recommend them. I have also consulted three M.A. theses: Thomas E. Templin, "Light Horse Harry Lee, Federalist" (University of Virginia, 1967), Philander Dean Chase, "The Early Career of 'Light Horse Harry' Lee" (Duke University, 1968), and Leonard E. Richardson, "The Military Career of Light Horse Harry Lee in the South, 1781" (University of Tennessee, 1966).

For the history of the Lee family, there is information in Burton J. Hendrick, *The Lees of Virginia; Biography of a Family* (New York, 1935), Ethel Armes, *Stratford Hall: The Great House of the Lees* (Richmond, Va., 1936), and Cazenove Gardner Lee, Jr., *Lee Chronicle: Studies of the Early Generations of the Lees of Virginia,* ed. Dorothy Mills Parker (New York, 1957).

My discussion of Robert E. Lee relies especially on Douglas Southall Freeman, *R. E. Lee: A Biography*, 4 vols. (New York, 1934–35), which also contains a brief biography of Henry Lee in Chapter 1, on Thomas L. Connelly, *The Marble Man: Robert E. Lee and His Image in American Society* (New York, 1977), and on Allen W. Moger, "General Lee's Unwritten 'History of the Army of Northern Virginia,' " *Virginia Magazine of History and Biography*, LXXI (1963), 341–363.

My understanding of the Revolutionary War was formed by writing *A Revolutionary People at War: The Continental Army and American Character, 1775–1783* (Chapel Hill, N.C., 1979). In that book, readers will find fuller treatment of some of the subjects discussed in Chapter 1 here, especially the political outlook of Continental Army officers. For general histories of the war, see Christopher Ward, *The War of the Revolution*, ed. John Richard Alden, 2 vols. (New York, 1952), and Don Higginbotham, *The War of American Independence: Military Attitudes, Policies, and Practice, 1763–1789* (New York, 1971). The officer corps is discussed in Richard H. Kohn, "American Generals of the Revolution: Subordination and Restraint," Don Higginbotham, ed., *Reconsiderations on the Revolutionary War: Selected Essays* (Westport, Conn., 1978), 104–123; in Gerhard Kollmann, "Reflections on the Army of the American Revolution," Erich Angermann, *et al.*, eds., *New Wine in Old Skins: A Comparative View of Socio-Political Structures and Values Affecting the American Revolution* (Stuttgart, 1976), 153–176; and in Don Higginbotham, "Military Leadership in the American Revolution," *Library of Congress Symposia on the American Revolution: Leadership in the American Revolution* (Washington, D.C., 1974), 91–111. For an insightful and suggestive brief study of the war in the South, read Russell F. Weigley, *The Partisan War: The South Carolina Campaign of 1780–1782* (Columbia, S.C., 1970). I am particularly indebted to John Shy's work on the Revolutionary War, published in *A People Numerous and Armed: Reflections on the Military Struggle for American Independence* (New York, 1976), and in "The Legacy of the American Revolutionary War," Larry R. Gerlach, *et al.*, eds., *Legacies of the American Revolution* (n.p., 1978), 43–60. Among the important studies of the militia in the Southern War are Robert C. Pugh, "The Revolutionary Militia in the Southern Campaign, 1780–1781," *William & Mary Quarterly*, 3d ser., XIV (1957), 154–175; Clyde R. Ferguson, "Carolina and Georgia Patriot and Loyalist Militia in Action, 1778–1783," in Jeffrey J. Crow and Larry E. Tise, eds., *The Southern Experience in the American Revolution* (Chapel Hill, N.C., 1978), 174–199; and John David McBride, "The Virginia War Effort, 1775–1783: Manpower Policies and Practices" (Ph.D. diss., University of Virginia, 1977).

The politics of the war years and the Confederation period, including the movement for a stronger national government, receive treatment from varied perspectives in Gordon S. Wood, *The Creation of the American Republic, 1776–1787* (Chapel Hill, N.C., 1969), E. James Ferguson, *The Power of the Purse: A History of American Public Finance, 1776–1790* (Chapel Hill, N.C., 1961), Merrill Jensen, *The New Nation: A History of the United States During the Confederation, 1781–1789* (New York, 1950), Jackson Turner Main, *Political Parties Before the Constitution* (Chapel Hill, N.C., 1973), H. James Henderson, *Party Politics in the Continental Congress* (New York, 1974), and Jack N. Rakove, *The Beginnings of National Politics: An Interpretive History of the Continental Congress* (New York, 1979).

The importance of the war years to young nationalist-minded revolutionaries is suggestively analyzed in Stanley Elkins and Eric McKitrick, "The Founding Fathers: Young Men of the Revolution," *Political Science Quarterly,* LXXVI (1961), 181–216. Thomas E. Templin, in his "Henry Lee: A Biography," 259–261, n. 20, convincingly defends the argument of Elkins and McKitrick against the criticisms in David Hackett Fischer, *Historians' Fallacies: Toward a Logic of Historical Thought* (New York, 1970), 104–106. For studies of Continental Army officers' role in postwar politics, see Edwin G. Burrows, "Military Experience and the Origins of Federalism and Anti-Federalism," in Jacob Judd and Irwin H. Polishook, eds., *Aspects of Early New York Society and Politics* (Tarrytown, N.Y., 1974), 83–92, William A. Benton, "Pennsylvania Revolutionary Officers and the Federal Constitution," *Pennsylvania History,* XXXI (1964), 419–435, and Sidney Kaplan, "Veteran Officers and Politics in Massachusetts, 1783–1787," *William & Mary Quarterly,* 3d ser., IX (1952), 29–57. Two important studies of revolutionary attitudes partly shared by Lee are Douglass Adair, "Fame and the Founding Fathers," in Trevor Colbourn, ed., *Fame and the Founding Fathers* (New York, 1974), 3–26, and Gerald Stourzh, *Alexander Hamilton and the Idea of Republican Government* (Stanford, Calif., 1970)

Among the general interpretative studies of the politics of the Early National Period, I owe an especially large debt to Drew R. McCoy, *The Elusive Republic: Political Economy in Jeffersonian America* (Chapel Hill, N.C., 1980), as well as to conversations with the author. Other important works include James M. Banner, Jr., *To the Hartford Convention: The Federalists and the Origins of Party Politics in Massachusetts, 1789–1815* (New

York, 1970), Lance G. Banning, *The Jeffersonian Persuasion: Evolution of a Party Ideology* (Ithaca, N.Y., 1978), Richard Buel, Jr., *Securing the Revolution: Ideology in American Politics, 1789–1815* (Ithaca, N.Y., 1972), David Hackett Fischer, *The Revolution of American Conservatism: The Federalist Party in the Era of Jeffersonian Democracy* (Chicago, 1965), Richard Hofstadter, *The Idea of a Party System: The Rise of Legitimate Opposition in the United States, 1780–1840* (Berkeley, Calif., 1969), John R. Howe, Jr., "Republican Thought and the Political Violence of the 1790s," *American Quarterly*, XIX (1967), 147–165, Linda K. Kerber, *Federalists in Dissent: Imagery and Ideology in Jeffersonian America* (Ithaca, N.Y., 1970), Shaw Livermore, Jr., *The Twilight of Federalism: The Disintegration of the Federalist Party, 1815–1830* (Princeton, N.J., 1962), and two articles by Marshall Smelser, "The Federalist Period as an Age of Passion," *American Quarterly*, X (1958), 391–419, and "The Jacobin Phrenzy: The Menace of Monarchy, Plutocracy, and Anglophilia, 1789–1798," *Review of Politics*, XXI (1959), 239–258.

The foremost book on postwar military questions is Richard H. Kohn's *Eagle and Sword: The Federalists and the Creation of the Military Establishment in America, 1783–1802* (New York, 1975). Among other issues important to Lee, Kohn discusses the controversy over the postwar militia, the Whiskey Insurrection, and the crisis of 1798. These and other concerns are analyzed for their ideological implications by Lawrence Delbert Cress in his doctoral dissertation, "The Standing Army, the Militia, and the New Republic: Changing Attitudes Toward the Military in American Society, 1768 to 1820" (University of Virginia, 1976), and in his revision of that work, now entitled "Arms and Ideas: Political Ideology and the Evolution of American Military Institutions to the War of 1812." The subject is treated briefly by Don Higginbotham, "The Debate over National Military Institutions," in W. M. Fowler and Wallace Coyle, eds., *The American Revolution: Changing Perspectives* (Boston, 1979), 154–168.

Southern Federalists are analyzed in Lisle A. Rose, *Prologue to Democracy: The Federalists in the South, 1789–1800* (Lexington, Ky., 1968), and James H. Broussard, *The Southern Federalists, 1800–1816* (Baton Rouge, La., 1978). For Virginia politics, I have relied on Richard R. Beeman, *The Old Dominion and the New Nation, 1788–1801* (Lexington, Ky., 1972), Norman K. Risjord, *Chesapeake Politics, 1781–1800* (New York, 1978), Norman K. Risjord, "The Virginia Federalists," *Journal of Southern History*, XXXIII (1967), 486–517, Norman K. Risjord and Gordon Den

Boer, "The Evolution of Political Parties in Virginia, 1782–1800," *Journal of American History*, LX (1974), 961–984, and two articles by Harry Ammon, "The Jeffersonian Republicans in Virginia: An Interpretation," *Virginia Magazine of History and Biography*, LXXI (1963), 153–167, and "The Formation of the Republican Party in Virginia, 1789–1796," *Journal of Southern History*, XIX (1953), 283–310.

Two important episodes in Lee's career, the Whiskey Insurrection and the Alien and Sedition Acts controversy, can be studied not only in Kohn, *Eagle and Sword*, but also in Leland D. Baldwin, *Whiskey Rebels: The Story of a Frontier Uprising* (Pittsburgh, Pa., 1939)—which should be compared with Jacob E. Cooke, "The Whiskey Insurrection: A Re-Evaluation," *Pennsylvania History*, XXX (1963), 316–346—and in James Morton Smith, *Freedom's Fetters: The Alien and Sedition Laws and American Civil Liberties* (Ithaca, N.Y., 1956), Marshall Smelser, "George Washington and the Alien and Sedition Acts," *American Historical Review*, LIX (1954), 322–334, and Adrienne Koch and Harry Ammon, "The Virginia and Kentucky Resolutions: An Episode in Jefferson's and Madison's Defense of Civil Liberties," *William & Mary Quarterly*, 3d ser., V (1948), 147–176.

Out of the large literature on the War of 1812, I owe the most to McCoy, *Elusive Republic*, and to Roger H. Brown, *The Republic in Peril: 1812* (New York, 1964), Bradford Perkins, *Prologue to War: England and the United States, 1805–1812* (Berkeley, Calif., 1963), Burton Spivak, *Jefferson's English Crisis: Commerce, Embargo, and the Republican Revolution* (Charlottesville, Va., 1979), J. C. A. Stagg, "James Madison and the 'Malcontents': The Political Origins of the War of 1812," *William & Mary Quarterly*, 3d ser., XXXIII (1976), 557–585, and Norman K. Risjord, "1812: Conservatives, War Hawks, and the Nation's Honor," *ibid.*, XVIII (1961), 196–210. Three studies by Donald R. Hickey analyze the Federalist opposition: "The Federalists and the War of 1812" (Ph.D. diss., University of Illinois at Urbana-Champaign, 1972), "Federalist Party Unity and the War of 1812," *Journal of American Studies*, XII (1978), 23–39, and "The Federalists and the Coming of the War, 1811–1812," *Indiana Magazine of History*, LXXV (1979), 70–88. Myron F. Wehtje, "Opposition in Virginia to the War of 1812," *Virginia Magazine of History and Biography*, LXXVIII (1970), 65–86, shows that other Virginians shared Lee's concerns. The Baltimore riot has recently been described in Paul A. Gilje, "The Baltimore Riots of 1812 and the Breakdown of the Anglo-American Mob Tradition," *Journal of Social History*, XIII (1980), 547–564, Frank A. Cassell, "The Great Baltimore Riot of 1812," *Maryland Historical Maga-*

zine, LXX (1975), 241–259, and Donald R. Hickey, "The Darker Side of Democracy: The Baltimore Riots of 1812," *Maryland Historian,* VII (1976), 1–19. For the political and social context of the riot, see L. Marx Renzulli, Jr., *Maryland: The Federalist Years* (Rutherford, N.J., 1972), and Gary Larson Browne, *Baltimore in the Nation, 1789–1861* (Chapel Hill, N.C., 1980).

The land speculation of the Early National Period receives brief treatment in several works: A. M. Sakolski, *The Great American Land Bubble* (New York, 1932), Curtis P. Nettels, *The Emergence of a National Economy, 1775–1815* (New York, 1962), Shaw Livermore, *Early American Land Companies: Their Influence on Corporate Development* (New York, 1939), and Kenneth P. Bailey, *The Ohio Company of Virginia and the Westward Movement, 1748–1792* (Glendale, Calif., 1939). The best background for Lee's involvement appears in the biographies of his fellow speculators: Robert D. Arbuckle, *Pennsylvania Speculator and Patriot: The Entrepreneurial John Nicholson, 1757–1800* (University Park, Pa., 1975), Roy Bird Cook, *Washington's Western Lands* (Strasburg, Va., 1930), Jacob E. Cooke, *Tench Coxe and the Early Republic* (Chapel Hill, N.C., 1978), Joseph W. Cox, *Champion of Southern Federalism: Robert Goodloe Harper of South Carolina* (Port Washington, N.Y., 1972), Ellis Paxson Oberholtzer, *Robert Morris: Patriot and Financier* (New York, 1968 [orig. publ. 1903]), Charles Page Smith, *James Wilson: Founding Father, 1742–1798* (Chapel Hill, N.C., 1956), and Samuel M. Wilson, "George Washington's Contacts with Kentucky," *Filson Club History Quarterly,* VI (1932), 215–260. Lee's Potomac ventures are discussed in Corra Bacon-Foster, *Early Chapters in the Development of the Potomac Route to the West* (Washington, D.C., 1912), Fairfax Harrison, *Landmarks of Old Prince William,* 2 vols. (Richmond, Va., 1924), and Ricardo Torres-Reyes, *Potowmack Company Canal and Locks: Historic Structures Report, Great Falls, Virginia* ([Washington, D.C.], 1970). Arthur G. Barnes has reconstructed Matildaville in his study for Southside Historical Sites, *History of Patowmack Canal: Matildaville* (1978). Virginia's laws on debt and insolvency are explained in Peter J. Coleman, *Debtors and Creditors in America: Insolvency, Imprisonment for Debt, and Bankruptcy, 1607–1900* (Madison, Wis., 1974).

Careful analysis of Thomas Jefferson's terms as governor of Virginia may be found in Dumas Malone, *Jefferson and His Time,* I: *Jefferson the Virginian* (Boston, 1948), Merrill D. Peterson, *Thomas Jefferson and the New Nation: A Biography* (New York, 1970), and the editorial notes in Julian P. Boyd, ed. *The Papers of Thomas Jefferson,* IV (Princeton, N.J.,

1951), esp. 256–258, 266–267n. I have also used Fawn M. Brodie, *Thomas Jefferson: An Intimate History* (New York, 1974). Jefferson's successor as governor is discussed in Emory G. Evans, *Thomas Nelson of Yorktown: Revolutionary Virginian* (Williamsburg, Va., 1975). For a discussion of the attack on Jefferson by Lee's oldest son, see Merrill D. Peterson, *The Jefferson Image in the American Mind* (New York, 1960). Jefferson's Republican historian is studied in Donald G. Morgan, *Justice William Johnson, The First Dissenter: The Career and Constitutional Philosophy of a Jeffersonian Judge* (Columbia, S.C., 1954), and A. J. Levin, "Mr. Justice William Johnson, Jurist in Limine: The Judge as Historian and Maker of History," *Michigan Law Review,* XLVI (1947), 131–186. Jefferson's attitude toward war as an instrument of policy is the subject of Reginald C. Stuart, *The Half-way Pacifist: Thomas Jefferson's View of War* (Toronto, 1978).

ACKNOWLEDGMENTS

I RESEARCHED AND WROTE THIS BOOK WHILE I WAS A FELLOW AT THE Institute of Early American History and Culture in Williamsburg, Virginia, from 1977 to 1979. The Institute gave me uninterrupted time for work and generous aid for travel and research materials. I am especially grateful to the director, Thad W. Tate, the editor of publications, Norman S. Fiering, and the visiting editor of publications, David L. Ammerman, for their support of the project.

In April 1979, I took various versions of parts of this book on the road and received helpful reactions from those who heard them. At the meeting of the Organization of American Historians, George A. Billias, John Shy, and Russell F. Weigley gave me valuable comments and encouragement. The people who came to an Institute colloquium suggested ways to improve the first two chapters. And a lively meeting of the King and Queen County Historical Society expressed an active interest in the Lees, which continued for several hours of a fine spring afternoon, thanks to the hospitality of the Society's current president, Donald Rhinesmith.

For help in obtaining sources, illustrative material, and special studies, I thank Arthur G. Barnes, Edmund L. Drago, Elizabeth Friedberg, Rachel Klein, Charlotte Partain, Jonathan H. Poston, Donald Sweig, and especially E. Wayne Carp. I am grateful to members of the Lee family who aided the work: Carter L. Refo provided a portrait of Henry Lee, and Anne Carter Lee gave me permission to quote from manuscripts in her possession.

In revising my first draft, I benefited from incisive readings and suggestions by E. Wayne Carp, Lawrence Delbert Cress, George M. Curtis III, Norman S. Fiering, Christian G. Fritz, James H. Kettner, Drew R. McCoy, Stephen Maizlish, Reid Mitchell, Merrill D. Peterson, W. J. Rorabaugh, Frank S. Smith, and Thad W. Tate. As an editor, Jane Garrett is my ideal.

While working on this book, I received hospitality for which I remain very grateful. No Californian could ask for a better introduction to Virginia than to see its land, churches, and estates with Thad W. Tate for a guide. The staffs of all the libraries mentioned in the notes helped me generously. I thank all of these manuscript repositories for permission to quote from documents in their possession. My visit to Stratford Hall was made possible by the Robert E. Lee Memorial Association, was made efficient by the Custodian of Records, Judith S. Hynson, and was made memorable by Fraser Neiman and Janet Long. In Durham, North Carolina, Reid Mitchell and Martha Reiner put me greatly in their debt. In California, I had the good fortune to be the guest of John, Marjorie, and Michael Edwards and the summer tenant of Morgan Doyle. In Berkeley, Christian G. Fritz has repeatedly been the best of hosts. Warren and Carol Billings in New Orleans and Frank S. Smith in New York made professional trips into pleasure trips. Among the most important instances of hospitality that furthered the completion of this book was a timely and warm invitation by the members of the Department of History at the University of Texas at Arlington and their chairman, Richard G. Miller, to join them, first as a visitor, then as a colleague.

My greatest gratitude and obligations are expressed in the dedication of this book. Philip and Charlotte Partain opened their home to me on my trips to the Washington, D.C., area and repeatedly ignored Poor Richard's warning that visitors, like fish, stink after three days. The pleasure of their company made my visits more frequent. Although Lester J. Cappon made only a few brief appearances in Williamsburg during my stay there, he was still my host for two years: looking out from a dozen photographs of the Institute council and staff over a period of thirty years, embodying the Institute's tradition of scholarship, taking an active interest in the work of the Fellows, filling the lead role in countless Institute anecdotes, and—incidentally—paying my rent. I cannot imagine those years or this book without these friends.

INDEX

A NOTE ABOUT THE AUTHOR

CHARLES ROYSTER was born in Nashville, Tennessee, in 1944. He received his A.B. from the University of California, Berkeley, in 1966 and his Ph.D. in 1977. From 1977 to 1979 he was a Fellow of the Institute of Early American History and Culture. He has taught at the College of William and Mary, at Berkeley, and in the University of Maryland's Far East Division. He is currently on the faculty of the University of Texas, Arlington. His first book, *A Revolutionary People at War: The Continental Army and American Character, 1775–1783,* which was published in 1980, won The John D. Rockefeller 3rd Award of the Bicentennial Council of the Thirteen Original States Fund.

A NOTE ON THE TYPE

THIS BOOK WAS SET, via computer-driven cathode-ray tube, in a modern version of a type designed by the first William Caslon (1692–1766), greatest of English letter founders. The Caslon face, an artistic, easily read type, has had two centuries of ever increasing popularity in our own country. It is of interest to note that the first copies of the Declaration of Independence and the first paper currency distributed to the citizens of the newborn nation were printed in this typeface.

Composed by American Book–Stratford Press, Saddle Brook, New Jersey. Printed and bound by Haddon Craftsmen, Scranton, Pennsylvania. Typography and binding design by Karolina Harris.

4/08